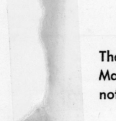

ERRATUM

The 1952 map on page 296 is in error. Massachusetts and Rhode Island should not be shown as Democratic areas.

REVOLT OF THE MODERATES

Books by Samuel Lubell

THE FUTURE OF AMERICAN POLITICS

THE REVOLUTION IN WORLD TRADE

REVOLT OF THE MODERATES

SAMUEL LUBELL

REVOLT OF THE
MODERATES

Harper & Brothers: New York

E
835
.L8

To my wife, Helen Sopot Lubell, in appreciation of conspicuous patience above and beyond the call of matrimonial duty in my three wars with three books

CONTENTS

REVOLT OF THE MODERATES

ONE

The Conservative Ordeal

1. Test of a Nation

On the eve of Dwight D. Eisenhower's inauguration one national magazine instructed its Washington staff to report the event through the eyes of spectators. In electing the first Republican president in twenty years the people had slammed shut one era of American life with unmistakable finality, or so the editors reasoned. What more penetrating way of capturing the significance of the new emerging age could there be than through what the crowds said and did as they watched one President retire and a new one take the oath of office?

Came Inaugural Day and the magazine's staff of twenty-six reporters and eleven photographers deployed themselves through the festive city, making the rounds of the state delegations, squeezing into the jam-packed ballrooms, mingling with the spectators along the three-mile parade route. But when the result of all this reportorial eavesdropping reached the editors it proved strangely disappointing. The reports were rich enough in the picturesque detail

1

which falls under the shop label of "human interest"—how eager parade viewers perched on kitchen ladders brought from home or bought the fat inaugural editions of the local newspapers not to read but to soften the bleacher seats . . . the anger of those onlookers who had to yield up seats because the inaugural planners forgot to provide aisle space to the comfort stations . . . how a screen cowboy tried twice before lassoing the President . . . Mamie's astonishing energy as she blew kisses at the passing floats . . . the live turtle waving an American flag in its front leg . . . the Confederate banners flaunted by Southern delegations . . . the almost guilty silence as veterans from Korea marched by . . . the even deeper hush that stilled the spectators when the first atomic cannon ever shown in public rolled into view . . . the final touch of the political ringmaster in closing the pageant with two lumbering elephants. . . .

But if there was no dearth of "color," nowhere in the reports could the editors find what they searched for—the chance remark, incident, or pictorial detail which could serve as an illuminating caption of what the entire epochal event portended.

Always in the past when American history had taken a crucial turn its significance could be read in the inaugural ceremonies. The leveling crush of the Age of Jackson had been foreshadowed by the moblike rush with which Old Hickory's followers took physical possession of the White House, upsetting pails of punch, smashing crockery and clambering on damask chairs with muddy boots to catch sight of the new President, who finally had to escape through a side window.

Similarly, grim forebodings of imminent civil war rustled in the rumors of intended assassination which caused Lincoln to slip into Washington in the secrecy of the night. On Inaugural Day sharpshooters squinted down from houses along Pennsylvania Avenue, while a military escort almost hid Lincoln from view as he rode to the Capitol.

There was the somber, sunless setting for Franklin Roosevelt's accession; the awkward silence with which Herbert Hoover stood on the inaugural platform waiting for his successor, the band's failure to accord the departing President a final salute of respect, the lights in the White House burning through the night as the new President prepared to close all the banks.

But what omen of things to come could one draw from the carefree gaiety of the Eisenhower jubilee? The news dispatches were pitched to the theme of a popular hero risen to answer a troubled nation's need for leadership at "a time of tempest." But little in the bearing of the inaugural throngs suggested such a fateful rendezvous with destiny.

Was it simply that the people had come to Washington to frolic and in this holiday mood had thrust aside all thoughts of the deeper historical meaning of the event?

Or could it be that the real significance of Eisenhower's victory lay so deeply buried beneath clashing hopes and fears that it had been unable to break through the carnival crust?

This book seeks to fathom the deeper recesses of the puzzle posed by that Inauguration Day. One reason the meaning of the Eisenhower Presidency has remained so elusive has been the dazzle of his personality. With no memoirs of disgruntled subordinates to thin or break the war hero's aura, it has been only too easy to think of Eisenhower as an embodiment of the theory that "great men make history." But, as I believe this volume will demonstrate, his has been a performance in which the play has been more significant than the star.

In essence the drama of his Presidency can be described as the ordeal of a nation turned conservative and struggling

—thus far with but limited and precarious success—to give effective voice and force to that conservatism. In this conservative ordeal will be found the frame for the innermost conflicts of the Eisenhower Presidency, both its torments and conciliations, as well as for the heritage with which his successors will have to deal.

If the heroic scale of this struggle for conservatism does not immediately leap to our attention it is largely because we have not yet rubbed our eyes awake to how much more difficult it has become to preserve order than to start a revolution in our chaotic world.

As children we were taught to look upon revolutionists as a heroic lot, suffering prison or even martyrdom for their beliefs. But at least for our age this notion that revolution is a signal achievement can be discarded. Of the seventy-six members of the United Nations, only nine have not experienced a change in their form of government since 1914, through either revolution, military occupation or newly won independence. The truly Homeric feat these days is the infinitely more torturous task of preserving a peaceful, stable government.

Rarely in American history has the craving for tranquillity and moderation commanded more general public support. In foreign affairs the gossipy myth that ours is a mercurial, impatient temperament has been belied by how steadfastly we have plugged away at the role of global, philanthropic policeman, trying now with dollars and now with guns to stabilize governments in lands many of us could not locate on a map.

At home, the New Deal generation, once so zealous to make America over, devotes its evenings to wrestling with mortgage payments and inculcating a respect for tradition and discipline in overly progressive children.

Even among the "younger" generation there is hardly a flutter of iconoclastic revolt. No collegians are swallowing goldfish or eating phonograph records; marriage has become a campus vogue, while the boldest collegiate exhibitionists can conceive of little that is more daring than growing a beard. Not too long ago a friend was interviewing a college graduate for a prospective job. Asked the youthful graduate in his first question, "What kind of pension plan does your company have?"

Why then, if this yearning for conservatism seems virtually unchallenged in the country, is it proving so difficult to give it effective reality?

Part of the answer is that intellectually all of us believe in ghosts, that our minds cling tenaciously to symbols forged by a past that is dead. Our political parties, in particular, are like haunted houses. To the extent that they have meaning to the voters it is mainly in terms of the animosities and loyalties, the medals and scars, of the political wars of Franklin D. Roosevelt. Yet the election returns show that neither the Democrats nor the Republicans can sustain a clean-cut majority in the country in terms of these ghostly mementos.

Before a decisive majority can be brought into being one—or both—of the major parties must come to mean something different from what it stood for during the age of Roosevelt.

Partly because of the illusion that conservatism and wealth are synonymous, many people still picture the politics of our time as a clash between "right" and "left." But the truly crucial struggle is being waged between the past and the future, between those who would continue to fight the battles of the 1920's and 1930's and those who would empty the parties of their old symbolism so they can meet the issues of what President Eisenhower once termed "not a moment but an age of danger."

Still, if the stakes were little more than party supremacy, the striving for conservatism could hardly be considered an epochal affair. The current state of American politics could then be summarized as a race between the two parties as to which can free itself first of the dividing distrusts of the Roosevelt period.

In this race the role assigned Eisenhower was that of a substitute for the realignment the parties have not been able to manage. His has been the mediating task of transition, reflecting the fact that the balance of political power rests with those moderate voting elements who are in restless revolt against both parties.

But what lifts this "revolt of the moderates" to worldshaping importance is the fact that the contest for domestic political power is being fought against the backdrop of a world in upheaval. The effort to refashion a new political majority at home comes at the same time that the United States, no longer able to wield a free hand in foreign affairs, has been striving to build a coalition of peace and order abroad. Only too often and too violently do the needs of these two coalitions clash.

When Eisenhower was inaugurated some commentators referred to him as "the President of the free world," without perhaps realizing the full implications of the phrase. The test that must be applied to the Eisenhower administration is its success—or failure—in striking a double balance, both at home and abroad.

Examined by this standard, the drama of the Eisenhower Presidency becomes transformed. Its true hero has been not the man in the White House but the American people. As this struggle to reconcile the needs of domestic and world balance has unfolded, it has become a testing of the entire American nation, at perhaps the most critical juncture in its history.

This was true even before Eisenhower's illness. The heart attack he suffered in Denver was but a reminder of what we should have known, that in any circumstances it is the

American people who will have to finish what President Eisenhower started.

As will be seen later in a more detailed examination of Eisenhower's personal role, the essential quality of his leadership has lain in the skill and faithfulness with which he has followed the public temper. Throughout his Presidency, Eisenhower has been the understudy for the people themselves.

The testing of any nation is a complex experience, involving many cross-tuggings and even contradictions. These more subtle nuances must be left to later chapters. Still, it may help bring into focus the essential nature of this testing if its main elements are outlined briefly at the outset, leaving their amplification for later.

The heart of the matter is what amounts to a running civil war between technology and government. With astonishing scientific ingenuity we have contrived to turn our globe into a technological top, which must be kept spinning to maintain equilibrium but whose whirlings threaten constantly to shake us to pieces.

How to reconcile political stability with this technology, which has made revolution almost a dime-store affair, is the crux of the conservative ordeal.

One agonizing illustration of this conflict can be seen in the futile efforts to devise some means of governmental control over nuclear weapons, with each failure spurring an arms race which makes control in the future ever more difficult. Another example is the maneuverings of various governments to keep their economies booming—without bounding out of control.

That the Republican party should have been the political means through which the Eisenhower Presidency sought to conciliate this duel of technology and government is in itself a symptom of the crisis. Sharp indeed has been the dilemma of the Republicans. Traditionally they have

fancied themselves as the torchbearers of an antigovern-
ment philosophy, which looks upon "the State" as man's
enemy. Yet the inexorable drive of technology operates to
make government the tool of survival in our world.

Whether that is how things *should* be is not at issue.
George Washington liked to call himself "a citizen of the
Great Republic of humanity at large," which was also the
outlook of other founding fathers like Benjamin Franklin
and Thomas Jefferson. But as technology has shrunk the
globe we have become increasingly citizens of one particular nation. More and more of our lives—the currency which
gives value to our labors and savings, the language in which
our myths are written, the passports upon which we travel,
the preparations against possible atomic attack—has come
to bear the stamp "Made in U.S.A." or in Britain, France or
Japan.

This sweep of nationalism bristles with its own terrible
dangers. One peril is the dogma Hitler sought to enshrine,
that a nation is an end in itself, to which individuals must
be subordinated. A second ambush lurks in the fact that
so many problems can be dealt with effectively only in a
frame of action which transcends national frontiers.

But these dangers merely define the gauntlet that must
be run in using our national governments. Whatever hopes
may be entertained for international agencies, the nation
remains the prime governing unit in our world, the instrument through which even decisions of international
co-operation must be registered. Nor, with weapons in existence capable of overwhelming a nation in a lost weekend,
can any people meet the threat of totalitarianism by weakening its own government.

The dilemma of the Republicans has lain in the fact that
their instinctive yearnings tug back to an age of simpler
government at a time when the dominant forces in the

world keep heaping ever fresh responsibilities and burdens upon government.

Nor is this solely a Republican dilemma. The prevailing attitudes toward government held by most Americans reflect their dislike or support of the New Deal. But the awesome issues of a nuclear age make the Rooseveltian quarrels seem almost like nostalgic footnotes to a time when the stakes of government had not yet become the stakes of survival.

As technology propels us, we have no alternative to some change in our concept of government—which makes the struggle for conservatism all the more agonizing. Stability is what every Western nation yearns for above all else, but that stability cannot be attained by clinging to the past, as the conservative-minded might be inclined to do.

New weapons and reshuffled power relationships are forcing profound adjustments upon every country. Britain, Holland, France and Italy have had to yield up at least part of their empires. The United States has been compelled not only to join "entangling alliances" in advance of war, but to break itself of a long habit of leisurely indecision in foreign policy. In both world wars we could debate among ourselves for almost two years before entering those conflicts. The Truman Doctrine to defend Turkey and Greece was settled upon in three months. The decision to intervene in Korea was snapped out in a matter of hours.

These global changes inevitably force far-reaching internal adjustments as well. The mere fact that a fifth or more of a nation's production goes for defense generates new problems and tensions in how this burden is shared at home. A military alliance must also be fed by the bread of economic co-operation, which requires balancing innumerable internal interests of many nations.

How high can tariffs be? Should currencies command a fixed value regardless of the domestic adjustments that may result? Are surplus farm stocks to be dumped abroad no matter what the effect may be upon our allies? Or is it wiser to put these surpluses into storage at the expense of the American taxpayer?

And even while we fight to bail ourselves out, the ceaseless workings of technology engulf us with fresh dislocations, with new products or techniques which disrupt established economic relationships, with new weapons which strip naked established defenses.

In short, whatever internal equilibrium may have been adequate in the past will suffice no longer. Whether we happen to believe in "one world" or "America first," whether we were "New Dealers" or "rugged individualists" in the past, does not alter the basic choice all of us face—of agreeing among ourselves upon a new role for government.

The inescapable fact is that no American action—or inaction—is without its global effect. An attempted "withdrawal" from world affairs would have as much impact, albeit with different results, as deeper involvement. Similarly, if "do nothing" government has become a meaningless abstraction, it is also true that simply "getting the government to do something" is no assurance that the right thing will be done.

How to make government effective is our problem. Is what government does or does not do to be left to chance or consciously thought through? Is it to be directed toward appeasing the ghosts of Politics Past or of meeting the needs of Survival Present?

Not only the United States but virtually every other country is confronted with this task of redefining what makes an *effective* nation.

Among the underdeveloped countries this testing is remarkably akin to the trial which parentless children undergo as they grow to adulthood. All of the newer nations in the Orient, for example, are products of the orphanage which was called imperialism. All show the marks of that foster parentage in their characters. Where the training was tempered by an emphasis on self-reliance, as in the Philippines, the transition to independence has seemed easier. Where the hatreds of the orphanage were particularly acute the urge for independence has become almost synonymous with delinquency.

What ideals and ideologies will these orphans of imperialism accept or reject as they achieve manhood? What disciplines will be incorporated in their governmental institutions? What skills and crafts will they learn to make themselves economically self-supporting?

Only lately have the Western powers come to appreciate how delicate is the task of rearing a good nation, and we have become so much busier with our educational aids, from ideological primers to Point Four erector sets. But whether we have acted in time—or will be proven too late— will not become clear for perhaps a generation.

In the Western countries the trial of what makes an effective nation is perhaps even more agonizing, for the testing is not one of children struggling to assert their manhood but of matured adults abruptly confronted by new demands which require a change in their most deeply rooted habits.

One result, the politics of every country is being revolutionized. Everywhere politics is being *internationalized* to become more and more alike in country after country.

The party labels differ, but if one peers beneath them in England, France, Germany, Italy or the United States one sees the same struggle to eliminate or subdue old sectional and class cleavages. In Britain the conflict is largely over wiping out the hatreds of the old depressed areas which suffered so much in the 1920's and 1930's. In Italy poverty-stricken Sicily must be revitalized and assimilated with the rest of the nation. In France one watches the sad inadequacies of a cultural unity which is not stiffened by the backbone of political unity.

In each of these countries the common issue is whether a new unity can be achieved which will enable these peoples to meet the trials of the cold war. And it is inherent in the very nature of this testing that in each of these countries some faction should arise to propose escaping from a world that seems beyond management by taking refuge in the "neutralism" of domestic disillusionment.

How profound this struggle is can be seen in the closeness of voting which has prevailed in nearly every Western country in recent years. Almost every new election has been advertised as one upon which the fate of a nation hinged. But these elections have brought only small shifts in voting. Even where governments have fallen and new ones have arisen there has been little change in basic policy.

The rigidity of these indecisions, the consistency of these waverings, are all the more remarkable when one considers how chaotic and unpredictable the postwar years have seemed.

In part this persistent uncertainty reflects the harsh choices posed by the cold war, choices which have often made inaction seem more desirable than action. But it also reflects the fact that these choices have had to be registered through political parties which still are wedded to perpetuating prewar hatreds and ideologies.

The whole of Western civilization is caught up in this same struggle between the past and future which is the essence of the American political trial.

That, in any case, is the perspective from which I have chosen to examine the current political scene in the United States. It is the drama, in miniature, of a world in transition, with every nation being forced to break free of the past so it can find a new internal balance that can be fitted into a new world equilibrium.

Human thought seems fated to follow a cycle of imprisonment and liberation. When first set forth, intellectual concepts free our imaginations. But as what once was new hardens into dogma, these same concepts become like so many prison walls that shut in our minds. In no field is the need for a mental prison break more urgent than in what we call "politics."

2. E Pluribus Politics

Antoine Pinay, France's seventeenth premier since liberation, had fallen seven days earlier. His successor had not yet been chosen that Christmas week in 1953 when *Le Figaro* appeared on Parisian newsstands with a front-page article by François Mauriac, who earlier that year had won the Nobel prize for literature.

Mauriac undertook to explain why French premiers changed as frequently as the seasons. The fault, he contended, lay not with the premiers but with the French people themselves, whose "bad political habits" permitted them to secrete only a certain species of parliamentarianism. Summing up his thesis Mauriac wrote, "If institutions do not change it is because men do not change. . . . The saying that character is destiny applies to peoples as well as individuals."

Although Mauriac did not intend it that way, his observation on the destiny of nations being shaped by their character provides the key to the changed nature of politics in this atomic age.

To many people, the term "politics" remains little more than a dirty word, which conjures up stuffed ballot boxes, intriguing political bosses and crooked deals. Others have tried to define politics as a struggle of rival interests—in Harold Lasswell's phrase, of "Who Gets What, When, How." These things will continue to be part of the "game of politics" yet they obviously fall short of the new decisive dimension which has been given to government, and therefore politics, in our time.

The position of every nation today makes one think of a novel or play whose plot is contrived to hinge upon some fateful choice the hero or heroine must make, a choice which is determined by the very character of the hero or heroine. Similarly, every people in the world is under siege, with all we prize most highly resting upon the decisions our governments make. Yet in making those decisions, try as we will, we cannot escape ourselves. For our governments can act only in terms of our national character, of the kind of people we are.

And it is in those terms that we must learn to view the politics of our age, as a testing of the character of nations while they struggle to make—or evade—the decisions on which survival hinges.

To see ourselves as part of this process, we shall have to break with at least two habits of American thinking.

One is the bureaucratic specialization which divides politics from economics, military strategy or foreign policy. The same men in the White House or in Congress decide all these things and the primitive urge for re-election affects their every decision. As government looms ever larger in importance, it becomes more urgent to focus upon the interplay of forces which causes even the highest strategic decisions to be influenced by perhaps the lowest of political considerations.

The second habit from which we must break free is that of thinking of ourselves as separate and apart from the politicians who represent us.

This detachment of the people from their government is one of the more deeply ingrained American traits. If something goes wrong, the sovereign people are never held at fault. Always it is "that man in the White House" or some other official who is accused of "betraying" the "public trust." The conscience of the "public" is left to slumber untroubled.

This myth of the "blameless public" has been indulged in too long. It is time that "we the people" realized that our politicians are what they are—for better or worse—because of ourselves.

The process by which we transfer our virtues and faults to our politicians is not unlike the interplay between an actor and his audience. When Martin Van Buren retired from the Senate and his household goods were sold at auction one shrewd observer noted that the carpet in front of Van Buren's looking glass had been worn threadbare. Figuratively speaking the carpets of all our political leaders have been worn thin through constant rehearsal before the mirror that is public opinion.

By subjecting our politicians to the box-office test of periodic elections we force them, consciously or unconsciously, to probe for all our weaknesses and strengths, our prides and prejudices, for the issues which will rouse us out of apathy or even make us so blind with rage that we cannot see our own interests clearly.

Election by election, this process of political selection continues until everything about us manages to find its image in some one or other of our politicians, every act of courage and timidity, greed or sacrifice, indignation or complacency. These and other traits register in the makeup of our politicians and through them are impressed upon our national character.

Of course, the representation is never mirror-perfect. Some Congressmen, who have not had to face a real contest for twenty years, may continue to reflect mental attitudes fashionable a quarter of a century ago, indifferent to changes in their own constituency. Every now and then, as well, a maverick will arise to defy the prejudices or even interests of his own constituents and still win re-election.

But the dominant trends seem to be running against such independence. More and more of our politicians are coming to be known as "types" or as recognized spokesmen for certain entrenched interests or prejudices. The contest between Eisenhower and the late Senator Robert A. Taft is one good illustration. If a playwright had tried to contrive a pair of characters to dramatize the isolationist-internationalist cleavage in the Republican party he could not have found two better prototypes.

We smile when we read of how the late Eugene Talmadge acquired the demagogic trademark of snapping his red suspenders. While campaigning on a hot day early in his career, Talmadge stripped off his jacket, baring his suspenders. A man in the crowd exclaimed, "Red galluses, by God!" That was all the cue Talmadge needed.

Since that incident our educational level has risen appreciably, but are today's campaigning techniques any further removed from popular prejudice than Talmadge's? More and more in recent years political campaigns have come to be directed by advertising agencies. The common practice is to begin by searching out the prevailing prejudices of the people through a public-opinion poll (cost $10 per prejudiced knee being tapped) and then to mobilize every Madison Avenue aid to "sell" the candidate in the light of these prejudices.

Nor can television be expected to make our politics any less theatrical or less steeped in appeals to prejudice.

What has happened to diplomacy also shows how irresistible our politicians find the passions of the people. From what once was a relatively private affair, conducted with the finesse and tempo of a Viennese waltz, diplomacy has become a virtual headline brawl. Statesmen like Winston Churchill have deplored this tactic of "open disagreements openly disagreed on," but even his great influence has been unable to change the practice.

Since the cold war is so largely a battle for the minds of men it is inevitable that our own prejudices and emotions will be used against us. Nor is there much use in taking up arms against the hucksters of what might be rechristened "Maddening Avenue." Our best self-defense is to "see ourselves as others politick us." By changing our own characters we can force our politicians to change.

Usually when writers talk of "national character" they try to search out those traits which can be applied to the whole country generally, as if in answer to the question, What is an American or Frenchman or Englishman?

But certainly in the United States varied traits have always been at conflict with one another and our "national character" can be understood best in terms of the balance of unity and disunity that is struck among these traits.

Significantly, this test of unity has also been the basic long-run test of American politics. In our history no party has been able to gain or hold ascendancy as the normal majority in the country unless it made itself the effective instrument for unifying the nation. Today three main issues divide the country—foreign policy, racial and religious tolerance and economic status. The famed Roosevelt coalition collapsed because it was unable to preserve sufficient cohesiveness among its supporters on these three issues. It is in terms of these same issues that I have tried to judge the progress—or lack of progress—which the Republicans have made in replacing the old Roosevelt majority with a new, conservative coalition.

Has the G.O.P. been remade sufficiently so that it can win and hold power without a popular hero like Eisenhower? Or is the Republican effort at unifying the country bound to fail? And if the task is to be taken up by the Democrats again will the defeat of 1952 have made them better able to succeed?

In searching for the answers to these and other questions

my technique has been to isolate the voting elements who are most sensitive to these issues and to follow them through the throes of the transition which they are undergoing, seeking to determine how much of the Rooseveltian memories still survives and how much adjustment has been made to the emerging issues of a new age. Naturally this examination has required an appraisal of the political effects of the major social and economic changes in the country.

To dramatize the forces involved and their interplay with our political character a variety of methods has been used. Senator Joseph McCarthy, for example, appears in these pages not as a witch hunter, but as the expression of the trait of disillusionment which lurks in every nation's make-up. Similarly the sketches included here of Richard Nixon, George M. Humphrey, Ezra Benson, Strom Thurmond and Eisenhower himself are intended as profiles less of men who happen to be in office than of certain enduring qualities in the American political temperament.

I have also tried to trace through the effects of more impersonal forces, such as how the desire to preserve the economic gains since the depression has brought a revival of a genuine two-party politics for the first time since the 1890's and how this operates against applying our economic power to winning the cold war. Other chapters analyze the role of business and whether it can be made into a truly conservative force; how the doctrine of "massive retaliation" grew out of the public's reaction to the Korean War; the two conflicting streams of interest reshaping the politics of the South; how the technological revolution unites the middle class, distracts labor and divides the farmer; also how the pace of possible realignment is slowed by two venerable American institutions, Congress and the small town.

In all this I have tried as far as possible to work within

the discipline of the actual election returns and of what the voters themselves have told me as I traveled about the country during recent elections. For every county in the country the Presidential returns have been analyzed at least as far back as the Civil War. Beyond that the voting of every major city and literally thousands of sensitive voting precincts has been studied.

As those who read *The Future of American Politics* may have sensed, I believe that voting returns are like radio-active isotopes through which one can penetrate to the dynamics of a nation and see how they are altered by social, political and historical change.

Coalition politics, by their very nature, tends to make Machiavellians of us all. Particularly in a country as big as ours, every coalition must aim at bringing into political alliance somewhat conflicting elements. While a genuine harmony of interests must underlie any successful coalition, less virtuous cements are usually applied as well—bargains of sundry sorts, the spoils of office, and ease of access to the Treasury, whether through open subsidy or tax favors. In short, coalition politics poses the constant trial of what people will do—or not do—to gain political power.

In this way all of us become accessories to one another's strengths and weaknesses, prejudices and enlightenments.

In the past, domestic temptations always dominated the forging of any political coalition. But the cold war has put a new cutting edge to all these temptations as it forces us to ask what profiteth a man or party to gain a political kingdom at the possible sacrifice of peace?

Let us see what balance Eisenhower struck between the needs of political coalition at home and allied coalition abroad.

TWO

===

Ye Compleat Political Angler

1. Dinner at the White House

No one touched the lone glass of tomato juice on the tray. As the White House waiters passed among the guests, the Scotch, rye and Bourbon drinks disappeared quickly. But the solitary tumbler of tomato juice, put out perhaps as insurance against the temperance convictions or ulcers of some one of the guests, stood untouched through the evening.

The President was in good humor, greeting each guest with warm enthusiasm. Earlier in the day he had sent a message to Congress. When someone told him that several Democratic Senators had commented ruefully, "There isn't much in that we can fight," he grinned with delight, like a boy scooping in all the marbles.

It was after dinner that the political talk started. The President had seated himself in one corner of the sofa of the Red Room, with his guests grouped in a semicircle around him. There was a moment or two of awkward silence. Then someone cracked the ice of reserve by asking whether his trick knee still hurt him while golfing. After that there was no let-up in the discussion.

It was in much this simple fashion that nearly all of the now famous Eisenhower stag dinners began. The things talked about would vary with the interests of those present or with the day's events. Some of the guests who were consulted in piecing together this sketch of a typical stag dinner recall a memorable exposition by the President of France's political problems. On another evening, when Walter Reuther and George Meany were among the invited, the discussion turned into a lively debate on what free enterprise meant.

But generally through most of 1955 the President's future political intentions were uppermost in the minds of his guests, and the scene in the Red Room tended to take on the quality of a tantalizing tableau in which the drama of a whole nation was laid bare through one man's struggle between a passion for active duty and a dream of quiet retirement.

The dream would appear first. Somehow the talk would drift around to "the farm" at Gettysburg. The President would respond with an animated discourse on the charms of country life.

If any of his guests happened to be interested in farming, he might confess that he had gone into raising black Angus cattle on the advice of friends, even though his own nostalgic preference ran to the whitefaced Herefords which he had seen around Abilene as a boy in Kansas. Then he would switch to the house itself and it would be like listening to a recital of Mr. Blandings building his Dream House.

With gay humor the President would tell of the curious problems that arose when one undertook to remodel a century-old farm dwelling. Unlike the antique the Blandings bought, the Gettysburg house had been of such sturdy construction that it seemed unthinkable to tear it down.

But after two wings were replaced, air-conditioning put in and enough new plumbing installed for eight and a half bathrooms, the President conceded "it would have been cheaper to have started from scratch."

Good-humoredly, Eisenhower would laugh it all off with some comment like, "It's our only extravagance" or by remarking jokingly, "Someday I'm going to have to get a job to pay for it all." He then would explain how much the house meant to Mrs. Eisenhower. Some friends had once presented her with photographs of seventeen different homes in which the Eisenhowers had lived since their marriage—various hotels, Army quarters, even a villa in France. The Gettysburg farm was the first home which had been their own. It had given Mrs. Eisenhower the joys of picking out her own furniture, planting her own shrubs and trees, fussing over the exact shade of green for the shutters and the colors in which each bedroom was to be painted; in short, of doing all those little things that every woman likes to do.

As they listened, his guests could not help feeling that the President was no less enamored of Gettysburg than was Mrs. Eisenhower. Usually, someone would bring up the subject agitating the group.

"Mr. President, you must run for a second term," a guest would urge. "Our party needs you. The whole world needs you."

Since this same question had come up at so many stag dinners, the President's response would show an almost practiced skill. He might talk of how much less influence he would command in a second term in view of the prohibition against any President having more than two terms. Not that he thought any man ought to have a third term, but it weakened the President for Congress to know he could not run again.

Although in good health at the time, the President would warn, "Don't rely on any one man." The Republican party had to be built around young men—"young in spirit"—not around "oldtimers like me."

He might go on to cite some of "the many fine young men we have in the party." The names would vary from dinner to dinner, but among those mentioned most often would be Richard Nixon, Herbert Hoover, Jr., Bob Anderson, Cabot Lodge, Charlie Halleck, Harold Stassen and Clifford Case. Sometimes he would top off the list by adding, "and some of the people right here tonight."

The guests would nod agreement to this accent on youth, but would argue back that "youth needs inspiration" and "you are the leader the young people of the country will follow."

And so it might go through the evening, with those present protesting Eisenhower's indispensability and the President parrying their compliments, without saying either "yes" or "no."

To most of his guests the ease with which the President left them pleasantly guessing seemed evidence of little more than political dexterity. His closest intimates, though, knew how deep ran the emotional conflict beneath the gay banter.

When World War II ended Eisenhower confided to close friends, "I've had all the glory I want. I'd like to live out my days as the head of a small college, doing some farming on the side." Actually, he became head of a rather big university. Still he never really was happy in the postwar years.

As one intimate recalls, "He was all frustrated inside watching how things were going in the world and not being able to do anything about them. He didn't regain his serenity until he became President."

To those who knew him best the rambling talk of Gettysburg was evidence of a renewal of this old conflict between a soldier's desire to exchange the rootlessness of public life for the quiet countryside, and the restless drive of a man of whom one close friend observed, "Maybe it's his sense of duty, but there is a passion in him that requires his being in the decisive center of things, giving his all."

Eisenhower's heart attack may have resolved this conflict; perhaps not.* Still, this account of a typical stag dinner is worth pondering for the clues it yields to one of the more intriguing mysteries of the Eisenhower Presidency—how a general who had never run for public office before and didn't even vote until he was fifty-eight years old could be transformed, within three years, into one of the most masterful politicians in American history.

Much of the public, of course, does not even think of Eisenhower as a politician. In my interviews with voters around the country, it was not unusual to hear him praised for being "clean of politics" or criticized as "just a soldier who lets the politicians tell him what to do." Some voters

* A few months after Eisenhower's heart attack I asked one White House intimate what he thought "would happen to the Republican party after Eisenhower is out of the picture." The carefully phrased reply was,
"I refuse to discuss things I don't believe will happen. Eisenhower will keep tacit command of the Republican party and will exercise responsibilities to measure up to his strength."
The only interpretation I could put on the remark was that the men around Eisenhower were determined to make every effort to have him continue at the helm of the Republican party even if he did not run for re-election.
This could be accomplished most dramatically by having Eisenhower serve as Secretary of State or in a new dramatic "peace" post in the Cabinet of the Republican whom he favored as his successor. The law forbids offering anyone a Cabinet post in advance of an election but the likelihood of such a development would become known publicly, of course. It could be dramatized to the country as insurance of carrying on Eisenhower's "peace" policy and of his efforts to remake the Republican party.

even term him "a pretty good Democrat." Many see him as "above both parties."

In part, this widely held image of Eisenhower as a five-star babe in the political woods reflects an extremely narrow definition of a politician as someone who is constantly running for office or managing the campaigns of other candidates. If, however, one defines "politics" in its broadest sense—as the art of governing people through other people—there is little question that Eisenhower must be rated as a highly skilled professional, as compleat a political angler as ever fished the White House.

Both as Supreme Allied Commander during the war and as NATO's commander Eisenhower had to exercise varied political stratagems to cajole the allied governments into co-operation. Similarly, the atmosphere of his Presidency has not been that of an uncompromising leader, defying what the public or his political associates might think. On the contrary, it would be difficult to cite any President, including both Roosevelts, who has been more adept in "giving the people what they want," or who has been more of a "party" man in patronage matters and in building a party organization, or even, considering how wide was the cleavage at the outset, who has done so well in bridging the rifts within his own party.

These being partisan times it may be worth stressing my own belief that considerable political skill is an absolute essential for an effective President. Myth makers like to make our heroes appear as demigods of perfection, ignoring that in any country with so many clashing interests only rarely is a straight line the shortest distance between two political points.

Moreover, the very affection in which the President is held emphasizes the importance of a candid examination of his role as a political leader. The deep anxieties that were stirred by his illness revealed the remarkable degree to which the American people have identified themselves with him. But how much of the Eisenhower Presidency mirrors the man and how much was contributed by the people themselves? Unless we understand the process by which the man and the people became one, both the public and his successor will be sorely handicapped in carrying out the tasks which will remain after Eisenhower has left the White House.

Perhaps it is too soon to attempt a definitive portrait of Eisenhower. Still, from talks with more than a dozen of his aides, four qualities emerge which, when tossed together, make up the recipe for what might be termed the Eisenhower magic political mix.

First, perhaps his strongest single characteristic seems to be a driving determination to win. Partly this reflects the sheer intensity with which he throws himself into everything he does, whether it be work or play. As one aide has observed, "The President doesn't even sign his name quietly."

While discussing something with a member of his staff he twirls his eyeglasses. Usually after a few minutes he is out of his chair and pacing the room. He seems to relax by turning from one form of intense concentration to another, as when playing golf or bridge.

Biologically, in other words, Eisenhower appears to have the temperament of a "free running horse," who is in constant need of working off an excess of nervous energy. Yet he also has developed a conscious discipline which enables him to exhibit unending patience when trying to conciliate conflicting viewpoints. Sometimes during such sessions he may grind his teeth, a tell-tale sign of repressed impatience. His famous outbursts of temper also seem a means of relaxing inward tensions. As one frequent target of such outbursts has noticed, "He goes up like a rocket and comes down as fast. He frets over small things and resents criticism but on big things can be as calm as a rock."

Coupled with this intense energy is Eisenhower's military training, which leaves little place for a loser. A revealing interchange with the press occurred in London shortly after he was named Supreme Allied Commander. A spokesman for the correspondents had assured him they would do anything necessary to win the war, within the bounds of truth and accuracy. Eisenhower replied, quite properly, that while he would deal fairly with his associates and allies, he would lie, cheat, steal—do anything—to beat the Germans.

Politics is a less mortal struggle than war, of course, and Eisenhower has publicly cautioned his fellow Republicans against forgetting that "our greatest enemy is not the Democrats" but "the Communists." Still, he definitely relishes a hard-hitting political campaign—when the Democrats are the target.

After the 1954 elections some Democratic leaders in Congress protested that the tactics which had been employed by Vice-President Nixon reflected on their patriotism. Eisenhower's private reaction to these protests was, "Nixon must have done a good job if the Democrats complain so much."

Washington correspondents have often pictured Eisenhower as shrinking from the things politicians are called upon to do. Yet, his aides agree that no matter how much he has fumed or grumbled in the privacy of his office, in the end he usually has gone along with what his political advisers felt needed to be done to win.

In 1954 he actually campaigned more extensively than any previous President had in a mid-term election—although this may be credited to a bit of mislaid research. When the campaigning question first came up, Eisenhower asked Leonard Hall, the Republican National Chairman, "What have other Presidents done?"

Without thinking, Hall replied, "Oh, they all stumped for their party."

Back in his office, Hall ordered some research into the question. When completed, it showed that virtually no President had ever done much in the way of mid-term campaigning.

After the election, at a breakfast session with some Republican Congressmen, Hall related what his research had shown, remarking, "Mr. President, that was one report I never showed you."

Eisenhower's second distinctive quality is his practicality. One can comb his speeches in vain for evidences of the brand of idealism which inspired the Atlantic Charter and "The Four Freedoms," or Woodrow Wilson's League of Nations. "Enlightened self-interest" is a favorite Eisenhower phrase in justifying our foreign policy. He is apt to emphasize the point by citing our dependence on raw materials imported from abroad.

His idealism appears to find its main outlet in such personal acts as churchgoing and in a sense of duty to a cause higher than himself. His intimates have learned that no appeal will move him more deeply than "This is a duty you owe the American people." When he was being pressed to run for the Presidency, one aide recalls that every possible argument and pressure was employed upon him, "but the only one that made any difference was that it was his duty."

In carrying out this duty, though, Eisenhower is coldly logical and realistic. This combination of an idealistic sense of duty implemented by practical means can be extraordinarily effective politically. Often, in fact, it may yield much the same end results as cynical maneuvering.

That, of course, was the criticism hurled against Eisenhower during the North African landings for dealing with Admiral Darlan, the notorious Vichy collaborator. To Eisenhower, though, the issue at stake was the intensely practical one of which French leader could halt French resistance and reduce American casualties—an attitude which was supported fully by both President Roosevelt and Winston Churchill.

Again, it is not generally known that Senator McCarthy offered not to ride into Wisconsin on the Eisenhower campaign train in 1952 if Eisenhower felt McCarthy's presence would be embarrassing. After pondering the question in solitude Eisenhower decided that the cause of party unity was too important and agreed to have McCarthy ride with him.

How to handle the Wisconsin Senator remained Eisenhower's most nettlesome political problem during his first two years as President. As one of his assistants recalls, "No other issue split the White House staff so violently." Those staff members who had been active in the Citizens for Eisenhower clubs pressed the President constantly to crack down on McCarthy. Equally strong for doing nothing were those White House aides who had to deal regularly with Republicans in Congress.

Confronted with this division within his own official family and a threatened split in the Republican party, Eisenhower did pretty much what any "practical" politician would be expected to do—he let the matter drift, assuring the more ardent anti-McCarthy members of his staff that "given time these things take care of themselves."

How wise Eisenhower was will be debated heatedly, depending on how people feel about the Wisconsin Senator. A later chapter deals with some of the deeper implications of McCarthyism. In the frame of this examination of Eisenhower as a politican, however, it is worth noting that his refusal to tangle openly with McCarthy was completely in character with his handling of the "tough ones" while in the Army.

"He will make decisions if he has to," explained one wartime aide. "But he prefers to case a problem from every angle before acting. If he doesn't like any of the proposed solutions, he can let something drag for months. He used to drive some of us crazy with his slowness in making up his mind."

Nor, in line with good military tactics, is Eisenhower given to frontal assaults upon people he disagrees with. If a Cabinet member takes a position the President dislikes, Eisenhower rarely rebukes him openly. After the Cabinet meeting however, the outspoken member may be talked to by Sherman Adams, the President's chief of staff, by Nixon or by some other Presidential assistant.

One aide who has watched this "softening up" technique employed repeatedly attributes the tactic to the fact that "Eisenhower likes people and tries not to hurt anyone." But others in the White House say quite bluntly, "The President is as skilled a maneuverer as the Army has produced."

Certainly it can hardly be coincidence that while Eisenhower is popularly pictured as the grinning image of goodwill, his staff chiefs—both Bedell Smith and Sherman Adams—have been portrayed as ogres of toughness.

The third key to Eisenhower's political effectiveness will be found in a strong sense of organization. In politics an "organization man" usually is someone who has worked himself up from lowly precinct levels and who has learned to vote a straight ticket almost as a religion. Eisenhower's own party affiliations were sufficiently nebulous for many Democrats, including President Truman, to want to run him for the Presidency. Being a general, though, Eisenhower regards it as axiomatic that no commander can function without a supporting organization. As a result, he probably has been more co-operative with Republican leaders on organization matters than any previous President.

Eisenhower has invited Leonard Hall to at least one Cabinet meeting to discuss the importance of patronage for the future of the Republican party. Beyond insisting that persons nominated to the posts be qualified, Eisenhower generally has gone along with the patronage requests of Hall and Sherman Adams.

At first Eisenhower's knowledge of organization politics was so slight he was only dimly aware of what a precinct captain was. But Eisenhower is a quick learner, particularly in picking up the lingo of anything that interests him. Not long after becoming President he surprised the businessmen attending one stag dinner by asking, "How many of you here can tell me what precinct you vote in?"

None of his guests could, of course. Eisenhower then confessed, "I was just like you," and launched into a lecture on how important it was for businessmen to interest themselves in the grubbiest details of political organization.

Not until after the 1954 elections, however, did he acquire an all-out zeal for revitalizing the Republican organization. Some of those close to him interpreted this as indicating he had decided to run for a second term. Others thought he wanted to build a strong enough organization so the Republicans could win without him.

Whatever the motivation, with characteristic intensity Eisenhower began demanding "a Republican party worker in every precinct in the country." Some veteran politicians tried to explain that no party has ever been able to recruit enough precinct workers to reach down to the last precinct. But the President brushed aside their objections impatiently. After one such session one aide walked out of the President's office muttering, "He thinks if the Army can be organized down to the smallest unit, a political party can be."

Told that a party chairman in some state was not too efficient, Eisenhower would retort, "Get rid of him. Get someone who will work." Since state chairmen are elected within the states, changing them is not quite so simple a matter. Still, by the summer of 1955 two-thirds of the forty-eight state chairmen were persons who had been named since Eisenhower became President.

At the 1952 Republican convention Senator Taft had the support of ninety-three of the 193 delegates from the Southern states. In nearly all these states Taft leaders no longer are in control. In Alabama, for example, the Taft leader was given a Federal post which, under the Hatch Act, disqualified him for political activity and opened the way for an Eisenhower man to move in. The 1956 convention will be recorded as the first public demonstration of how effective an organization steamroller the Eisenhower forces have fashioned.

The fourth ingredient in the distinctive Eisenhower political mixture is a remarkably acute sense of public relations. Here, as well, his Army training has served him well. At West Point the tactical textbooks emphasized that a good commander always visits his troops to inspire them to fight and Eisenhower has applied this lesson to Republican party workers. While stationed in the Philippines for three years, he also served as a ghostwriter for General Douglas MacArthur, who was not unaware of the political facts of life. Eisenhower was selected for the post of Supreme Commander in Europe by George Marshall, who liked his generals articulate and who, himself, was a shrewd publicist.

As Chief of Staff, for example, Marshall made it a rule never to appear before a Congressional committee or a press conference with a written statement—a tactic Eisenhower has often utilized. As Marshall liked to explain to the officers under him, "You lose much of the impact of conviction when you talk from a press release. A Chief of

Staff ought to know his business well enough to answer any questions a Congressman or newspaperman might ask."

But where MacArthur and Marshall were both quite formal in their approach to the public, Eisenhower is the epitome of informality. All his aides agree, "He has a natural gift for doing the right thing." During a tour of New Hampshire the Eisenhower party was having dinner at the home of Sinclair Weeks, the Secretary of Commerce. Weeks had planned on serving charcoal-broiled steaks, but the open-air fireplace would not draw properly.

Eisenhower, who delights in demonstrating his culinary ability, waved Weeks aside and, with the aid of a cook and another servant, fixed the fireplace and proceeded to broil steaks for everyone.

The next morning, as the Eisenhower party was about to drive off, the President ejaculated, "I forgot to say good-by to my friends in the kitchen!"

Jumping out of the car he dashed back into the kitchen to shake hands with the cook and servant who had helped him with the steaks.

Such warming gestures, invaluable in American politics, come spontaneously. Still Eisenhower has a lively appreciation of the value of his own personality. In discussing what moves people to vote he has remarked, not boastfully but as if stating an objective fact, "Think how many votes that 'I like Ike' slogan was worth to us."

The President has his grumpy days. Tom Stephens, his former secretary, noticed that on such days Eisenhower usually wore a brown suit, which led to these off days being referred to in the White House as his "brown suit mood." Basically, though, Eisenhower is an optimistic person. "I've never heard him say that something couldn't be done," recalls one aide. Eisenhower rarely misses an opportunity to try to infect those around him with this "nothing is impossible" feeling.

His heavy reliance on personal charm is also apparent in the impressive number of persons he has entertained in the White House. The guests at his stag dinners alone had passed the twelve-hundred mark by the summer of 1955. He had also lunched or breakfasted with nearly every member of Congress at least once and with some hundreds of Republican functionaries.

Eisenhower has developed the politician's knack of calling a person by his first name on a second meeting. He will refer to even slight acquaintances as "my friends." One person who watched Eisenhower at a gathering with Congressmen observed, "He's a great one for cottoning up to someone who's been giving him a little trouble. He'll do everything but embrace the man."

Some of his critics have tried to picture Eisenhower as being manipulated by Madison Avenue advertising agencies, citing such actions as his efforts to improve his television delivery by calling in screen star Robert Montgomery. But this charge misses the essential point, which is Eisenhower's complete readiness to use every kind of publicity appeal.

Once one of his aides remarked casually that the American people had never seen a Cabinet session in action. The next day Eisenhower had Jim Hagerty, his press secretary, working on the idea of televising the Cabinet.

Again, Eisenhower co-operated wholeheartedly with the effort to swing the 1954 elections by a last-hour appeal to ten Republicans to phone ten other Republicans in chain-letter fashion urging them to vote. The persons Eisenhower telephoned were selected with all the care of a TV give-away program. His mail for three weeks was gone through. The likeliest prospects among the letter writers then were interviewed personally to make certain they would publicize well. Through the whole telephoning stunt Eisenhower was as relaxed as if talking to old friends.

The many facets of Eisenhower's political character are not easily summed up. But the more important faculties are revealed perhaps in Eisenhower's oft-expressed admiration for Oliver Cromwell, who, as Eisenhower once told a G.O.P. pep rally, "sent his Roundheads into battle singing hymns and chopping off the heads of their foes." In his own approach to politics Eisenhower has managed to combine Cromwell's zeal to win and sense of a Heaven-bound mission with a keen sensitiveness to the psychological intangibles that make for good organization and effective public inspiration.

One further aspect of Eisenhower's evolution as a politician should be noted. Although the qualities we have cited were part of the man all along, it took him almost two years to learn how to apply them.

At the start of his administration some of his aides felt "he was frightened to death of politics." This fear apparently was transmitted to the White House staff. In those early months virtually everyone in the White House seemed to have two dominant concerns. One was to say nothing publicly—the President had made clear he would crack the military whip on possible "leaks." The other was to avoid stubbing their political toes, particularly in dealing with Congress.

One person who worked with some of Eisenhower's key aides at the time recalls, "I never heard anyone defend a proposal by saying it was the right thing to do. All the talk centered around what was politically smart."

This period of fumbling by "too many political cooks" tended to fade as the President's confidence in his own judgment grew. What impressed his staff most as they came to know him was his remarkable energy and intellectual curiosity. When a new problem arose he would press questions on even minor details with the avidity of a student cramming for an exam. Nor would he rely on his staff alone.

Through stag dinners and visitors he would search out other opinions. Often after such conversations his aides would get a note from the President demanding, "What about this?"

But the real turning point in his political growth seems to have come with the change in his relations with Congress. These hit bottom during the spring of 1954. In drafting his 1954 State of the Union message Eisenhower had put forward what he and his staff considered a "bold new" program of what the Republican party should stand for. He had called for a liberal foreign-trade program and continued foreign aid, a tax structure to stimulate consumer and business spending; also a four-year public housing program calling for thirty-five thousand units a year, liberalization of the social security system and the expansion of health insurance by guaranteeing private insurance companies against loss.

Instead of organizing to put through this program, however, the Republican leaders in Congress made the Bricker Amendment the first order of business. Then came the Army-McCarthy tangle. By spring the President's program seemed virtually forgotten. Pacing his office angrily, Eisenhower would demand of his aides, "What does the Republican party want to do—commit suicide?"

As the 1954 election drew near, however, many of the Republicans in Congress were reminded that they would need Eisenhower's support in the campaign. Congressmen and Senators began drifting into the White House to have their pictures taken with the President.

Politicians are like women in that nothing improves their morale more than a little courtship. With a sense of his own political appeal quickened, Eisenhower's spirits perked up. Then came the cheering evidence that the famed Eisenhower "luck" was still working.

Instead of being weakened by the Democrats' winning

control of Congress in the 1954 election, Eisenhower found his own position strengthened. Freed of having to rely on the so-called "right wing" of his own party for legislative support, he acquired a new maneuverability. The closeness of the 1954 election also convinced him that the public supported his "middle of the road" program.

By the spring of 1955, as one assistant recalls, "the President was feeling that he was a hell of a good politician." Not long before his heart attack, in talking with friends he remarked, "I know what the people want and my program gives it to them."

2. *"Blood Money" and Apples*

During the French Revolution a foreign ambassador was lunching with one of the Revolution's leaders when a mob came tearing by. Leaping to his feet, the leader hastily excused himself. "I must catch up with that mob," he explained. "I am their leader."

That legendary anecodote is worth bearing in mind in any appraisal of the Eisenhower administration. Eisenhower was elected in 1952 to fill a deeply felt need for leadership. Many persons saw him, in the words of one elderly widow in Jacksonville, as "the man God always sends this country in time of need." Some cynically sophisticated observers credited his victory to a Freudian yearning for a "father image."

But if the Eisenhower landslide reflected a widespread desire for a hero who would hoist a standard and proclaim, "Follow me," that is not what Eisenhower has done. On the contrary the essential quality of his leadership has lain in the skill with which he has followed the public mood. Like our French mob leader, he has led the people by moving in the direction toward which they were already inclined.

Such a pattern fits neatly, of course, with Eisenhower's own belief in the warmth of conciliation. Early in his Presidency, when many commentators were urging him to get rough with Congress, he would protest to intimates, "Some people think that to be a leader you must pound on your desk and show people who is boss. But that's not my way of working."

But perhaps more important than personality has been one impersonal fact—an acute consciousness, shared by the whole White House staff, that the G.O.P. still is the minority party in the country.

To friends Eisenhower has repeatedly voiced his determination to do everything possible to restore the Republicans to their old position as the majority party. Eisenhower has done things which he knew would cost the Republicans votes, as with his veto of the pay increase for postal workers. Still, few administrations have given more thorough attention to the political effects of their actions or have been more zealous in courting the public.

Perhaps the best evidence supporting this conclusion will be found in the faithfulness with which Eisenhower's more important policies have reflected the desires of the electorate. One can turn back to the 1952 election and find, in what people said and felt as they voted for Eisenhower, a virtual outline of what later became the Eisenhower policies. What is more, the conflict which tore at the emotions of the voters in 1952 still defines the choices between which people's voting is being pulled today.

During the whole campaign I traveled through the country, covering thirty cities and seventeen rural counties, asking persons of every description whom they were going to vote for and why. From my first day of interviewing to election day there was no basic change in the mood of the country.

Everywhere I found only one issue was helping the Democrats—the memory of the depression. Twenty years had passed since the depression low. Yet the fear of a return to "those Hoover times" still dominated the thinking of millions of voters. Repeatedly people said in effect, "There are lots of things I don't like about the Democrats but I remember those soup lines."

In Cleveland one worker declared bluntly, "The Truman administration stinks! They put people in jail for stealing a loaf of bread and look what they get away with in Washington. But," he went on, "I don't know how to vote. I went six years without a job in the last depression. I think another bust is coming. I'm afraid of the Republicans. I don't know what they would do."

In Miami a young widow sat down on the front steps of her house, apparently happy to be able to air her troubled feelings. "It would be a crime to continue the Democrats in power," she said, "but I remember the depression. We were living in Cleveland then. Father was on WPA. Mother had to go to work. It almost broke up their marriage. It was terrible."

On the Republican side a number of issues were winning them votes, from charges of Communism and corruption in government to Eisenhower's personality and a sheer weariness over the Democrats' having been in power so long. But the angriest condemnations of the Truman administration from traditionally Democratic voters were provoked by the grievances that rose out of the Korean War—higher taxes and higher prices and the drafting of "our sons" for "a useless war."

Typical of the economic complaints were comments like these:

"I figure Eisenhower will throw those grafters out and that way cut taxes."

"These price rises are eating me up."

A gray-haired widow in a poor district of Los Angeles protested, "I've had enough giveaway government. They say we've never had it better. How can you be better off if your savings are cut in half?"

Even more vehement were the outbursts of parents whose sons had been drafted. From the Korean outbreak to election day more than one million youths were drafted and nearly one million more Reservists and National Guardsmen were called back into active duty. Most of the families affected were bitterly resentful.

A construction worker in Manhattan turned up the palms of his hands as he exclaimed, "I'm a laborer. I work with my hands. But the Democrats have sold Christian civilization down the sewer! My son is missing in Korea. There was no reason for that war!"

To anyone interested in human psychology it was fascinating to watch how these two sets of emotions—the dread of another economic depression and the frustrations over the seemingly endless stalemate in Korea—came to grips with one another. Like two powerful wrestlers they grappled in the arena that was the voter's mind. When the struggle was over the back of the Democratic political power in the country had been broken.

"No one shoots Santa Claus," runs the old political adage. Yet what happened was that surprising numbers of voters came to resent the prevailing prosperity as being "bought by the lives of our boys in Korea." The feeling was general that the Korean War was all that stood in the way of an economic recession. From accepting that belief, many persons moved on emotionally to where they felt something immoral and guilt-laden in the "you never had it better" argument of the Democrats.

In Weatherford, Texas, one farmer told me this revealing incident. Near the campaign's end several elderly pensioners were discussing politics in the public square. One or two talked of voting for Eisenhower. A Stevenson supporter stopped to argue, "If the Republicans win, they'll cut your pensions. You'll all be selling apples again."

Retorted one pensioner, "Maybe so, but at least it won't be a bloody apple."

The same grim phrase "blood money" was used by voters in Texas and Iowa, Detroit and Los Angeles. To many voters, in fact, the election actually became a choice of voting for war or hard times. The fact that both world wars were fought under Democratic Presidents caused many people to feel "the Democrats always get us into war," while the memory of the 1930's linked the Republicans emotionally with hard times.

Near Dyersville, Iowa, I called on George Recker, a prosperous farmer. I found I had stumbled into a small family reunion. Recker's oldest boy, still in uniform, had just been discharged from the Army and his relatives and in-laws had come to welcome him back.

The elder Recker was sitting on the porch alone in a rocker with a pillow behind his head. Asked how he felt about the election, he replied angrily, "It's all right having all this prosperity but the price is too high."

Leading me into the living room, Recker told his son, "Show the man your legs." The boy, who had been in Korea, lifted his trousers, baring an ugly black scar on each leg.

"For a time we didn't know whether he would walk again," interjected Mrs. Recker.

"My other boy has also been wounded!" Recker stormed. "It's not worth it. Why can't we have good times without wars? If this is the price we have to pay for prosperity, I'd rather have hard times."

During the last weeks of the campaign, to fight down the effects of Korea the Democrats drummed hard on the dread of another bust. The responses given me after the election indicated this "scare" drive may have boomeranged.

One Texas farm wife had been undecided until three

days before voting. She felt Stevenson "made better speeches" and "was even the smarter man." What finally swung her to Eisenhower was the depression talk. "I was through the last one and know how bad it was," she recalled. "But my nineteen-year-old boy is going into the Army soon. The Democrats seemed to be saying prosperity was more important than the life of my boy."

Many families with sons in the service or nearing draft age actually felt they were being tested before God as to which they valued more highly—dollars or lives. Some feared their loved ones might be struck down if they made the callous, materialistic choice which to them seemed implied in the Democratic campaigning.

But if many persons who voted for Eisenhower wanted only to see the Korean War ended, others were prepared to go to war with Russia. Early in the summer the voters I interviewed divided about evenly over having "a military man" as President, with many fearing Eisenhower because "war is the only business he knows." But as hopes for a ceasefire in Korea waned the sentiment in favor of a general as President grew stronger. In mid-August, for example, Fred Myers, of Houston, Texas, with two draft-age sons, felt, "If the war is settled by November, I'll be for Stevenson. If not it's Ike. If we can't get a truce I figure we'll need a military man around to clean things up."

Throughout the country the predominant feeling was one of impatience with "a war that's getting nowhere." In Kansas City, Clarence Melton, a Truman voter who shifted for Eisenhower, expressed the sentiment I heard more often than any other.

"I'm against this idea that we can go on trading hills in Korea indefinitely," he declared. "My boy is in the Air Force. Naturally I'd like peace. But if it's a war that we're in let's fight it with everything we've got. If it's not a war, let's get out of there."

The mood of the electorate, in sum, was one of mixed frustrations. Mingled with a natural desire for peace was a deep sense of guilt over "war prosperity" and a resentment, as expressed by one soldier stationed at Columbus, Georgia, that "no one is paying any attention to the men fighting in Korea."

Not a person interviewed credited Russia with any desire for peace. The general expectation, in fact, was that Korea would be followed by other aggressions. If a peaceful settlement was the first preference of the public, then all-out war was their next best choice. But the one thing the voters generally were agreed on was that they did not want to pay heavy taxes and have their sons drafted for a "police action" that "isn't getting anywhere."

As mandates go this one obviously was shot through with its own contradictions. Still, the Eisenhower administration managed to make it the basis of our foreign policy.

3. Strategy by Public Opinion

It had been biting cold in Korea and the warm sun at Guam was a relief. Eisenhower had not been aboard the cruiser *Helena* long before he changed into a gray sport shirt and tropical slacks. Relieved of the pressure of time and wearied from three days of hopping around the Korean battlefront, he spent most of the first two days at sea sleeping and reading Westerns.

At Wake Island, some of his key aides and newly named Cabinet boarded the ship. As they clambered aboard, each man was introduced to the President's systematic nature by being handed a mimeographed sheet listing the appointments and conferences the President-elect had scheduled for the three-day run to Honolulu.

The cruise soon turned into a kind of floating "bull session." In Korea, Eisenhower had listened to General James Van Fleet argue vehemently for a summer offensive. The

President sympathized with the general's anger at not being allowed to bomb behind the Yalu River. Several times during the talks on the *Helena* Eisenhower exploded, "Why it's elementary military tactics that you chase a plane to where it comes from even if you cross a border!"

But Eisenhower was reluctant to light anew the flames of a war that had been smoldering so long.

This still unsettled conflict in his mind was embedded in his first State of the Union message. The speech bristled with phrases which appeared to promise tougher action— the order to the Seventh Fleet "unleashing" Chiang Kai-shek and the hint of a blockade of Red China, the reference to liberating the countries of Eastern Europe, the announced goal of a "new, positive" foreign policy which would end the "posture of paralyzed tension" in which the free world found itself.

But these hints of stronger action were contradicted by other passages in the message which promised a quick end to all mobilization controls and which declared "the first order of business is the elimination of the annual deficit . . . and to ease taxes."

Actually the President was gambling that a truce would be reached in Korea without further armed action. A number of warnings were being conveyed to the Chinese, including the conspicuous shipment of atomic material to Okinawa, that if no truce was forthcoming, we would take stern measures. Whether it was because of these warnings or Stalin's death, the truce was reached.

Had this gamble failed, as Secretary of State John Foster Dulles has conceded, the administration would have had to "retrace its steps." Instead of being reduced, military expenditures probably would have had to be increased. Sterner military measures would also have required reimposing the mobilization controls which Eisenhower had dropped as evidence of his faith in a free economy.

The whole course of the Eisenhower administration flowed out of this initial decision to seek lower taxes and a lessened military program. What this State of the Union message boiled down to was that we had set out to have a tougher foreign policy at less cost in taxes and without the use of American manpower. Those objectives sound contradictory but, as we have seen, they were the contradictions people had voted for in electing Eisenhower.

These contradictions were bridged by the doctrine of "massive retaliation." When this "new strategic look," with its prime reliance on atomic weapons, first was set forth, quite a furor was kicked up. In allied countries fears were voiced that we might commit other countries to an atomic war. Many Americans felt it immoral or unwise to threaten atomic warfare.

What has largely been overlooked in the discussion of this new strategy is how closely it corresponds to the impatient demand expressed by so many voters during the election—"Let's fight the war in Korea all-out or pull out."

To the extent that public opinion was allowed to shape our military policy the popular reaction to Korea could be expected to have this effect:

First, if our armed forces were to be reduced to make possible tax cuts, ground troops would certainly be cut most drastically in favor of the military services which did not rely so heavily on drafting American boys.

Second, in any future crisis, our political leaders could be expected to be slow in taking military action but, once involved, to lash out with every weapon available.

The same dread that the American people might not support a prolonged attrition which would prompt our politicians to try to avoid involvement could be expected to spur them to get any war over with quickly once we were engaged.

In his conduct of the Korean War, President Truman

fought to preserve the concept of a limited war, in which atomic weapons would not be used. The political effect of the 1952 election was to repudiate that concept.

It may be argued that the public did not knowingly vote for a strategy of massive retaliation. Many persons may have thought that with the Korean War "out of our system" we would be able to pick up as if Korea had never happened. But the shaping of a nation's character does not proceed in such an obliging way.

Our first reaction to the invasion of South Korea was that it was a test of our determination to resist aggression. But the morning after election day we had shown that although we would fight against aggression there were also conditions under which we would not see the fight through. After that demonstration nothing could be quite the same again, since neither the enemy nor our own military planners would forget.

Two other factors which led to our reliance on massive retaliation should be noted. For some years, at least since he became Thomas E. Dewey's chief foreign-policy adviser, Secretary Dulles had been trying to bridge the conflicting views of the internationalist and isolationist wings of the Republican party. The favorite isolationist doctrine, of course, was the so-called "Fortress America" concept, which would have concentrated military spending on sea and air power, with little reliance on allies.

Dulles was too confirmed an internationalist to believe we could establish ourselves as an armed Gibraltar encircled by a hostile world. Besides, a spin of the globe would show that while the Soviets could strike directly at any part of the United States by crossing the polar regions, we could not reach the truly vital areas inside Russia except from bases outside this country.

Still, in his mind Dulles had revolved the concept of centering our primary deterrent power in this country, leaving the countries along Russia's borders to be guarded by smaller forces supplied by these nations themselves. Such a concept seemed to promise a reduction in our commitments abroad, particularly in ground troops.

The final push which led to this concept being adopted as the basis of our strategy was the driving insistence by Secretary of the Treasury George M. Humphrey upon a sharp cut in arms spending. If there were to be any sizable budget cuts we could not equip ourselves to fight in varied parts of the world with both atomic and pre-atomic weapons. Between the two the choice was made to rely primarily on nuclear weapons.

The chief risk in this new strategy was that in breaking with the concept of a limited, non-atomic war we might drift into a situation where our only choice would lie between no action and the use of nuclear weapons. And if that happened, would we actually use nuclear weapons in situations short of all-out war?

Something like this tormenting dilemma threatened to develop in Indo-China but military events moved too rapidly. For a time, some Pentagon strategists argued that the beleaguered French garrison at Dienbienphu could be saved by dropping a ring of atomic bursts around the city. But before any final decision was made, the Communist forces had moved in so close to the city that atomic weapons could no longer be used.

To a considerable degree as well, the choice of "no action or nuclear war" threatened in the crisis over the islands of Quemoy and Matsu, near Formosa. The islands could be defended relatively easily through nuclear weapons, but most of our allies objected to their use.

The essential weakness in the doctrine of massive retaliation, in short, is that while it may provide an adequate deterrent against all-out, full-scale world war it leaves in some doubt our ability to meet "small wars," of the kind which the Soviets have organized in several areas in recent years.

This weakness is pretty generally conceded in Washington. In fact, it was largely in these terms that the issue was debated in the National Security Council.

At one extreme, the most forceful spokesman for the "No more Koreas" viewpoint was Humphrey. Blunt and forceful, Humphrey minced no words in contending that "the United States has no business getting into little wars. If a situation comes up where our interests justify intervention, let's intervene decisively with all we have got—or stay out."

The most sharply opposed view was championed mainly by the Army, which bore the brunt of defense cuts. On his retirement as Army Chief of Staff, General Matthew Ridgway wrote Secretary of War Charles Wilson, warning that the "day of nuclear plenty" for Russia as well as the United States "draws nearer."

When that day comes, possibly between 1958 and 1962, Ridgway feared an atomic stalemate in which neither side would dare employ nuclear weapons for fear of retaliation. The Soviets might then seek to create situations where they could profit from their superiority in ground troops and conventional weapons. The Western allies, Ridgway argued, needed balanced forces capable of meeting any type of military threat.

Our actual "military posture," to use a favorite term of the Joint Chiefs of Staff, seems one of leaning between these extremes. Our arms budget provides for a sizable Marine force and enough Army divisions so we would not be powerless to deal with a "small war." Perhaps the best way of viewing the Humphrey-Ridgway difference is as a struggle over the direction in which we are moving. Generally speaking, as military spending is cut we move closer toward an "all or nothing" reliance on nuclear weapons.

This danger may be compounded by the effects of our

own example upon our allies. Each time we have cut our military effort, the Western European nations, all of whom are worse off economically than we, have reduced theirs.

When NATO first was set up in 1951, our European allies agreed to furnish forty-three divisions by 1954. Early in 1952, when Truman ordered a stretchout in our arming, NATO's arming was also slowed. Again in 1953, when Eisenhower cut the military budget, NATO's arming was slowed still further. Toward the end of 1955 the best available estimate was that another five years would be required to bring into being the minimum number of divisions which had originally been planned for 1954.

If this same pattern persists in the future, the whole of NATO could be lost.

To sum up, one way of visualizing both where we stand and the trial ahead is to fix in our minds what might be called the Eisenhower Balance. This label can be attached to the balance struck by Eisenhower between the risks of war and the many domestic pressures for reduced spending and lowered taxes.

Politically, that balance represents no small feat of conciliation. At their famous "Morningside Conference" during the 1952 campaign Eisenhower and Taft agreed on a goal of reducing expenditures to $70 billion in 1954 and to $60 billion the year after. During the fiscal year which ended in June of 1955 slightly more than $65 billion were spent. Eisenhower, in other words, has carried his party along with much lower reductions in military spending and foreign aid than many Republicans had hoped for.

Even at that, however, the Eisenhower Balance represented a considerable gamble that the cold war would slacken rather than intensify.

By training, of course, no President could have been better equipped to appreciate what was at stake in this gamble. But that only poses two questions which caption the whole of the Eisenhower Presidency and which will largely determine the place that history assigns to him:

First, did the times require that Eisenhower ask more of the American people?

Second, will the Eisenhower Balance be maintained in the years ahead?

After his landslide victory Eisenhower could have asked almost any sacrifice of the American people and they would have responded. A harsher burden would have meant sharper political frictions, perhaps even a loss of some of his popularity. As it was, his immense military prestige helped persuade many people to accept defense reductions that might otherwise have been opposed.

Did Eisenhower's military experience enable him to gamble shrewdly and wisely? Or did it lull the American people into an unfounded reassurance which they accepted all the more readily since it satisfied their desires for lower taxes and for keeping their sons at home?

Time—and the Russians—will decide whether the price of conciliation was too high.

The second question—whether the Eisenhower Balance will be held or upset—is one which the American people will answer. In fact, one might say that our political battling in the years ahead will revolve around this balance which Eisenhower struck, not only in defense and foreign aid but in all our other problems, from balancing the budget and maintaining the economic boom to farm subsidies and aid for education.

None of these problems have been finally resolved, of course, but in every case, as later chapters will show, Eisenhower has managed to impart to them a new quality—of transition through moderation.

Whoever is in the White House after 1956, whether Republican or Democrat, will have no choice but to continue with this search for a new middle-of-the-road conservatism.

Why that is the likely shape of things to come will be brought out more fully as we examine the raging struggle between moderation and extremism in the three crucial arenas of foreign policy, economic improvement and racial tolerance. Everywhere but in the South the moderate elements have gained the upper hand politically. Still, the more extreme elements are far from being beaten finally. If anything, one can expect them to return to the fight with even greater intensity after the 1956 election no matter who wins.

How much strength do the extremists still command? What could revive their waning power?

For some years the strongest single pressure for extremism has been the sense of disillusionment over foreign policy which so many Republicans have harbored for so long. It may help us to determine how much of this disillusionment still survives if we look at the relations of the United States and Great Britain through the two men who have made themselves the most controversial politicians in the two countries.

THREE

The Politics of Revenge

1. Birds of Ill Weather

The McCarthy-Army hearings had been running for six weeks when the Wisconsin Republican Convention met in Milwaukee. As the Senator walked onto the flood-lit platform one delegate started grinding a hand siren. Other delegates surged into the aisles in a clamorous parade behind a huge, gilt-framed picture of McCarthy labeled "For America." Earlier in the day an effort to read a "Joe Must Go" resolution had been drowned out. Now the convention roared its approval of a vote of confidence in McCarthy after hearing him vow he would persist as in the past "even if I leave a few scars on my own party."

A month earlier a more restrained meeting took place in a workmen's hall in South Wales. For fifty-five minutes the assembled trade unionists listened to Aneurin Bevan defend his splitting with the Labour party's leaders over German rearmament and Far Eastern policy. When Bevan finished, his listeners cheered a resolution honoring him for twenty-five years of service to his constituency.

In setting and audience these two meetings, four thousand miles apart, differed markedly. Yet they were dramatically linked. For of all the politicians in the English-speaking world, no two are more alike in temperament and historical significance or have careers more inextricably bound together than Joseph Raymond McCarthy and Aneurin Bevan.

That this rebellious pair should be defying their party leadership at the same time was no accident. Inherent in the type of politicians they are is the fact that they should rise and fall together. Nor does the failure of their bid for power lessen the importance of understanding their strange affinity. For each is an embodiment of those angry traits of disillusionment in his own country's makeup which, if ever let loose, could wreck the Anglo-American alliance which is the cornerstone of all hopes for peace.

In temperament and political tactics both men seem stamped out of the same "bad boy" mold. Each clearly belongs to the school which believes that the way to attract someone's attention is to poke a finger in his eye. Belligerent, vituperative and intemperate, the one thing neither appears capable of is restraint.

With Bevan, this extremism seems at least partial compensation for childhood frustrations. Through infancy and adolescence he stuttered badly. To cure himself he would go off onto a nearby hillside and orate aloud. His free-hitting vocabulary reflects the diligence with which he searched for words free of stumbling letters. Not until he was past twenty did he discover that the impediments in his speech vanished if his oratory was sufficiently passionate or caustic. To be calm and reasonable may be psychologically impossible for Bevan.

McCarthy's energies, as well, appear to have been wound into tensely coiled springs by youthful shyness. In the one-room Wisconsin schoolhouse which he attended, he sometimes found it so difficult to recite in class that he would run home to the comfort of his mother. Called upon to make his first public speech while in college, he mumbled a few words and fled panic-stricken from the stage. Characteristically, though, the next day he decided to join a debating society.

But it is when one looks beyond their tempestuous personalities to the impersonal backdrop of a world in crisis that the historic parallel between McCarthy and Bevan emerges. One then sees that each man stands for roughly equivalent forces in terms of American and British political life.

In essence, both men are politicians of revenge. Theirs are the voices of a wrathful, disillusioned past.

If their viewpoints seem to differ so drastically, as toward economics and Russia, it is because of the different forms that political vengeance takes in Britain and the United States. In Britain, the forces of disillusionment are primarily economic in origin, twisting up out of the obsolescences of an empire struggling to retain its competitive vigor and out of the impact of that struggle upon too rigid a class structure.

The vengeful streak in the American political makeup springs mainly from the vexations of our reluctant involvement in two world wars and, as we shall see, its impact upon our ethnic structure.

Uncompromising zealots, it is part of their avenging role that each man should see himself locked in mortal combat with a world-choking conspiracy. In Bevan's case, reflecting the nature of potential disillusionment in Britain, the devil to be exorcised is an economic one, with Britain being "sold out" by a Foreign Office which has made itself the hired tool of American capitalism.

With McCarthy, the serpent of all conspiratorial evil coils back to the alliance that brought us into World War II on the side of Britain and Russia. His villains are also nested in the agency handling foreign relations, the State Department, which is pictured as "betraying" America through either Communist sympathies or through being hoodwinked by our British ally.

Starting from such seemingly opposite views, in short, each man comes out at the same point of sullen rebellion against the role his country is playing in the world. That one should be so anti-British and the other so anti-American is inherent in the forces driving the two men, as is the fact that they should have seemed strongest politically when Anglo-American relations were so sorely strained by the Korean War.

In fact, if allowance is made for the different election calendars in the two countries, the coincidence in timing of their thrust for power is startling. It was when political tensions over Korea were touchiest, immediately after Truman's dismissal of MacArthur, that Bevan chose to declare open war on his own party by resigning from the Labour Cabinet. Less than two months later—while the Senate was still holding its hearings on MacArthur's dismissal—McCarthy made his extremist plunge with his "treason" attack on General Marshall.

The invasion of South Korea had forced the Western powers to rearm. For Britain this meant tightened economic pressure, and Bevan set about systematically to exploit the widespread feeling in his country that Britain was being asked to do too much. McCarthy, in turn, was equally energetic in trying to attract the grievances that rose out of the common resentment in this country that Britain was doing too little. Each man, in a sense, fished the waters the other troubled.

Although both men seem finally to have been defeated by their own excesses, what really overcame them was the triumph of moderation in their own countries. Once the

Korean War was settled, the frustrations and tensions which had nourished their political strength faded. When McCarthy chose the anniversary of Pearl Harbor to "apologize to the American people" for supporting Eisenhower, he had already been driven into the corner of defeat. Similarly, Bevan's open attack upon Clement Attlee the following spring was the desperate fling of a beaten man.

It is indicative of the self-destroying nature of disillusionment as a political force that each of these rebels set out cockily to remake his party in his own image only to find that he had to help defeat his party to survive politically.

McCarthy and Bevan, in short, are truly birds of a feather, but they are like those birds on sticks which children buy and which flutter and whirl when moved about but which are lifeless if no wind agitates them. The power demonstrated by "McCarthyism" and "Bevanism" was evidence far more of the force of the ill winds that bore the pair aloft than of the men themselves.

What is of enduring significance in the two men is not the zeal and energy with which they sought to make themselves the magnetic center for the many grievances that were astir in Britain and the United States during those years. An appeal to prevailing frustrations is the constant occupational role of politicians generally and is probably essential for the active workings of democracy. What is worth exploring, though, is the basic source of their animus —the hard core of the disillusionment they personify—and why its dynamics should propel each man to champion a form of "go it alone" isolationism which would upset the strategic balance in the world.

2. Britain's Unreconstructed Rebel

The dreary mining town of Tredegar in which Bevan was born lies in one of those ironically green valleys of South Wales of which Richard Llewellyn wrote so graphically, where the contrast between the verdant countryside and the gray slag heaps is a constantly bitter reminder of what was sacrificed to the industrial revolution.

Aneurin was the third or fourth of nine or ten children— his mother once confessed to Bevan's biographer that somewhere in the struggle to get along on a miner's pay she lost count of how many children there had been—only seven surviving. In the pressure of caring for this brood, Phoebe Bevan also forgot the knack of reading and writing. But neither she nor her husband, David, ever lost the drive to rise to something better.

In the Tredegar social scale, the Bevans were "respectable chapel" people in contrast to the "boozers," who dissipated their earnings in the pubs. Into the four-room stone-floored Bevan cottage, already cramped with nine sleepers, two bachelor uncles came to live. The added income they provided, with little increase in overhead, enabled the Bevans, when Aneurin was about nine, to buy their own home for the equivalent of about $600. This new home had a small garden and the only gas stove on the street.

As in all of the Welsh valleys, strikes flared intermittently —one, in 1910, breaking out the year Aneurin, then thirteen, went down into the pits. The people of Tredegar had also developed a tradition of almost socialist co-operation in meeting their problems. In the 1870's the Tredegar workers began their own health-insurance system—A. J. Cronin was one doctor later employed. They built their own temperance hall and movie house, hospital and a library, through which Bevan was introduced to books on socialism.

Still, if the sense of class conflict streaked through the seams and veins in every mining area, the waters of disillusionment did not really flood the pits until after World War I. Prior to the war the booming coal and steel industries of South Wales had drawn thousands of workers from other parts of Britain. During the war itself Tredegar was so prosperous the shops often stayed open till midnight on pay day.

Between 1920 and 1937, though, employment in the Welsh mines was slashed in half. Bevan, who had returned home after a stay at the London Labour College, went unemployed for eighteen months.

There were other experiences to serve as an apprenticeship for a future Minister of Welfare. He dug trenches and laid pipes on make-work relief projects; he led a march against the board administering the poor law; once he was refused relief because his sister was working. In 1925 his father died "in my arms," as Bevan later wrote, "choked to death by pneumoconiosis. No compensation was paid him by the mine owners; in those days it was not scheduled as an industrial disease under the Workman's Compensation Act."

Bevan's own family experiences were part of the community pattern. As a member of the town council, he once inspected a number of families on relief. So miserable was the plight of one family that Bevan left a half-pound note and, rushing out of the house, walked rapidly down the street. Stopping abruptly he turned to a companion and swore, "I'll make those——pay for that!"

Given this conditioning of class conflict it is not surprising that politics to Bevan should seem a ruthless struggle for power, or that he should feel that "socialism and more socialism" was the only solution to Britain's troubles.

But there was at least one crucial weakness in this dream of socialist castles in Spain. It assumed that Britain's economic crisis revolved around who owned her factories and how their profits were divided, when her problem was how to regain her competitive standing in world markets.

Who owned the means of production might have been decisive if Britain had command of all the raw materials, food and factories she needed for survival. But in achieving pre-eminence as the world's greatest trading power Britain made herself sorely vulnerable to imports for half of her food and most of her raw materials. More important than whether her industries were privately owned or nationalized was whether they had the competitive ability to gain access through trade to the food and materials Britain had to have.

The prolonged economic crisis which dragged on through Bevan's formative years—from 1920 through 1938 Britain never had less than a million unemployed and in four of those years as many as two million were jobless—reflected the heart-rending slowness with which Britain adjusted to the emerging industrialization of Germany, the United States, Japan and other countries.

What needed to be done can be seen in the economic recovery Britain has achieved since the end of World War II. The outstanding feature of that recovery has been the *new* exports that have been developed, like automobiles, pharmaceuticals, aircraft and machinery products, in place of coal and textiles on which Britain's trade supremacy originally rested.

Through the 1920's, however, the development of new industries went forward with mangling slowness. As late as 1929 coal and textiles still accounted for 40 per cent of all of Britain's exports, compared to 17 per cent in 1954. What new industries were developed were established mainly in other parts of Britain and failed to ease the plight of the older industrial areas like Wales.

There really were two Englands, as W. H. B. Court has described them, "the spreading suburbs of the prosperous centres of the new industrialism, and the disorder, the dirt and the gloom of the dying sections of the old."

This failure to make the necessary adjustments to a changing world was largely a failure of government. Under the laissez-faire tradition then in vogue, governments were not considered responsible for reorganizing a nation's productive efforts to bring it into balance with new competitive needs. These adjustments were supposed to be left to the workings of free competition.

The net effect was virtual economic civil war inside Britain.

The war was fought most bitterly, of course, in the areas of sorest vulnerability to sharpened world competition—the textile areas and coalfields. One government study showed that in 1925 three-fourths of Britain's coal was being mined at a loss. After the bitter 1926 mine strike wages were reduced and hours were lengthened. But Britain's basic competitive position was not improved and the hatred left behind has remained a drain on her unity.

On one postwar trip to England I interviewed some miner families to learn why they would not let their sons be miners even though the mines had been nationalized.

One woman replied, "I was carrying my baby all through the seven months of the 1926 strike. I swore if it were a boy I would kill him rather than let him go down into the pits."

Bevan can perhaps be understood best as the unreconstructed rebel of that civil war. That, as well, is the source of both his strength and weakness as a politician. To the extent that socialism provided a form of direction which would help Britain adjust to her altered trade position in the world it was a more realistic philosophy than the drift of laissez faire. But socialism tended to defeat itself when it became an attempt to avoid the need for adjusting to world competition. And it was precisely this flaw in the character of British socialism—*the inability to see Britain's interest in world affairs*—that dominated Bevan's own outlook.

When, for example, Mussolini invaded Ethiopia in 1935 Bevan argued against imposing economic sanctions upon

Italy, contending that Britain's policy was that of the successful burglar turned householder who wants a strong police force. "If I am going to ask any worker to shed his blood," declared Bevan, "it will not be for medieval Abyssinia or for Fascist Italy, but for the making of a better social system in this country."

Again, when the Spanish Civil War broke out, Bevan and Jennie Lee, his wife, both ardent disciples of the Popular Front, fought against the embargo on arms sent to the Spanish Loyalist Government. When the news of Hitler's invasion of Poland came over the radio, Bevan and his wife celebrated by playing some old phonograph records of the marching songs of the Spanish Republican Army. As his wife later wrote, "Now we may listen to them again. We need not be ashamed. . . . Our enemy Hitler has become the national enemy."

And yet, five months earlier, when the Chamberlain government had introduced conscription as a tardy offset to Hitler's armies, Bevan had declared in Parliament, "We have lost, and Hitler has won. He has deprived us of a very important English institution—voluntary service. . . ."

Bevan's friends usually have explained his opposition to arming against aggression as a typically Marxist attempt to draw a distinction between "a worker's" and "a capitalist's war." But this picture of Bevan as a slave to Marxist convictions doesn't hold up.

In his book, *In Place of Fear*, Bevan admits that what attracted him to Marxism was its usefulness as a weapon in arming the working class against the upper class. To Bevan, socialism has always been a means of blinding himself to those realities in the outside world which, if he admitted their existence, might have interfered with the war of domestic retribution he was fighting.

Certainly, this escapism is the key to Bevan's anti-Americanism and is the shadow of significance he casts into the future. The cold war, as we have noted, has forced every nation to strike a new balance between home and foreign needs. In Britain this balancing ordeal is most agonizing in the perpetual economic crisis it has brought.

A whole host of factors has made balancing Britain's domestic and foreign economic needs more difficult than at any time in her history—an extreme dependence on imports, the loss of investments during the war which necessitates a prodigious export effort, the loss of parts of her trade empire, the sharpened technological competition of other nations, the cold war itself, in the resources it takes for defense.

Essentially Bevanism reduces itself to proposing that these economic strains be eased by turning Britain's back on the risks of war. When, as during the Korean War, Bevan minimized the danger from Russia and pictured the United States as the source of international tension it was not because he really believed such nonsense. He had to deny the existence of a real threat of aggression to justify his insistence that domestic welfare objectives be given priority over defense.

A high degree of calculated shrewdness entered into his effort to make himself appear as simultaneously the chief critic of the United States and the champion of greater welfare benefits for the British people. At the 1952 Labour party conference Bevan drew considerable applause when he pictured the United States as being "hagridden by two fears: the fear of war and the fear of unemployment." In that speech, Bevan was also laying bare the flesh and bones of his own political reasoning. Privately he explained to friends that a bust or war had to come, and he was maneuvering to be able to profit from either event.

Bevan lost his gamble, of course. His maneuverings support the judgment that to him Marxism has become more of a political tool than an ideology.

This distinction is important in focusing on the real threat to Anglo-American unity. It does not lie in a more embittered class conflict inside of Britain. Internal class antagonisms are being moderated steadily and nothing like the bitterness of Bevan's youth now exists. The main danger comes from the adjustments forced upon Britain to maintain her position as a competitive state. As long as these adjustments go tolerably well, Bevan has little political future. He can come to power only if domestic economic disillusionment deepens sufficiently so that sheer escapism could sweep Britain.

Currently the danger of Bevanism is not that it will dominate the British political scene but that it will remain a dragging burden on Britain's unity for some years to come. Nor should this be attributed to Bevan personally. The character of nations like the character of individuals is shaped by their experiences. The trauma of the 1920's and the depression left a flaw in the British character, which to this day limits the economic pressure that Britain can stand.

But if the bitterness of those days still burns in British memories, time has brought some healing of the old scars. When the Conservatives returned to power in 1951, they were wise enough not to try to go back to the laissez faire of the 1920's—had they done so they would be through politically today. Instead they continued the processes of readjusting Britain's economy to world conditions which Labour had begun. In doing so they helped push back into partial forgetfulness the dividing conflicts of Bevan's youth. What had once been a veritable civil war between two extremes—that of no government versus all government—is being changed to a contest over different means of governmental direction.

The diversification of Britain's industries is also building a base for renewed economic courage. In Tredegar, today, for example, four new factories relieve the old dependence on coal. During the 1955 campaign Bevan made his usual talk on the hill between Ebbw Vale and Tredegar which was a favorite rallying point during the depression.

"It was here we held our demonstrations," Bevan reminded his listeners, "when I marched with you during the dark days. Let us not forget that the better times of now had to be struggled and fought for."

From his audience came cries of "Hear, hear." But if some persons in Tredegar remember "we'd all have starved if we hadn't grown our own cabbages and potatoes," a whole new generation is growing up to whom those "dark days" have no meaning.

The transition is far from completed. Setbacks are always possible. Still, enough change has taken place so it seems clear that Bevan symbolizes not the "wave of the future" but the receding tide of the past. This holds for McCarthy as well.

3. From La Follette to McCarthy

Few communities could differ more from Tredegar than Grand Chute, Wisconsin. Lying just north of Appleton, part of this rustic township has been swallowed into the city in recent years. But in 1908 when Joseph McCarthy was born there, Grand Chute was entirely rural, twenty-odd square miles of flat countryside, broken by scattered clumps of trees and clusters of farm buildings, a cemetery and nine one-room schoolhouses.

Outagamie County in which Grand Chute lies has been described as a "farmed-out stretch" of cut-over timberland. Still, its pink sandy loam was sufficiently fertile to reward hard labor with a comfortably rising living level. Joe's grandfather, Stephan, an Irish immigrant, had toiled for ten years on New York farms before saving enough money to buy his own land in Wisconsin. By 1911 two of his sons

were sufficiently well-to-do to have their biographies included in a history of the county.

The fact that Joe's father, Timothy, did not rate a biography might indicate he was less successful than his
brothers. However, he was able to improve his economic
status steadily. The first McCarthy children were born in a
crude, log-hewn house. By the time Joe came along
Timothy had built an eight-room, white clapboard house.
Joe and a younger brother, Howard, shared one room. In
later years the children had the use of a Dodge car for
their own pleasure.

Family friends have described Timothy as "a little man,
spare and reserved," and Joe's mother as "buxom and full of
steam." The example the frugal couple set their children
was one of devout Catholicism, strict discipline and driving
perseverance. Once while loading hay, according to a
neighbor's recollection, Joe had to lead a team of horses
through a ditch of water and a boot fell off. Instead of
stopping to pick up his boot Joe kept driving the team until
all the hay was in.

In short, while McCarthy's childhood was not one of
economic ease, he never experienced the grinding poverty
that Bevan underwent. For an understanding of McCarthy's political beliefs one must look at the cultural, rather
than economic life of Grand Chute.

Predominantly German, with a sprinkling of Irish and
Dutch families, Grand Chute was a clannish community.
The church and family were the centers of social life, with
many of the families interrelated. At the Underhill school
which Joe attended, there were eight children who bore the
McCarthy name; five Ruschers, five Hegners and three
Plamanns—these four family names accounted for all but
four of the twenty-five children at the school.

Many of the families had brought with them the Ba-
varian tradition of hereditary family farming—less than 10

per cent of the farms in the county were operated by tenants—and the feeling was widespread that too much education only made children unfit for farming. Joe himself quit school after the eighth grade, resuming his schooling in later years after he left home. In the early 1920's Outagamie County spent only $46 a year educating each child, the tenth lowest expenditure among Wisconsin's seventy-one counties.

Reflecting this cultural isolation, the politics of the community was that of a minority island in a hostile sea. Wisconsin in those years was staunchly Republican, of course. Grand Chute was as devoutly Democratic.

From 1860 through 1892, there was only one Presidential election in which Grand Chute failed to vote more than 60 per cent Democratic. The first Democratic candidate for President to lose the community was William Jennings Bryan, whose dry leanings and loose-money agitations alienated the thrifty Germans, but even he lost by only three votes.

This Democratic allegiance seems mainly to have been a religious and ethnic matter. During the 1840's when the heavy German and Irish migrations to this country were under way the Jacksonian Democrats befriended the immigrants while the Whigs, who were the antecedents of the Republicans, tended to play along with the nativistic Know-Nothing movement.

Lincoln made strenuous efforts to court "the German vote" in 1860. He was a part owner of a German-language newspaper and traveled about with a German dictionary in his bag. He scored some successes since the Germans did not like slavery. But after the Civil War, the periodic anti-Catholic and temperance agitations of Republican voting elements kept the bulk of the Germans and Irish in the Democratic party.

In Wisconsin the area of heaviest German-Catholic settlement, stretching from the northern shores of Lake Winnebago, south to Milwaukee, constituted the bulwark of Democratic strength. In all but four of the elections from 1862 until World War I, this eastern Wisconsin area sent a Democrat to Congress.

Today these same counties are among the strongest Republican areas in the whole state. Eight counties can be taken as typical of largely Catholic German-American voting—Outagamie, Calumet, Manitowoc, Kewaunee, Dodge, Ozaukee, Jefferson and Marathon. All were Democratic from 1864 through 1892, while two—Ozaukee and Calumet —did not even break against Bryan. In 1932 these counties voted 74 per cent Democratic compared to a state average of 67 per cent. By 1952, the Democratic vote in these counties had dropped to 32 per cent, appreciably below the state average of nearly 39 per cent.

So astonishing a shift, of more than 40 percentage points between 1932 and 1952, means a change in party loyalty of more than half the Democratic voters in these counties. It is in this startling political conversion that one will find the key to McCarthyism, both to the political forces he personifies and to why Eisenhower found them so difficult to deal with.

A simple election table tells much of the story:

Democratic Per Cent of Presidential Vote in Grand Chute

1912	58%	1936	68%	1948	45%
1920	31%	1940	43%	1952	23%
decline	27%		25%		22%

Three wars—the two world wars against Germany and to a lesser extent the Korean War—caused this angry political shift which took place in German-American communities all over the country. In Ohio, for example, nine heavily German counties had voted unbrokenly Democratic for

President from 1836 through 1916. Seven of the nine counties broke in 1920, returned to the Democratic fold, to break again in 1940. In 1948 these counties swung back to the Democrats again, providing the votes which enabled Truman to carry Ohio. In 1952 these counties gave Eisenhower two-thirds of their vote.

The far-reaching political significance of this change can be judged from the fact that as the second most numerous foreign stock in the country, the German-Americans constitute the balance of voting power in many states, particularly in the Midwest.

It would be a mistake to regard the reaction to these wars as evidence primarily of divided loyalty between Germany and this country. As we will see a bit later the dynamics of Americanism are much more complex. More to the point is the fact that just as the unemployment of the terrible twenties and thirties was like a virtual civil war in Tredegar, so World War I was an emotional civil war to the German-Americans. A few items from the Appleton newspapers show why the "loyalty" struggle of World War I burned so deeply into the ethnic consciousness of German-Americans.

A certain Appleton German with anarchist instincts today is suffering from bruises which he received yesterday afternoon when he attempted to expound his views regarding President Wilson and his policy to a number of men at the Potts-Wood Company plant on Pacific Street. This German started the argument by abusing the President and wound up by saying that his greatest desire was to be in a position where he could place a bomb under the President and blow him to kingdom come. His auditors stood his tirade until the climax and then the fireworks started. By the time it was over the German resembled nothing more than a pound of chopped beef and it was with considerable difficulty that he found his way home. He had little difficulty leaving the building, however, a couple of boots helping him on his way. [April 4, 1917]

Appleton people in habit of giving loud expressions to "anti-American talks" should take care since Federal agents are in city. [April 27, 1917]

John R——, 34, of K——, was overheard in a tavern exclaiming "the Kaiser is the man." He was arrested, charged with drunkenness, and given five days in jail. [April 23, 1918]

Another picture of the German Kaiser was taken from an Appleton home by police. [July 11, 1918]

To demonstrate its loyalty the local German-American Alliance sponsored a gigantic Americanism rally. At St. Joseph's, the principal German church in Appleton, a new flagpole was erected and conspicuously dedicated. But the pressure of the community forced the church to disband its organizations.

During the Fourth Liberty Loan Drive in 1918, when bond sales sagged, possibly because the war was over, some of Appleton's best citizens undertook to stimulate bond sales with a series of night raids. The "night riders" dragged one German farmer, still in his nightgown, out of the house, threw a rope around his neck, and yanked it hard. When the farmer's son grabbed a baseball bat and knocked two men down, the "night riders" left. But for some time after the farmer's neck showed the markings of the rope.

These rope burns probably would have been forgotten if there had been no second war against Germany. Although World War II brought no vigilante actions or open incidents, it scratched open old wounds. The political effect was virtually to destroy the Democratic party locally.

After World War I hatred of Wilson was so intense that Outagamie Democrats did not even put up a slate of candidates for the county offices, while Harding swept Grand Chute two to one. Two years later, when Senator Robert La Follete, who had opposed entering the war, ran for re-election, he got 96 per cent of Grand Chute's votes. In 1900 when La Follette first ran for Governor, he lost Grand Chute, while in 1904 he barely won with 53 per cent.

This change in La Follette's popularity took place in all the German counties. Prior to World War I, his worst showing had come among the German-Americans, while his main political strength had centered among the counties which were Scandinavian in background. Dane County, where he was born, was largely Norwegian, and "Fighting Bob" learned to speak some Norwegian. Having settled on poorer lands than the Germans, the Norwegian farmers also seemed quicker to protest against economic conditions. Their general cultural outlook seems to have been more liberal. When woman suffrage was put to a referendum in 1912, for example, the strongest Scandinavian counties voted 49 per cent in its favor, while the strongest German counties were only 25 per cent in its favor.

In waging his fight against the First World War La Follette won over the German-Americans to where, as the table below shows, he ran as strong among them as anywhere in the state.

La Follette Per Cent

Year	German Counties	Scandinavian Counties
1900 (Gov.)	53	72
1902 (Gov.)	46	66
1904 (Gov.)	47	69
1916 (Sen.)	59	73
1922 (Sen.)	85	86

Al Smith brought a good many of the German-American counties, along with Grand Chute, back to the Democratic party, while Roosevelt, in 1932, scored a record 71 per cent of Grand Chute's vote. After 1940, however, local Democratic officials could not even find enough persons who were willing to act as paid election judges.

That McCarthy should emerge as the spokesman for these resentments provides a revealing illustration of the curious dynamics of coalition politics in this country. McCarthy himself was only eight years old when World War I broke out and, of course, neither he nor his family suffered the indignities to which their German neighbors were subjected. In fact, the years in which McCarthy grew up were years of steady Democratic ascendancy.

When, as a young man, McCarthy's fancy lightly turned to thoughts of political love, he first registered as a Democrat. In 1936 he ran the Roosevelt Birthday Ball in Waupaca, where he had gone to begin his practice of law. Later that year when he moved to Shawano, another German-American community forty miles from Appleton, he became president of the Young Democratic Club. That fall he ran for District Attorney on the Democratic ticket but drew only 28 per cent of the vote to 22 per cent for the Republicans and 50 per cent for the La Follette Progressives.

Not until 1939 did McCarthy run for office again. This time he emerged as a Republican. What had happened to convert him politically?

Between 1936 and 1939 one election intervened, one of the more important votes of our generation. It was in the 1938 election that the anti-New Deal coalition first took shape in Congress. This was also the year in which the Progressive movement, which the elder La Follette had fathered, was torn apart. That coalition, as we have noted, was composed of two different streams of voters, of those drawn to La Follette by his fight for economic liberalism and those who were attracted by his opposition to the war. The New Deal and the rise of Hitler subjected this coalition to intolerable strains. While Roosevelt drew the economic liberals into the Democratic party—and this happened all through the Midwest—the German-Americans were tugged into the Republican fold in opposition to Roosevelt's foreign policy.

Many people have wondered how McCarthy could represent the same state which backed La Follette for more than a quarter of a century in a reformist crusade that made Wisconsin the symbol of everything progressive in American political life. The explanation is that there were two sides to the La Follette heritage. When the 1938 election tore this heritage apart, McCarthy cast his political lot with the people among whom he had been born and lived his entire life—the German-Americans. In doing so he rejected La Follette's economic liberalism but fell heir to La Follette's role as the father of modern American isolationism and as a politician of revenge.

La Follette's desire for revenge, his admirers may contend, was largely a matter of principle. During the war he had been burned in effigy, threatened with expulsion from the Senate and had been the target of scores of hostile resolutions. Considering how bitter were these attacks, it was only human that he should have sought vindication when the war was over.

McCarthy's role as the politician of revenge, on the other hand, seems mainly a development of expediency. Despite the differences in personal motivations, however, the two men wound up espousing much the same viewpoint toward world affairs.

Each set out to turn himself into an avenger of "a war that had been fought in vain" and "a peace that was lost at the conference table." La Follette, in line with his leftist economic bias, blamed the First World War on a conspiracy of munitions makers and bankers. McCarthy, facing "right" economically, has tried to blame the Second World War on a "conspiracy" of Communists and New Dealers.

In his attack on General Marshall, who had been the architect of the defeat of Germany, McCarthy blamed

"America's Retreat from Victory" upon a "conspiracy on a scale so immense as to dwarf any previous such venture in the history of man. . . ."

La Follette's assault on the Treaty of Versailles was almost as indiscriminate—"a treaty that is without parallel in all history as a spoils-grabbing compact of greed and hate."

How far this passion for revenge blinded La Follette can be seen in his attack on the International Labor Organization. One of the earliest champions of labor legislation in the country, La Follette opposed the I.L.O. on the ground that it would have power to enact domestic legislation, despite the plain prohibition upon such power in the I.L.O. Charter. His argument against the I.L.O. parallels the accusations hurled today against UNESCO and other UN agencies.

Clearly, what gave both La Follette and McCarthy flame and substance was the prejudices and emotions of the people they represented. One can go into any German-American community in the country and find that a talk with typical residents becomes a virtual playback of Mc-Carthy's speeches. In all of these communities the belief is generally accepted that "the big mistake" of American foreign policy was "in getting into the two world wars." This sense of disillusionment is sharpened by the widespread feeling that we were "tricked into" both wars "against America's real interests." Usually people feel we were "hoodwinked by propaganda" but many persons are inclined to believe "there really may have been a conspiracy" at the bottom of it all.

In such communities the Democratic party is commonly assailed as "the party which can't stay out of war." One often runs into expressions of violent distrust of both Russia and England. In all of these communities one also finds a burning desire to vindicate their opposition to the last war. The way the peace has turned out is often cited as proof that "Germany and Russia should have been allowed to fight it out between themselves without our getting involved." McCarthy and his investigations are welcomed by many voters as proof that they knew all along who America's real enemies were.

To sum up, both Bevan and McCarthy have really been engaged in trying to rewrite history. Each has been driven by a burning sense of what should not have happened.

But it is important to note that their vendettas with history point to strikingly different sources of disillusionment and disunity.

The nature of Bevanism reveals that the problem of British unity is primarily economic. If Britain's cold war policy is ever fundamentally shaken, it will be because of the stresses and strains of the adjustments she is forced to make to remain a competitive state.

In the United States, McCarthy's career indicates, the main danger to our foreign policy is ethnic disunity. Our struggle with Russia is supposedly over our capitalistic system, but it is not on the economic front that we find the prime source of disillusionment over foreign policy.

Why should ethnic tensions be so critical an American weakness? What part have they played in Eisenhower's efforts to remake the Republican party?

FOUR

Remaking the Republican Party

1. The Dynamics of Americanism

In the spring of 1952 I tried a little experiment in fathoming the psychology of voting. I had long been interested in the Stuyvesant Town housing project because it comes close to being a cross-section of New York City's varied ethnic elements and because its vote tends to break almost even in Presidential elections. Learning that Louis Harris of the Elmo Roper organization lived there I asked him to bring together several neighbors for a political bull session.

Three of the persons he invited showed up: two were white-collar workers, while the third was a storekeeper.

Before they arrived, I had told Harris that, after learning how his neighbors intended to vote, I would ask one question which I thought would reveal why they felt as they did.

What was that question?

It was "How did you feel about the Civil War in Spain which Franco won?"

Almost fifteen years had passed since General Franco overthrew the Spanish Republican government. Yet the responses of the three men fell into a remarkably precise pattern.

The storekeeper, who had announced he "never" would vote Republican, felt "the Spanish Civil War was when World War II really started."

"It was the first test of Democracy against Fascism," he argued. "We should have helped the Loyalist government against Hitler and Mussolini, who were on Franco's side."

One of his two neighbors disagreed vehemently. To him the Spanish Civil War had been a struggle of atheism versus Christianity with Russia as the enemy. "We should never have recognized Russia," he contended. "It was a mistake to have gotten into the last war as an ally of Russia. I was born a Democrat but I'm voting Republican this time. I want Acheson and those Reds cleaned out of Washington."

The third man, who was not a native New Yorker, wavered between these extremes. He had sided with the Spanish Loyalist regime against Franco. He also felt that Russia had been a valuable ally during the war, though he distrusted her now. A staunch Roosevelt supporter, he was ready to vote for Eisenhower but "not for a Taft Republican."

The reactions of these three Stuyvesant Town residents is a fair indication of the extent to which nearly all of us are prisoners of the past in matters of foreign policy. Although we may not be conscious of it, much of our thinking on events abroad still is dominated by attitudes formed in the 1935–40 period when World War II was brewed.

Nor is it only the old "isolationists" who remain dug in behind the mental trenches of the Hitler decade. Consider, for example, the uproar that was kicked up over General MacArthur's views on how the Korean War should be fought.

The loss of much of Indo-China following the truce in Korea and the war threat that clouds the islands off Formosa indicate there was considerable strategic merit to Mac-Arthur's contention that the issue with Red China should have been fought through in Korea. A sizable part of the population, however, attacked—or supported—MacArthur less because of the strategic merits or faults of his views than because of how these people felt about Adolf Hitler.

As our Pacific commander during World War II, Mac-Arthur became a symbol of the strategy which proposed defeating Japan rather than Germany first. This "Asia First" strategy appealed to the old "isolationists" partly because it enabled them to give expression to their hostility to Russia. Also the ethnic elements which resisted entering a war against Germany and Italy preferred to focus upon Japan as the chief enemy. Opposing this strategy and its symbols were those who thought that Hitler was the prime enemy to be crushed.

By the time of Korea the whole world strategic situation had altered. Yet the "Europe First" and "Asia First" concepts, which took shape during World War II, remained the rallying slogans of many persons in the Korean controversy.

After World War I we acted in much the same way. From Warren Harding to Gerald Nye the debate over American foreign policy was dominated more by a vengeful desire to fix blame upon who and what had gotten us into World War I than upon what needed to be done to prevent a new war.

Why this curious American passion for refighting wars that are past?

That riddle is worth intensive study since it could compel us to revise much of our thinking about why the American people have had so much trouble adjusting to their changed world role.

Because in its youth the United States adopted a tradition of aloofness from Europe's wars, historians have written of "isolationism" as if it were a problem in immaturity. We have been pictured as slow to outgrow the attitudes which may have suited the "Young America" of a century or more ago but which can no longer be reconciled with our global interests.

But the tradition of revenge in American foreign policy did not appear until after World War I. Far from being a hangover of national adolescence, it has been a quite *modern* and *adult* manifestation.

The question arises whether the isolationism of our national youth has not been dead for a considerable time and whether what troubles us now is not something quite different, even if, at times, it comes costumed in the silken breeches of Washington's admonition against entangling alliances.

Significantly, this passion for refighting past wars has not always characterized the American temperament. We have been able to fight several wars—the highly unpopular conflict of 1812, the Mexican and Spanish-American Wars—and let them slide into history once they were over.

Only the Civil War and the two world wars have lain like indigestible lumps on the American stomach.

These three wars were long, bloody, costly affairs. But our diagnosis of McCarthyism points to another feature common to these struggles—each was something of a civil war to at least part of our population.

The conflicts which were easily assimilated into our historical bloodstream did not outrage any important ethnic element in the country. By contrast, the wars with Germany—as well as the Civil War—upset the ethnic balance in the country. Each of these three Armageddons left behind an element in the population whose feelings rendered them ripe for a politics of revenge.

If this analysis is sound, then the making of our foreign policy is not being obstructed, as is so widely believed, by a lack of public awareness of our responsibilities of world leadership. The essential difficulty is that our interventions in world affairs tend to drive some part of the population into revolt against the results of those policies.

If Senators like McCarthy, Jenner, Welker or Bridges try to discredit every form of international action, it is not because they believe we can live apart from the rest of the world. Primarily it is because their political appeal is aimed at those who are disillusioned by the failures or frustrations of our foreign policy. Perhaps we should stop calling such politicians "isolationists." A more meaningful and accurate term would be to describe them as the "disillusionists."

Ethnic tensions are not, of course, the sole source of this disillusionment. Later we will see why the structure of our parties aggravates this sense of disillusion and also how it has become a weapon of economic conflict as well. Still, there is no understanding American politics without a lively appreciation of the importance of ethnic influences.

My own studies of election returns since the Civil War indicate that *at all times* in our history ethnic tensions have been almost as important a voting force as sectional and economic conflicts. The successive immigrations to this country have made us a nation of divergent cultural streams, each with its own distinctive political flow, predispositions and even versions of history.

From the election maps one actually can trace the routes of settlement which each of these varied elements followed across the country. Whether in Michigan, Ohio, Iowa or Oregon, counties settled by New Englanders have held to an identical voting pattern for more than a century. The same persistence of voting habits can be seen in counties which were settled from the South or by some immigrant group. Often in these counties which have always swung together politically although hundreds of miles apart, one finds that the same family names dominate.

Particularly in recent years ethnic characteristics have shown a special sensitivity to foreign policy. In the 1940 election, for example, Roosevelt gained percentage-wise over 1936 among voters of Jewish, Polish and Yankee descent—all of whom had emotional ties with peoples Hitler was fighting. Roosevelt's heaviest losses came among voters of German, Italian or Irish ancestry, where there were strong resistances to a war with Germany and Italy on England's side.

It was not that the members of any of these ethnic groups voted as a "bloc" under instructions from leaders. People do indeed vote as individuals. But it is also true that no individual can avoid being influenced by his cultural conditioning. Just as income and occupation give shape to conflicting attitudes on economic issues, so ethnic characteristics can be viewed as the carrier traits through which agitations over foreign policy make themselves felt most dramatically.

These conflicts that are stirred by events abroad—to repeat—do not reflect divided patriotism between this country and ancestral homelands. Instances of genuine disloyalty are exceptional. The main problem, I believe, is one of assimilation and racial and religious tolerance here at home.

The strongest single force driving every immigrant group is the desire to be accepted as Americans. This drive is the key to their politics. Whatever helps—or hurts—the assimilation of the group will determine eventually its party allegiance. Until World War I this struggle for acceptance as Americans was primarily a domestic affair. Since 1914, though, the wars abroad and our own military involvement in those struggles have had a heavy impact in helping or hurting the assimilation of many ethnic elements. This is the prime reason why these groups react so strongly to events abroad.

During World War II, for example, in Hamilton County, Illinois, an elderly farmer with a German accent said something which a younger man near by interpreted as being pro-Hitler. The younger man knocked the farmer down. Such incidents may not make the newspapers but they are typical of the countless tensions that build up when the patriotism of any immigrant group becomes even remotely suspect.

The discriminations generated by such suspicions affect the descendants of these immigrant groups regardless of how they conduct themselves as individuals. To cite one example, the fact that so many Jewish names appeared as the targets of McCarthy's investigations undoubtedly led government agencies into an extra degree of screening of job applicants bearing Jewish names. Much the same thing must have happened with job applicants bearing German names in both world wars. One unavoidable effect of "loyalty" agitations, during or after war, is that they revive the unjust discriminations which immigrants generally suffer.

Since the impact of such discriminations is brutally intimate, it is not surprising that the political party which seems to champion their cause often wins a lifetime loyalty among these groups.

The emotional chain reaction set off by such discriminations also goes far to explain such surges of super-patriotism as those which followed both world wars. European writers have often joked about the fondness of Americans for considering themselves "more equal than anyone else." Because of our heritage of immigration, most of us are also under some compulsion to demonstrate that we are "more American than other Americans." It would almost seem that the more painful the frustrations endured by any immigrant group in its efforts to be Americanized, the more violent is its recoil of patriotism.

The Second World War, for example, served as a tremendous emotional release for ethnic groups such as the Polish-Americans and Jews. Hitler's invasion of Poland lifted everyone with a Polish name from the ranks of "poor Polacks" into the very forefront of the defenders of liberty. For Jews their age-old struggle against anti-Semitism became identical not only with the cause of Americanism, but with that of democracy and freedom all over the world.

Currently, the very fact that the patriotism of some groups was suspect during the war appears to strengthen their desire to seek vindication, with the war over, through demonstrations of super-patriotism.

Viewed in this emotional frame, one can also appreciate why the "red" issue exerts so powerful a political appeal among Catholics. Their religious teachings, of course, would tend to range Catholics in militant opposition to anything associated with Communism. In addition, the Communist issue is almost the first political cause which has given Catholics generally the chance to feel more American than other Americans. In the past, the social and economic status of Catholics was hurt by their religion. In terms of the cold war, however, Catholicism and the American struggle against Russia merge as one.

This change emerges dramatically if one contrasts the writings of two Catholic leaders, Bishop John Ireland, whose influence was so great roughly sixty years ago, and Francis Cardinal Spellman.

Ireland, whose jurisdiction embraced much of the Midwest, was constantly on the defensive. He preached temperance to refute the widely held belief that all Catholics liked whiskey; he voted Republican to challenge the stereotype that all Catholics were Democrats. Denouncing pacifism, he urged that Catholics prove themselves "the first patriots of the land." The one theme that dominated his writings was this need to show other Americans that Catholicism was not an alien force, hostile to American institutions.

In the postwar writings of Cardinal Spellman, though, one finds an untroubled identification of Catholicism and Americanism. In *What America Means to Me,* Spellman ends his eulogy of this country with a "land of loveliness which by the providence of Almighty God, is the last unfailing hope of embattled humanity struggling against the menace of atheistic Communism." In one revealing poem in this book Spellman urges the "Lord of Free Men's Souls" to:

> Grant that thy America may be a light
> Dispersing the shadows
> Of Darkness and doubt.

Later in the poem he continues:

> Our foes are thy foes
> They plot to destroy Thee
> They fight to fetter us.

Historians writing in the future may look back on the "treason" agitation of recent years as a manifestation of a nationalistic hysteria, which distracted and divided us at so critical a period. These historians should not overlook that much of the "loyalty" battle has really been a clash of conflicting ways of showing one's patriotism. It has been motivated largely by the drive to be accepted as Americans, which must turn out to be a unifying force in the long run.

The upsurge of anti-Western nationalism in Asia and Africa has prompted many writers and educators to stress the importance of the example of racial and religious tolerance which we set in this country. The truth is that a fuller measure of tolerance is needed not simply to influence world opinion but to achieve the domestic unity necessary for an effective foreign policy.

Unfortunately, while our political parties have often served to moderate our intolerances, they also help perpetuate them, as will be seen by examining the curious dilemma that confronts Richard Nixon.

2. The Nixon Dilemma

One of the odder features of the Eisenhower Presidency has been the fact that it has had a Vice President who was so much more controversial politically than Eisenhower himself.

During both the 1952 and 1954 campaigns, in my talks with voters, the comments voiced about Eisenhower were always good-humored. Hardly anyone questioned his sincerity. Even persons critical of his administration were more likely to blame the Republican party or the "people around him" than Eisenhower personally. Each section of the country seemed, in fact, to cherish its own favorite scapegoat, Sherman Adams in New England, Charles Wilson in Detroit, Ezra Benson in the farm belt.

When Nixon's name was brought up, though, it generally was with considerable vehemence—both by those who were for and those against him.

Characteristic comments ran:

"I don't think too much of Eisenhower but he'll get my vote because Nixon is running with him."

Or "I like Ike but I'm not taking a chance on Tricky Dick becoming president."

That Nixon could win the votes of persons who were cool to Eisenhower and alienate many who liked the President is all the more surprising when one considers how lightly we take our Vice-Presidents. Thomas Marshall, who was Woodrow Wilson's Vice-President, probably caught the prevailing attitude with his habit of calling out to Capitol visitors who peered into his office, "If you're not coming in, throw me a peanut."

What is the explanation of this Eisenhower-Nixon paradox?

Basically, it is that in the minds of many voters Nixon sharpens the very issue that Eisenhower has blurred. That fact, in turn, is one of the keys to the larger dilemma that Eisenhower has had to overcome in remaking the Republican party.

It was the "red" issue which first soared Nixon into the publicity firmament. On the surface this issue appears deceptively simple. Virtually everyone agrees that Communists should not be employed by the government. The controversy seems mainly over the procedures that should be employed in purging Washington of Soviet sympathizers.

But if differences over method were all that were at stake, the "red" issue would not be fought over so fiercely. Certainly, for example, Nixon's part in flushing out the perjury of Alger Hiss would not justify the bitterness of the "liberal" attack on Nixon.

Actually, only a small part of the "loyalty" battle has been over method. In my interviewing I find almost invariably that the angriest outbursts against Communists are voiced in areas where opposition to our entering World War II was strongest. Invariably as well, the loudest outcries against "McCarthyism" and "witch hunting" come from those who were most ardent for our intervention in that war.

In short, what makes the Communist issue so explosive politically is that it revives all the animosities and loyalties of the 1935–40 period, when the American people were debating so furiously among themselves whether Hitler's Germany or Stalin's Russia was our mortal foe. In the end, of course, Pearl Harbor forced the decision but long before that millions of Americans aligned themselves on one side or the other. And those who felt most strongly about the issue have been at political odds since.

Nor are ethnic emotions alone at stake. The long debate over our involvement in the war coincided with the period of fiercest agitation over the New Deal's domestic economic policies. Inevitably the two struggles merged. As a result, two conflicting chains of emotional symbols were left in people's minds—two streams of memories which even today are still like so many positive and negative particles of political energy. Any politician—or issue—who electrifies these memories causes them to polarize in antagonistic directions.

Since the same political magnetism which attracts one stream automatically repels the other, it is virtually impossible for someone to be a hero to one side and not something of a villain to the other.

Eisenhower has been insulated from this conflict by the fact that he is both a Republican and is identified in people's emotions with the war against Germany and Roosevelt's foreign policy. Nixon, though, was picked for the vice-presidential nomination largely in the belief that as "the man who put Alger Hiss in prison" he would help the G.O.P. dramatize the Communist-in-government issue.

It is as a symbol of that issue that Nixon has won for himself so loyal a following—and equally loyal an opposition.

The extent to which Nixon has become more symbol than flesh and bones to American voters was first impressed on me during the 1952 campaign when the news broke of his special expense fund. Both before and after Nixon's spectacular television defense, I spent several days interviewing people on how they felt about the fund.

What struck me most was how few persons cared whether corruption actually was involved. Most of the voters interviewed sided with or against Nixon on the basis of whether they sympathized with the purposes for which the fund was used.

As a forty-year-old musician in New York put it, "Nixon's expense fund doesn't bother me. All politicians have such funds. I'm against Nixon because he is a witch hunter."

Exemplifying the contrary view was the comment of a lawyer's wife: "I don't see anything wrong in what Nixon did. Anyone who has been doing as much as he has in fighting the Communists needs every help. More power to him."

Nixon, naturally, has sought to win public recognition as something more than a "red hunter" and, in that course has had White House backing. Even before his heart attack, Eisenhower, when out of Washington, had Nixon preside over the National Security Council and the Cabinet. Nixon made good-will tours on behalf of the President to both the Far East and Latin America. As chairman of the President's Committee seeking to reduce racial discrimination in employment, Nixon came into intimate contact with the most ardent advocates of civil rights.

But the effect of these activities has been undercut by the fact that Nixon has been the member of the Eisenhower "team" usually called upon when the White House sought to take the play away from McCarthy on the "Communist" issue. When McCarthy charged that Eisenhower was "soft" on Communists, Nixon was chosen to refute the accusation publicly. During the 1954 elections he was sent into New Jersey to counter the effects of McCarthy's attack on Clifford Case in his race for the Senate; it was Nixon who was used to play up the "red" issue in Colorado, Montana and Idaho.

Nixon's efforts to gain recognition for his non-Communist activities are, in many ways, a small-scale model of the problem which confronts the whole Republican party. Largely because the last three wars were fought under Democratic presidents the Republicans have won the support of nearly all of the disillusioned elements who opposed those wars. The Republican dilemma is how to keep the votes of this following, without becoming a prisoner of the disillusionment it harbors.

Usually this conflict is pictured as a clash of personalities, as if it could be resolved by reading McCarthy out of the party or by changing the views of Senator William Knowland, or Styles Bridges and others. What is generally overlooked is that every political party is shackled to its own following, and that no party can be remade much faster than the minds of its supporters.

As a result of the "twenty-year revolution" over which Roosevelt presided, each party acquired its own distinctive orbit of prejudices, reflecting the emotions and interests of the voters who were drawn to its banners. Within both parties today the struggle rages between those "die-hard" elements which would perpetuate these old prejudices and the moderate elements who are trying to break free of those symbols.

The "liberal" coalition of prejudices sought mainly to link support of the New Deal's economic measures with opposition to Hitlerism. The depression-born antipathy to business was sandpapered by the false charge that all business was "Fascistic," a misconception which was nourished by the fact that some Rhineland manufacturers financed the Nazi movement. The fact that Hitler suppressed the trade unions was linked with the rise of labor's power under Roosevelt and with progress in civil rights. Along with all this went some sympathy with Russia since, at least before the signing of the Nazi-Soviet pact in 1939, Russia was opposed to "Fascism."

On the "conservative" side, the effort was made to link all the resentments stirred by these "liberal" stereotypes into an opposing coalition of symbols. Almost from its inception the New Deal was assailed as a "socialistic" betrayal of the American Way of Life. The new power of labor, particularly of the C.I.O., was ascribed to "Communist" influence. Just as those who hated Hitler were ready to apply the adjective "Fascistic" to everything they disagreed with, those who were particularly hostile to Russia were inclined to label anything they disliked as "Communist."

After the outbreak of World War II, the expansion of government power necessary to win the war came to be condemned as a dictatorial projection of the earlier New Deal reforms and as the product of our wartime alliance with Russia. When the war ended, this chain of anti-Roosevelt symbols was linked emotionally with opposition to the UN, Red China's victory and "the lost peace."

The political importance of the conviction of Alger Hiss and the spy charges against Harry Dexter White lies in that they can be pointed to by the disillusionists as proof of their efforts to montage the New Deal and the war into "twenty years of treason." To those who still revere Roosevelt's memory, the Communist issue seems a red herring that is being used to discredit all "liberal" thought.

Any rational person could put together a thick book of factual evidence showing how unfounded were the stereotypes that went into both these "liberal" and "conservative" chains of prejudice. The links in both chains were truly hammered together by a process that can best be described as "guilt by association." Also, of course, all of these symbols were never accepted by all Democrats or all Republicans. Many liberals, for example, hated Russia and everything it stood for. Many anti-New Deal businessmen were ardent supporters of Roosevelt's foreign policy. Still, it was largely in terms of these prejudices that the Roosevelt and anti-Roosevelt coalitions took shape.

And it is in terms of these old symbols that the conflict within the Republican party over foreign policy can best be understood. One G.O.P. faction is dedicated to strengthening the coalition of disillusionment which was forged during the years of opposition to Roosevelt. Hence their constant efforts to extend the old anti-New Deal symbols into attacks on UNESCO, or to weaken the Presidency through the Bricker Amendment, or to impose a ceiling on the federal government's taxing powers, or to link all these causes with a new "states' rights" philosophy, as espoused by Clarence Manion.

But disillusionment is not the stuff of which responsible government is made. Keeping alive the anti-Roosevelt symbols also keeps alive the distrusts of Britain and other of our allies. It militates constantly against the management of a constructive foreign policy. If the Republican party is to regain its old status as the majority party in the country, the moderate Republicans feel the G.O.P. must break out of this old orbit of negativism and stand for a positive foreign policy.

Eisenhower, of course, has aimed at this latter effort and, as will be shown a bit later, he has made appreciable progress. But the claims of the past have been too strong to permit an overnight, revolutionary overhauling of the G.O.P.

Once in Houston when I asked a worker whom he favored for President he snapped back, "I haven't voted since they shot Huey Long. He was my man."

That may seem like a quaint reply but it also illustrates the almost unbelievable tenacity with which people cling to their political loyalties. The political force of such symbols as "Yalta" or "Big Business," or of names like MacArthur and Roosevelt, or of issues like the "Communists in government" lies in the fact that their mere incantation will touch off a whole chain reaction of emotional feeling. Nor is this any indication of a lack of intelligence on the part of voters. All voting is an emotional experience, for ditch diggers and professors alike. The strength of these symbols of the past reflects how deeply people were affected by the issues which evoked those symbols originally.

One dramatic case history can be seen in New York City's

voting. Nearly half of Gotham's population is Catholic, while another fourth is Jewish. Threatened as they were by Hitlerism, Jews generally were among the most ardent supporters of Roosevelt's foreign policy. Among Catholics, on the other hand, were many of the elements who were inclined to "isolationism" or who were most strongly opposed to Soviet Russia.

One would expect these conflicting feelings over foreign policy to be evident in voting for national offices. But the election returns show it has affected even the voting for municipal posts as well.

The two tables which follow rank the assembly districts in Brooklyn in the order of strength they showed in five elections, spanning the 1946–51 period. As Table 1 shows, the districts giving Eisenhower his highest percentages were those where Senator Irving Ives did best against Herbert Lehman in 1946 and where Vincent Impellitteri ran best for mayor in 1950. All but one of these eight districts are also among the eight Brooklyn districts which turned in the lowest vote for both Henry Wallace in 1948 and Rudolph Halley in his 1951 race for president of the City Council.

The second table shows where Eisenhower fared worst. All but two of the districts are also the poorest for both Ives and Impellitteri. All but two are among Wallace's and Halley's highest districts.

In ethnic makeup this second group of assembly districts is predominantly Jewish, while the group in Table One covers the most heavily Catholic areas in Brooklyn.

The remarkable consistency in voting for such varied candidates which is shown in these two tables explodes a number of widely shared illusions about the psychology of voting.

For example, there is the myth of the so-called "independent" voter. Both Halley and "Impy"—as Impellitteri

Ranking of Brooklyn Assembly Districts
Table One

Highest Districts			Lowest Districts	
1952	1946	1950	1948	1951
Eisen.	Ives	Impel.	Wallace	Halley
9	9	15	9	8
10	20	9	20	15
20	10	8	8	20
7	5	3	3	5
8	8	20	15	3
3	3	7	5	9
15	15	5	10	10
5	7	10	7	4

Ranking of Brooklyn Assembly Districts
Table Two

Lowest Districts			Highest Districts	
1952	1946	1950	1948	1951
Eisen.	Ives	Impel.	Wallace	Halley
24	23	23	23	2
23	24	24	24	24
17	19	2	19	23
2	2	18	2	19
19	16	19	18	18
18	18	16	16	21
16	14	11	13	16
14	4	4	11	1

came to be known—were elected on independent tickets in revolts against Tammany Hall. Most New Yorkers have assumed that the same "independent" voters elected both men. Although a few voting precincts can be found where both men ran strong, in the main Impy was strongest where Halley was weakest and vice versa.

Of the fourteen assembly districts in the whole city which Halley won by a clear majority in a three-way race, all but four fall among Impellitteri's lowest fourteen districts.

Clearly, two conflicting streams of insurgency were at work, one stemming primarily from Catholic voting elements, the other mainly from Jewish areas. The widely held image of the free-wheeling "independent" voter, who is above partisan emotions, fits neither group. The returns show that even when voters turn "independent," they do so within the pattern of their cultural conditioning.

This rule can be applied to all third-party elements in our history. All were insurgents within the particular voting orbit which was followed by the voting group to which they belonged.

Most people who type themselves as "independent" voters today really are part of some voting stream and they shift with that stream.

A second widely held belief that is challenged by these tables is that our party system is so managed from behind the scenes that voters get little opportunity to express their own will. In this case, however, in election after election, the Democratic leaders tried—but failed—to dam back the ethnic emotions dividing Catholics and Jews.

So much has been written about how our politicians manipulate the voters that it is often overlooked that the voters also manipulate their politicians. When people feel deeply enough about something they will attach those feelings to some candidate, often with little regard to whether the candidate shares these beliefs.

Going back into the election returns, one finds that this Catholic-Jewish hostility *first* shows up in 1936, when the Spanish Civil War was raging and Father Charles E. Coughlin tried to defeat Roosevelt by backing William Lemke on a third-party ticket. Since then some portion of New York City's Catholics and Jews have shifted their voting in mutual hostility to one another, regardless of who happened to be running. The one Democrat in recent years who has been able to win both groups was Mayor Robert A. Wagner, who is of German-Catholic descent but a strong New Dealer.

This case history of New York's voting undercuts still another widely held illusion— that Eisenhower's 1952 victory was primarily "a vote for the man." Certainly Eisenhower gained votes because of personal popularity. But the close parallel between his support and that of Ives indicates that the 1952 break among Democrats reflected a resurgence of many of the grievances of 1946. Of the eighteen New York assembly districts where Eisenhower gained more than 10 per cent over 1948, twelve show a difference of only 3 per cent or less from the Ives 1946 vote.

The extent to which Eisenhower's victory tapped the old "isolationist" well springs through the country can be seen in how he fared in areas where Lemke ran strongest and in how closely the Eisenhower vote matches Wendell Willkie's vote in 1940.

The thirty precincts in Ohio and Wisconsin which Lemke won in 1936 gave Truman 53 per cent of their vote in 1948. Stevenson sank to 30 per cent in 1952, which was not too different from the 25 per cent that Roosevelt pulled in 1940.

In the thirty-nine counties, outside of his own state of North Dakota, where Lemke drew at least 10 per cent of the vote, Eisenhower got 58 per cent to 44 per cent for the Republicans in 1948 and 54 per cent in 1940.

In 1948 Truman carried more than 250 counties which

Roosevelt had lost in 1940. Eisenhower won back all but 6. In many of these the 1952 election paralleled the 1940 voting precinct by precinct. Mercer County, Ohio, for example, shows 13 precincts which went for Willkie in 1940 and which swung for Truman in 1948. Willkie drew 63 per cent in these precincts, Eisenhower 65 per cent.

In Iowa, to cite just one more example, Al Smith won 500-odd precincts in 1928. These precincts reflected two main sources of Democratic strength, German-Americans, who were largely Catholic, and areas which had been settled from the South.

In 1940 these two voting streams divided sharply, with 175 of these precincts swinging Republican. Truman won back 130. In 1952 only 5 of these 130 precincts were won by Stevenson.

Since Eisenhower cracked the Democratic ranks all over the country, his election cannot be attributed to any single voting element. Still, it is something of an optical illusion to see his election as a victory for the internationalist viewpoint in foreign policy. Eisenhower's nomination, it is true, was engineered by the "internationalist" Republican wing, but some of his most spectacular gains came in areas which have been the strongest centers of isolationist sentiment in the past.

It is against this background of "isolationist" support that one must measure how much Eisenhower has accomplished in converting the Republican party to a new outlook in foreign policy.

3. Conversions Come Hard

Within the Republican Party, foreign policy might be said to play almost the same part that the civil rights issue does inside the Democratic party. The Democratic emphasis on civil rights grew out of Roosevelt's success in winning the support of Negroes and other elements sensitive to discrimination. The issue both won votes for the

Democrats and divided the party internally at the same time. This, of course, is precisely what the "isolationist" issue does with the Republicans.

The Democrats held power so long that the civil-rights cleavage became institutionalized, giving rise to what I have described as the "border state" politicians, who made a virtual profession out of conciliating the Northern and Southern wings of the party.

If the Republicans continue to hold the Presidency, they also can be expected to develop their equivalent of the "border state" brokers. Nixon, in fact, has exercised just that role. He can be described as perhaps the first of the mediating "broker Republicans" who sought to be the instrument through which both party wings could compromise.

He has performed this role consciously and skillfully. Along with William Rogers, the Deputy Attorney-General, Nixon was perhaps the strongest force urging Eisenhower to avoid an open break with McCarthy. On the other side, Nixon has done yeoman work on Capital Hill in tempering the opposition of all but the most extreme Republicans to some of Eisenhower's foreign-policy measures.

When such issues came up, Nixon's tactic would be to argue, "Maybe you don't agree with the President on foreign aid, but on the main issue of stopping the trend toward socialism, he's shown he's with you."

This tactic of weakening the extremes by "in-the-middle" compromise has harmonized with both Eisenhower's personal temperament and foreign policy.

In broad outline Eisenhower, of course, has followed pretty much the policies laid down by the Truman Administration. What is not so widely appreciated is that he also has moved closer to the viewpoint of the old "isolationists." The doctrine of "massive retaliation" is a sizable stride toward the reliance on sea and air power which Hoover and Taft sought to popularize. Also, while Eisenhower has avoided any drastic repudiation of our internationalist role, he has pointed American policy in the direction of "disengaging" ourselves from some of our commitments abroad.

Perhaps the fairest way of summing up the Eisenhower foreign policy would be to say that it reflects a "slow double turn." Eisenhower, himself, has turned somewhat to meet the "isolationist" viewpoint in the Republican party, while the disillusionists have turned somewhat more to meet him.

The net result is that the danger that a Republican victory would bring an abrupt reversal of our foreign policy has been averted, which is an important achievement. Whatever changes may be effected in our foreign policy in the future are likely to follow a slow, evolutionary pace, rather than any extremist somersault. What will not become clear for some years is how much more change the Republicans may continue to press for, even if in small steps.

Numerous evidences of this "slow double turn" can be cited. Perhaps the most marked single change is evident in the Republican attitude toward foreign aid.

When Harold Stassen appeared before a Senate committee to be confirmed as Foreign Overseas Administrator the first question shot at him by a ranking Republican was: "When are you going to end all this foreign aid?"

While Stassen was trying to reply, another Republican threw a second barb: "I hope you realize you're only being confirmed for a six-months' job."

At that time the foreign-aid agency was scheduled to expire the following June. While the extension of the foreign-aid and reciprocal-trade programs was effected largely through Democratic votes and only after concessions to opponents of the measures, more than a majority of the Republicans in the House voted for foreign aid in 1955.

How much of this change can be credited to the expectation, at the time, that Eisenhower would be the G.O.P.

standard bearer in 1956? How much of it represents a lasting change?

A rough judgment can be drawn perhaps from an intensive analysis of Congressional roll calls since 1941. In that year more than 85 per cent of all the Republicans in the House voted against both Selective Service and Lend-Lease. Since 1953, as the table below shows, the proportion of Republicans voting "no" on foreign aid has been more than halved.

Both in the East and on the Pacific Coast, the "no" vote among the Republicans had dropped below 20 per cent by 1955. In the Midwest it still hovered around the two-thirds mark.

Republican "Isolationist" Vote in Congress

Per Cent "No" of Total Voting

Region [1]	Selec. Serv.	Lend-Lease	Marshall Plan	1952	Foreign-Aid Bills 1953	1954	1955
Midwest	98	97	47	76	70	69	65
East	70	68	4	24	13	13	19
Pacific	60	80	4	30	18	20	19
All Rep.	89	86	25	53	40	40	40

[1] Other regions were omitted from this sectional breakdown; since they had so few Republicans a change of one or two votes jumped the percentages out of proportion to their significance. These roll calls are analyzed in more detail in the Appendix, p. 274.

In nearly all of the Midwestern states every Republican voted against both Selective Service and Lend-Lease. If one contrasts the districts in these states which now favor foreign aid against those in the nay column, three general influences seem at work—party support for Eisenhower, the degree of urbanism and the ethnic makeup of the district.

In Ohio, for example, all but one of the eight yes votes in 1955 came from predominantly urban districts, while five of the six no votes were cast by Congressmen from largely rural districts. At least three of these are heavily German in makeup. Much this same correlation shows up in Iowa, where three of the four no votes came from heavily German-American districts. The most consistent support for foreign aid is given by the districts embracing the city of Des Moines and southern Iowa, which has the lowest proportion of foreign born in the whole state.

In Minnesota the only Republican voting yes in 1955 was Walter Judd from Minneapolis. The urban Republican districts in the Midwest which have opposed foreign aid include one of the two Cincinnati seats, four in Chicago, where the influence of the Chicago *Tribune* has been so strong, and three in Indiana, all heavily German or heavily Catholic in background.

The lineup of individual Indiana seats provides another clue to why Eisenhower has been able to convert some Republicans but not others. The four districts which have voted no on all three of the 1953, 1954 and 1955 aid bills were lost by the Republicans in 1948. The two Indiana districts which have voted yes on foreign aid since Eisenhower became President stayed Republican in 1948.

The 1948 contest was the one vote in recent years in which the "isolationist" elements had no war grievance and they returned to the Democratic party in spectacular numbers. This return in fact provided the balance of votes which elected Truman (as I have shown in *The Future of American Politics*). To many Republican politicians the big lesson of the 1948 election was how heavy was the Republican party's dependence on the disillusionments of foreign policy to offset the G.O.P. weakness on economic issues.

When the Marshall Plan was enacted in 1948, the Republicans, then in control of Congress, were cockily confident they would win the Presidency in 1948. Only a fourth of the Republicans in the House voted against the Marshall Plan.

Some of this showing must be credited to the influence of Senator Arthur Vandenberg, who had been converted from his own old isolationism. With Vandenberg's death, Taft became the recognized Republican leader on foreign as well as domestic policy. Still, of the counties where Truman gained heaviest over Roosevelt's 1944 showing, fifty-seven are in Congressional districts where the Republicans have continued to vote against foreign aid, while only sixteen counties are in Republican districts which favor foreign aid.

The economic makeup of many districts is such that a Republican can figure on winning only by exploiting the frustrations stirred by our foreign policy. In Chicago, for example, the third district, which went Republican in 1946, 1950 and 1952, is inhabited mainly by moderate- to low-income workers. However, the district—which is the locale for many of James Farrell's novels—has a heavy concentration of Irish families. Fred Busbey, the Republican who has won the seat three times, has relied mainly on the emotions stirred by "Communism" to overcome the area's pro-Democratic economic bias.

This seat-by-seat analysis of Congressional roll calls leads to four main conclusions as to the political nature of "isolationism" today:

1. Much of it represents nothing more than the opposition of members of Congress to whatever a President of another party proposes. Between 1952 and 1953 the proportion of Republicans favoring foreign aid jumped from 47 to 60 per cent. On the Democratic side, opposition to foreign aid rose sharply after Eisenhower's victory. Thirty-eight per cent of all the votes against the 1955 aid bill were cast in the South, compared to only 19 per cent in 1952.

2. Despite this change, a Democrat still is more likely to favor foreign aid than is a Republican. In the 1952 and 1954 elections forty-six different seats shifted between the parties. In thirty-seven districts the shift brought no change

in how the district was voted on foreign aid. In eight of the nine remaining seats the change from Republican to Democrat brought a more favorable attitude toward our foreign policy. In only one case—the ninth district in Virginia—did the defeat of a Republican bring a shift from a yes to a no vote.

3. Generally speaking "isolationist" sentiments linger most strongly in rural rather than urban areas. Some of this may reflect a hangover of the old Populist agitations against "the money trust" and the international gold standard. Dan Reed's district in western New York was a Populist stronghold as was Dewey Short's district in the Missouri Ozarks. But other strong Populist areas divide about evenly between districts which are for and against foreign aid.

4. At least a third of the rural districts voting against foreign aid show heavy concentrations of German-Americans. In 1940 there were 146 counties outside the South where Roosevelt's vote dropped at least twenty percentage points from 1936. In all but about 20 per cent, the census showed German as the first or second strongest nationality. Of these 146 counties 121 are G.O.P.-held districts which have been against foreign aid. Only 15 counties are in Republican districts which favor foreign aid.

The "hard core" of Republican "isolationism," in sum, will be found in districts with a heavy German-American background or where the Republicans have come to rely on disillusionment over foreign policy as a weapon against the New Deal's economic appeal. In line with this analysis, as long as the Republicans remain victorious "isolationism" should decline steadily. But it can be expected to revive with a G.O.P. defeat.

Many observers feel that the future of the Republican party hinges upon who wins the struggle for Presidential succession after Eisenhower leaves the White House. My own judgment, though, is that further progress in remaking the Republican party hinges primarily on its success in strengthening its appeal in the country on economic issues. Until the G.O.P. establishes itself as the "party of prosperity" extremist Republicans are likely to continue to look to disillusionment in foreign policy to compensate for economic weakness.

FIVE

The Return of Two-Party
Politics

1. The "New Look" in Voting

In the fall of 1945 an obscure official in Washington scribbled his signature to a sheet of paper which was to prove something of a modern equivalent of the shot that opened up the Oklahoma strip. The paper he signed was a government order removing wartime controls over new residential construction. With its publication in the *Federal Register* the starting gun resounded for the biggest home-staking rush in American history.

By mid-1955 more than ten million new homes, involving an investment of roughly $100 billion, had been erected. In seven of those years new housing starts topped the million mark, making home construction the nation's biggest single industry. Perhaps a fifth of the whole population had been rehoused, much of it in wholly new towns, like Levittown, Park Forest, Lakewood Park, or Midwest City, which had been flung up over abandoned farmland or old potato patches and golf courses.

Propelling this housing boom along has been an equally spectacular expansion of the nation's middle class. In 1929 hardly one-sixth of all American families had a purchasing power in excess of $4,000 a year. By 1955, the Department of Commerce calculated, more than a half of all American families were earning $4,000 or more a year.

Nor had the seventh of advertized heavens been reached. Speaking at Columbia University's Bicentennial celebration, Arthur R. Burns, head of Eisenhower's Council of Economic Advisers, foresaw national production rising to $440 billion by 1960, which would average out to better than $6,000 income per family.

Such predictions may remind some people of the old promises of "a chicken in every pot" and "two cars in every garage." Still, there is little question that this burgeoning middle class holds the key to G.O.P. hopes for regaining ascendancy as the normal majority party in the country.

For a full generation the Republicans have suffered from an inferiority complex, reflecting a painful awareness that they lacked political sex appeal on economic issues. After each of the five Roosevelt-Truman victories, for example, Republican leaders found that the voting returns of any city pretty much matched its income map. In silk-stocking neighborhoods the Republicans would do well, but the lower down the economic ladder one went, the thinner the Republican vote got.

Since the depression Republican political strategy has been dominated by *one* driving motive—a hunt for issues or candidates which would divert popular attention from this weakness on bread and work issues. This lack of economic confidence, as has been shown, largely explains the eagerness with which so many Republicans have capitalized on the disillusionments of foreign policy. Until the G.O.P.

regains its economic nerve it is doubtful that it can serve as a truly stable and constructive party.

Even Eisenhower's landslide sweep of thirty-nine states did not erase the line of economic cleavage which Roosevelt drew. Eisenhower, it is true, cracked some of the strongest Roosevelt citadels. He won San Francisco, Bridgeport and New Haven, which had not voted for a Republican President since Calvin Coolidge; also Los Angeles, Minneapolis, Seattle, Buffalo and Rochester which had been Democratic since 1932. In our twelve most populous cities, Eisenhower lifted the Republican share of the total vote from 38 per cent in 1948 to 44 per cent.

But when one examines the Eisenhower vote in the major cities ward by ward, it still stratifies consistently along income lines. Gaining at all income levels, his vote overrode rather than wiped out the economic cleavage.

What happened was summed up by a Detroit worker. A lifelong Democrat, he was explaining why he favored Eisenhower. Mainly he was "sick of having politicians running the country" and wanted "this inflation stopped." His ten-year-old son interrupted to ask, "Daddy, what is the difference between a Democrat and a Republican?"

"That's a good question, son," the father replied. "The Republicans are for people with money and the Democrats are for us poor people."

The fact that this man was marking his ballot for Eisenhower had not wiped out his consciousness of a class conflict between the "common man" and "economic royalist," which Roosevelt had etched so sharply in the minds of millions of Americans. His sense of economic interest had simply been subordinated temporarily to other grievances.

In brief, that was the pattern of the whole of Eisenhower's victory. Warren Harding and Herbert Hoover had both won a higher percentage of the popular vote, but Eisenhower was the first Republican President since the

Civil War to draw substantial electoral support from every section of the nation, from grandchildren of both Union and Confederate veterans, from both farms and cities, suburbs and slums.

He won 31 of the 57 counties which had been Democratic since Al Smith's candidacy and 278 of 366 additional counties which had been Democratic since 1932. He carried counties like Brown and Union in Illinois, Brown and Dubois in Indiana and Queen Annes in Maryland which had never voted for a Republican President before.

But if the historic significance of Eisenhower's vote lay in just this fact, that it was a truly national vote which surmounted the many bitter, partisan cleavages of the past, it also posed one question for future elections to decide:

Could these old antagonisms be subdued for good? Or would the past rise to reassert itself?

The first voting test—in 1954—was generally interpreted as a victory for the past. Actually, it marked the emergence of a "new look" in American voting which is likely to dominate our elections for some years to come.

Many Democrats, of course, returned to their old ballot markings. Some had voted for Eisenhower in conscious defiance of what they considered their economic interest. Others had used the Eisenhower "crusade" as a means of purging their own party. As a lawyer in suburban Riverside, near Chicago, put it, "I'm not sorry I went for Eisenhower. The Democrats were in too long. But we've had the change and I still feel the Democrats are more the party of the little fellow."

But the 1954 voting also tore loose old allegiances. A cheesemaker in Des Moines, a railway express worker in Boston, a television shop owner in Minneapolis, a clerk in Detroit, a used-car dealer in Columbus, a Negro factory worker in Newark—in nearly every city I sampled during the campaign some persons told me, "There was so much depression talk in 1952 I was afraid to vote for Eisenhower, but I'd go Republican in 1956."

Others, like Joseph Schultz, a young Cincinnati salesman, had feared "a military man might get us into war." In 1954 Schultz swung Republican, explaining, "I'm better off than ever. I like being out of war for a change."

The closeness of the 1954 voting led to much talk of how confusing the election seemed. By and large, though, the results were a remarkably accurate reflection of economic conditions as they varied in different parts of the country. Where the downturn from 1952 was sharp, as in Michigan and Minnesota, the Democrats swept in. Where the level of prosperity was high, the Republicans held their own or even picked up voters.

In the shuffle of ballots, one item of striking significance was widely overlooked—*in a vote dominated by pocketbook considerations the Republicans had come close to running the Democrats a dead heat!*

The booming prosperity since 1954 has strengthened further the Republican economic appeal. Among farmers the Republicans have been weakened appreciably by the decline in farm prices. But in urban and industrial areas the old "hard times" imprint that has been the chief Republican liability has been ebbing—just how fast is the question that probably will decide the 1956 election.

Younger voters, in particular, who did not live through the depression, are inclined to credit the G.O.P. with their economic advancement of recent years. In one middle-class neighborhood in Detroit, a young man was loading his wife and two children into a car when I asked whom he voted for in 1952?

"Stevenson," he replied. "That was my first vote, but I'm going Republican now.

"We've just bought a new home," he went on. "Besides I've been promoted to the administrative side of my company. It's shown me that there's another side to the story of how a company is run besides what the workers see. I never appreciated that before."

There has been enough shifting of this sort so that in a talk before the National Editorial Writers Conference in the fall of 1955 I expressed the judgment that the odds favored a Republican victory in 1956. That did not mean the Republicans could win with any candidate, I explained, but if the boom continued they would be able to go to the country with the economic edge in their favor for the first time since "those Hoover times."

Still, it is also my judgment that neither party is likely to win a truly decisive majority before 1960 and possibly not until 1964.

That may seem to be peering pretty far into the future. Part of the Republican problem, of course, is the wide gap between Eisenhower's personal popularity and how people feel about the Republican party. On one Cleveland street in 1954, three voters declared, "I'd vote for Eisenhower but I have no use for the Republican party." One of these persons went so far as to say, "I'm for Eisenhower because he's a pretty good Democrat."

But my main reason for feeling that a decisive victory lies beyond either party's reach has little to do with Eisenhower personally. The judgment is based on what seem the main forces behind the truly "big news" of the 1954 election—the dramatic reappearance of a real, nation-wide two-party politics.

Only rarely has the United States had two evenly competing parties. The usual pattern has been for one clearly dominant party to hold office until its following divided, as with the Republicans until split by the Bull Moose Roosevelt. The advent of the New Deal did not alter this pattern but switched the role of the parties, with the Democrats becoming the majority sun in our political solar system and the Republicans the minority moon.

But the 1954 voting demonstrated that there no longer was a "normal," decisive majority on which either party could count. In New Jersey and Connecticut only 3,000-odd ballots provided the margin of victory; in Oregon less than 2,500; in New York Averell Harriman won by 11,125. In all, fourteen senatorial and gubernatorial contests were settled by less than 2 per cent of the vote. Outside the South 34,000 votes was the difference between the Democratic * and Republican totals for Congress.

To find a period in our history when the major parties were so jealously close, one would have to turn back beyond the voting span of all but a few venerable octogenarians. Between 1877 and 1896 the national political balance was so precariously poised that no party could win the Presidency twice in succession or hold control of both houses of Congress for two terms running.

"This country needs two parties" has long been a favorite agitation of reformers. Yet hardly any of us have had any living experience with such a political situation. So novel a development merits further scrutiny. Why should a genuine two-party politics reappear in the United States at this time? Does it promise to aid or obstruct us in meeting the tests of world leadership?

2. A Case of Political Insomnia

From its name—Centennial Road—one would have expected some semblance of a modern highway. But the centennial after which this six-mile stretch of rural Pennsylvania was named marked the one-hundredth anniversary of the Declaration of Independence. Whatever the visions of grandeur originally projected for this thoroughfare, I found

* Includes 171,000 Liberal party votes for Democratic candidates in N.Y.

it mainly a succession of bumps and ruts which would have made an ideal proving ground for testing a jeep.

For years the farmers living along Centennial Road had vainly pressured the courthouse crowd in nearby Bedford to get the road hard-topped. Brooding over repeated rebuffs, many of the farmers finally decided they were being too Republican for their own good. Because the G.O.P. enjoyed a virtual monopoly locally, these farmers reasoned, the party leaders assumed they would always win regardless of what grievances were left unattended.

Came election day of 1954 and farmer after farmer bumped down Centennial Road to a nearby lodge hall to cast a protest ballot for George Leader, the Democratic candidate for governor. To their amazement, when the votes were totaled, Bedford County, which had not gone for a Democratic President or governor since Grover Cleveland's day, had landed in the Democratic column.

The unpaved troubles of Centennial Road were not the only reasons for Bedford's historic switch. Dairying provides the county's main flow of income and in the 1954 election normally Republican dairy farmers all over the country boiled over like unwatched milk.

Most observers assumed that the 1954 standoff vote was brought about primarily by a resurgence of Democratic strength. But if the returns are examined county by county and ward by ward, one finds that through most of the country the Republicans actually held a good part of Eisenhower's gains over 1948. At the same time, though, they failed to hold their strength in areas considered as religiously Republican.

Of the five states where the G.O.P. Congressional vote fell 10 per cent or more from 1952—Kentucky, Wisconsin, Vermont, Maine and North Dakota—three have regularly ranked among the top Republican states in the nation. Of thirty-two contested districts where the G.O.P. candidates for Congress dropped at least ten percentage points from 1952, five never voted Democratic through the entire New Deal period, while another ten have been Republican since 1940.

Puzzled at what stirred behind this shift, I visited three staunchly Republican counties—Geauga in Ohio, Isabella in Michigan and Bedford in Pennsylvania—where the Democratic percentage jumped considerably above 1948. This meant that in each of these counties not only had the Democrats who voted for Eisenhower swung back but they had been joined by normally Republican voters as well.

In all three counties, Eisenhower voters who had gone Democratic offered the same explanation. "The Republicans around here have been in too long. We wanted a change."

"This county is ready for two-party politics," declared John Gore, who edits the weekly Geauga *Record*. "We're tired of being taken for granted any more. This county got on the Republican bandwagon during the Civil War and has never been off it since. The local machine thinks we have to vote for anyone they put up. It's time we were given a real choice."

This desire for an alternative party through which voters can make their interests felt has gained surprising force since the war's end. In some cases it reflects the feeling that "the only way to prevent corruption is to change parties regularly." Even in overwhelmingly Republican suburbs, as in Bergen County, New Jersey, Democratic mayors have been elected in revolts against the corruption of local Republican machines. Similarly in Boston one city employee confessed, "I used to think I had to vote the Democratic ticket even if the biggest horse thief was running. But by splitting my ticket I figure we get more honest men."

With many more voters, though, the turn toward a two-party politics reflects the effects of the vast economic changes which have been transforming the country. Particularly since the end of World War II there has been a dramatic upgrading in the economic status of most Americans. The decentralization of industry is shooting shafts of industrial feeling into the hitherto rustic countryside. With the power of government growing ever more important, every economic group has become more sensitive to the need of making its interests felt in Washington.

Thus far, at least, the net political effect of these and other changes appears to be a trend toward evening out the strength of both parties.

The spectacular population shift to the suburbs, for example, has thrown up Republican bulwarks which come close to counterbalancing the Democratic strongholds in the cities. In 1952, in fact, for the first time since the New Deal the commuter country around New York, Chicago, Cleveland, Detroit and Milwaukee rolled up heavier majorities for the Republicans than these cities gave the Democrats.

Close to half of Eisenhower's total plurality in Illinois, Pennsylvania and New York State was furnished by the suburbs around Chicago, Philadelphia and New York City. In 1920, as can be seen below, these same suburbs furnished less than 10 per cent of the total Republican plurality in the three states.

Per Cent of Republican State Plurality Cast by Suburbs

	In 1920	In 1952
Phila. suburbs	8	52
N. Y. suburbs	8	44
Chicago suburbs	7	40

In the decisive industrial states, in other words, the rural-urban cleavage of the 1920's is being replaced by a new struggle of the suburbs against the cities.

This change, in turn, reflects a growing tendency for all voting throughout the country to divide along economic class lines. The New Deal unloosed powerful trends, which have been working to nationalize the basis of American politics. These trends, as later chapters will show in more detail, have been quickened and extended by the Eisenhower Presidency.

But if considerations of economic class are becoming more not less important in American politics, it should be noted that this "class conflict" is more a "war of movement" within a mobile social structure than one of trench attrition between rigidly, unchanging social halves.

The table which follows profiles the distinctive nature of

A Profile of Class Solidarity

	Per Cent Republican		
	1936	1948 [1]	1952
New York			
Vote in city	24	35	44
Nearby suburbs	54	66	69
Philadelphia			
Vote in city	37	48	41 [2]
Nearby suburbs	52	64	63
Cleveland			
Vote in city	30	35	40
Nearby suburbs	54	62	63
Chicago			
Vote in city	33	41	45
Nearby suburbs	50	64	66
Los Angeles			
Vote in city	28	42	52
Nearby suburbs	36	51	59

[1] Wallace vote is included in N.Y., Pa. and Calif., other percentages are of major party vote.

[2] Why Philadelphia was the one city in the country to show a lower G.O.P. percentage in 1952 than 1948 is explained in my clinical notes, p. 278.

class conflict in the United States. It shows that changes in
the relative solidarity of the upper- and lower-income
groups move together. In 1936 the workers in the cities
were militant in their unison, while the better-income elements in the suburbs were divided almost evenly. By 1952 a
complete about-face had taken place. The center of gravity
of class solidarity had shifted to the suburbs and the cities
were divided within themselves.

Compared with 1948, Eisenhower gained more heavily in
the cities than in the suburbs, indicating that many of the
newer suburbanites whom the G.O.P. won in 1952 would
have voted Republican even if they had stayed in the cities.
In fact, this table shows that the same forces which have
solidified the well-to-do have simultaneouly divided the
workers.

My talks with numerous voters in recent years leave little
doubt that economically this change reflects mainly a growing sensitivity to inflation and, with it, a stiffened resistance
against "government going too far."

In 1936, of course, there was nothing to distract the mass
of workers from a single-minded devotion to the New Deal.
Fresh in their memories tingled all the depression grievances. More than $500 million were still frozen in locked
banks. Of the total national tax burden only 5 per cent was
borne by incomes under $5,000, which was where Roosevelt
drew his greatest political strength.

By 1952 roughly a third of the tax burden was being
borne by incomes under $5,000. This new tax consciousness
was stimulated further by the sizable migration out of
apartment houses, where taxes are hidden in the rent, to
home owning with its sundry local taxes. By 1952, as well,
the volume of savings held by individuals and subject to
depreciation by inflation had more than tripled, soaring
from $60 billion to $216 billions.

In short, the main force generating the current trend

toward conservatism will be found in the economic gains since the depression. These gains hold the secret to the puzzle of why neither the Democrats nor Republicans are able to achieve a decisive majority.

For to some millions of voters both parties symbolize a threat to these gains in different ways.

Many commentators and scholars, of course, contend that "there isn't any real difference" between our two parties. Certainly there have been times in the past when, as Matt Quay, the old Pennsylvania boss, observed, a Democrat seemed like "only a left-handed Republican." But at least since the New Deal the voting public has not shared this belief that our parties provide little more choice than between Tweedledem and Tweedlerep.

Over the last decade I have asked thousands of voters in every part of the country—just what difference do you see between our two parties? The striking thing that emerges is how uniform is the consensus on what the parties stand for.

On foreign policy, as earlier chapters showed, the Democrats are considered the party of foreign intervention even, as some persons feel, to "always getting us into wars," while the Republicans are regarded as the party of "isolationism" or less involvement abroad.

Economically, the Democrats are looked upon as "the party of the working man," inflation and government spending, while the Republicans symbolize "big business" and "people with money," deflation and less government spending.

Another difference commonly cited is that the Democrats are the favored political home for Catholics and other minority groups, while, at least in the North, the Republican party is still seen as largely a Protestant bulwark.

Each party's following cuts across these battle lines, of course. Still the strength these stereotypes exert can be seen in how readily people align themselves according to these images almost without second thought. Asked why he had switched to being a Republican, one Minnesotan grinned and replied, "I'll tell you the truth. I married a wife with some money."

Again, one Milwaukee housewife remarked that she was shifting to Eisenhower because she was tired of arguing with her husband. "He's a Republican and I'm a Democrat. Every four years I've had to listen to him tell me what's wrong with the Democrats. I finally told him all right, have it your way. Lets see what your Republicans will do."

"Why do you and your husband differ so strongly in politics?" I asked.

"Oh, his father is in business so he thinks he has to be a Republican," she retorted. "I come from a family where everyone had to work hard for a living. We're all Democrats."

The depth of emotion behind these attitudes largely explains why so many voters find it so difficult to choose decisively between the parties. For if the Republicans remain the "party of bad times" to many voters, others feel "the Democrats can't stay out of war." Similarly, farmers or workers will remark, "The Democrats have always done more for people like us," only to add, "But they don't know when to stop spending." Or the same man or woman will complain, "There's too much money in Eisenhower's Cabinet," and then observe, "But the Democrats lean too much to labor."

Caught among these conflicting fears, a sizable part of the electorate has developed what might be described as a strong case of political insomnia, tossing from one party bed to another. Many voters have told me they shift their votes from one election to the next to "keep either party from getting too strong." Other voters have swung between the parties as their fears of inflation and depression have risen and fallen.

At least since 1948 this inflation-depression equilibrium has constituted the balance of political power in the country. When the threat of another depression has seemed the chief threat to the gains of recent years, as in 1948, the dominant voting trend has favored the Democrats. By 1950, and even more so by 1952, the inflationary impact of the Korean War had swung the balance against "too much spending" and "too much government." In 1954 the scales tipped back again, coming to rest in almost dead-weight evenness.

In areas of economic distress as in Evansville, Indiana, where a tenth of the workers were jobless, the sentiment for increased government spending bounded. As the wife of an unemployed painter remarked, "Maybe the Democrats put the country into debt but there was work for everyone."

Similarly, a construction worker in Malden, Massachusetts, who had voted for Eisenhower, remarked, "They say when the Democrats were in there was a lot of corruption. That may be true but there was also more work. I'll take the old gang back with all that goes with it."

Through most of the country, however, there was more of a "wait and see" attitude. On one side of the scales, I found that most voters were balancing their gratitude to Eisenhower "for ending that murder killing in Korea." Generally, as well, people expected "with the war over things must come down some." Weighing against these sentiments were how hard hit people were individually by the post-Korean economic adjustment and an uneasiness over "how much further things might slip."

Some families, unable to resolve these clashing feelings, split their votes. In Detroit one tool-and-die worker went back to the Democratic party "because so many people were being laid off." His wife stuck with the Republicans, explaining, "My son who was in the Army is back home. I felt I owed them a vote."

Many observers attributed the change between the 1952 landslide and the 1954 standoff to Eisenhower's not being on the ticket in 1954. But the real difference between the two elections was not one of personalities.

In 1952 the public's thinking was dominated by the bloody stalemate in Korea. On that issue the popular mood was to demand a decision—to get the war over with one way or another. In 1954, however, the dominant issue was economic. On that issue millions of voters did not fully trust either party.

As one Illinois farmer commented, "I voted for Eisenhower to turn the tide of too much reliance on government. Now I'm voting Democratic again to see that things don't go too far the other way."

In the same distrustful vein, a Jersey City bus driver was trying to figure out which party was likely to win the House before deciding whom to vote for in the Senate race. "I'd like to see a different party in control of each part of Congress," he explained. "Then they'll watch each other and won't let either party have things too much its own way."

What the decisive margin of voters wanted was clear enough. They wanted to stay squarely in the "middle," avoiding depression and war, deflation and inflation, too much or too little government, too heavy a preponderance of influence for either business or labor.

This, of course, adds up to the same goal of "moderate government" which Eisenhower professed during the 1954 campaign. But where Eisenhower sought to convince the public that moderation could best be attained through the Republican party, the people preferred to seek it by using each party as a check upon the other.

Near McLeansboro, in southern Illinois, to give one example, Carroll Phillips, who combines preaching in a Baptist church with farming, felt Eisenhower was doing a "fine job" and deserved re-election. But when I asked about Eisenhower's campaign arguments that a President should have a Congress of the same party, Phillips replied, "It's better to have it split up so neither party has too much say."

This widespread distrust of both parties, I suspect, explains why so many people have talked of Eisenhower as being "above both parties," despite his strenuous activity on behalf of the G.O.P. It is not that the people are being fooled but that they want a President before whom they can deposit their mistrusts of both parties.

That this feeling does not reflect Eisenhower's personal charm is indicated by the popularity of many other politicians who are "liberal" on some issues and "conservative" on others, like Senators Paul Douglas, Stuart Symington, Irving Ives or Governor Frank Lausche. Through such "hybrid" candidates the voters pick what they like about both parties.

Since 1954 this desire for two evenly balanced parties has grown stronger in the farm belt, as will be seen in a later chapter. In the urban areas the conservative yearning to "hold on to what we have" can be expected to help the party in power as long as economic conditions are good. Still, booming prosperity does not seem to have overcome the desire to hedge one's fears of the uncertain future by balancing one party against the other.

This mistrust of both parties helps explain why the realignment now under way differs so markedly from that which followed Roosevelt's rise to power.

The reshuffling of party loyalties precipitated by the New Deal was a mass affair, with whole groups of voters swinging virtually en masse. Basically this was made possible by the fact that when Roosevelt came into office he quickly transformed what the Democratic party meant to people.

Negroes, for example, had remained loyal to the party of Abraham Lincoln in 1932, despite all their depression hardships. By 1936, however, they had swung with equal solidarity to the party which had introduced WPA and given every Negro a minimum standard below which his wages could not be cut since he could then go on relief.

Similarly, the bulk of workers, who had never felt there was too much choice between the parties during the 1920's, marched virtually as a bloc into what many termed the new "labor party."

In contrast the Republican gains of recent years have come through a shifting of individuals, not groups. At every income level and among all social classes one finds some families who have turned Republican, but there has not yet been any dramatic conversion of whole blocs of voters.

This slow tempo of realignment can be attributed largely to the curious paradox that both the voters and the country have changed so much more than have the symbols attached to the parties.

To sum up, the usual agitation for a "real two-party politics" has come from those who wanted to draw a sharp line of cleavage which would force all "conservatives" into one party and all "liberals" into the other. But the reappearance of a two-party politics at this perilous point in our history has virtually nothing in common with any such motive. Instead of seeking to sharpen the party cleavage, it is aimed at moderating both parties and using them to preserve the gains of the last two decades.

What has happened, in short, is that the moderate elements, by refusing to cast their lot with either party, have forced both the Democrats and Republicans to turn their backs on the extremists in their ranks and to fight for the middle ground where the balance of victory lies.

3. *"Two Fat Men in a Narrow Hall"*

Nothing quite like this revolt of the moderates has ever taken place before, and it may be several years before its full and novel implications are fully understood. Usually in the past when large numbers of Americans became dissatisfied with both parties, they gave vent to their grievance through third parties. From 1876 until McKinley's election the numerous third parties, from Greenbackers to Populists, prevented any President from gaining a full majority of the popular vote. In both 1876 and 1888 the winner actually got fewer votes than the loser.

These third-party insurgencies were sparked by a belief that the only real difference between the Democratic and Republican parties was that each was a custodian of different feelings toward the Civil War. Apart from that, many persons felt the parties were so alike that the truly crucial economic issues of the day could not be brought to conflict.

Today's revolt against both parties is clearly a quite different affair. It comes after a bitter period of party strife, during which the Democrats and Republicans differed sharply on both economic issues and foreign policy. If the 1876–1896 period could be said to have been marked by a search for ideological issues which would draw the parties apart, the dominant trend today can be visualized as a struggle to shed old ideologies.

On the whole, this rebellion against extremism seems a good thing. Certainly it is a necessary stage of transition that must be gone through before the country can be reunified politically. But this reappearance of two-party politics also brings a double danger.

With both the Democrats and Republicans committed to preserving the gains of the last generation, our parties have become, as one voter pictured them, "like two fat men in a narrow hall." They cannot squeeze past each other. Either they move in the same direction or remain stuck in unbudging deadlock.

One danger, in other words, is of stalemate rather than

balance. The second risk is that both parties may indeed move in the same direction—but against the interests of peace.

The closeness of the voting balance tends to enhance the bargaining power of every major voting interest. Each is in a position to threaten to upset the party in power by withholding or swinging its support. While these rival pressures offset each other to some extent, they tend to elevate the needs of domestic conciliation over the needs of waging the cold war abroad. To avoid upsetting the delicate political balance at home, *both* parties may shy from the military or economic actions which might be needed to meet new developments in the cold war.

As one illustration, take the raging argument over how much of a defense expenditure we can afford. The contention that our economy "cannot stand" more is certainly not valid in any physical sense. Industrial production has been pushed a full tenth higher than during the peak of World War II, while our labor force has been expanded by several millions. Obviously, the resources and facilities are available for an even heavier defense effort than was undertaken in World War II. No proposed program of defense and foreign aid combined calls for more than a part of what was done during the war years.

The ceiling on how much of a cold war effort we can stand is political not economic. It is set primarily by how urgent the American people feel is the crisis before us and how much political will power can be marshaled to see through the costs of what is undertaken.

It is at this sticking point of political will power that the delicate party balance exacts its price. With inflation made a constant threat by the domestic boom, it does not take much to upset the balance among various segments of the economy. Yet, as the 1954 election revealed, voters have become so sensitive to their economic interests that even moderate changes in economic conditions can shift the party balance.

It is through the threat of inflation that the domestic economy fights against what may be needed for the cold war—which is true not only in the United States but in Britain and every other country. To the degree that any nation's resources must be kept at home to conciliate domestic tensions, that country is able to do less abroad.

These internal resistances limiting the power we can exercise in foreign affairs have been strengthened by a curious illusion that has developed in recent years—that no one needs to pay for the cold war.

That, at least, is the implication of the attitude which has been adopted by all of the major pressure groups in their economic and political bargaining. All have taken as the measure of their well-being the income left them *after* taxes are paid. Labor, for example, contends that a steady rise in its take-home pay is needed to keep mass purchasing power high; business has insisted that higher earnings and dividends are necessary to continue a high rate of investment in new plants.

But if everyone is to be better off, net, after taxes are paid, who is to foot the bill for the cold war, which has been taking about a seventh of our national income?

One result, of course, is a struggle among the various segments of the economy to shift the cost of the cold war elsewhere.

Up to now these internal conflicts and distrusts have been tempered by the obviousness of the Soviet peril. If, however, the Soviets cut off this service of alarm, it is likely to become more difficult to divert our economic resources to the needs of peace. This prospect becomes all the more ominous if the cold war shifts to areas where economic weapons may be as important as military strength.

Stiffened resistance to unbalancing the budget must be

expected if the danger of war seems to recede. The pressures for reducing taxes are also likely to mount.

Nor in view of the prevailing temper of "moderation" can we even count on our politicians giving us the opportunity to take the harder choice of a more strenuous cold-war effort. The same competition of the parties to become accepted as the vehicle of "middle-road conservatism" also puts a premium on domestic conciliation even at the expense of the interests of peace, particularly if those interests seem less immediate than the next election.

And so, in the period ahead, it will be by our very gains of recent years that our national character will be tested. We cannot assume that what is good for each of us—the preservation of our individual gains—is necessarily good for the country as a whole. Situations will arise in which we will be torn by a considerable conflict between preserving our gains at home and winning the cold war abroad.

In part, of course, this testing is the age-old one of how greedy a people we are. But the desire to preserve the gains of recent years involves much more than a selfish desire for material possessions. Far more important, in fact, is a deep yearning for security which affects every segment of society and every nation in the world.

This search for security does not reflect any dread of a failure of production or of the traditional scourges of human society like pestilence, disease or starvation. Mostly this insecurity is the outcropping of uneasiness over changed political, social and economic relations, both between nations and, inside this country, between different groups of Americans.

Behind the restless tossing between the two parties stirs a profound indecision over the crucial question of what kind of government is needed for the kind of world we live in.

Usually when this question is debated it is in terms of

whether we should have more or less government. But the effective quality rather than quantity of government is decisive. The main problems of this age of danger cannot be met by any ideological formula, by either a blind curtailment of all government power or by its blind expansion for the sake of expansion.

Eventually the newer, emerging issues, rather than the old feuds, will give shape to this new role of government. In the years ahead, as the chapters which follow will show, we shall have to reconsider how the gains of various segments of the economy can be kept in balance; also how to reconcile the growing disparity between our normally relaxed ways and the increasing destructiveness of modern weapons.

We shall also have to take a new look at the relationships of Congress and the Presidency and what happens when the two branches of government are not in control of the same party. We will also have to ask ourselves how long we are to continue to deny both parties a clean-cut majority and just what must happen to bring about a decisive realignment of the parties.

Today both parties are on trial. But that means the people as well are on trial, for how are our parties to remake themselves if the people do not change their thinking?

How much progress have we already made in adjusting to the newer issues of our time? To begin with, let us see what business has learned since it was in political power last.

The Education of George Humphrey

1. The Issue Changes

George Humphrey had not been Secretary of the Treasury long before he moved some pictures. From the wall behind his chair he took down the portrait of Harry Truman which had been put up by Humphrey's predecessor, John Snyder. In its place Humphrey hung a painting of Andrew Mellon, which had been cooling its oils in an outer office through the twenty Democratic years.

It was a time of picture changing in all the government agencies, with Democratic saints coming down and lithographed icons of Eisenhower and Nixon, Hoover, Coolidge and even an occasional McKinley print going up in their stead. But none of the changes was as symbolic as Mellon's restoration to a place of honor, marking as it did the comeback of the businessman to the seats of governmental power.

The businessman has been called the key figure of American society. Certainly he is the frame and shoulders of the Republican party. Asked what the G.O.P. stands for, most voters respond, "It is the party of business." Even if Eisenhower had not run up a new record in the number of businessmen appointees, his administration would have been regarded largely as a trial of American business.

Generally, this testing has been pictured as one of the businessman's skill in acquiring the political know-how to recognize how different running a government agency is from managing a corporation. The biggest headlines have gone to a Harold Talbott, indiscreetly mixing private business interests with government connections, or to "Engine Charlie" Wilson, expounding what is good for the country with the maladroit directness that has made him seem like a businesman's edition of the late General George Patton.

But what has really been at stake in the political comeback of the businessman is whether business can be made into a truly conservative force in American life.

That statement may seem surprising, particularly to business leaders who assume that conservatism and business are identical. But this assumption does not square with the feelings of the millions of Americans who blame the last depression on business leadership or who wonder whether a business-run government can be counted on to preserve the hard-earned gains since that depression. When Mellon's picture was hung behind Humphrey's chair many people wondered, was it merely a gesture of respect to a past which was recognized as beyond recapture? Or did it mean that the Republicans actually were intent upon returning to the 1920's?

For the first few months of the Eisenhower Presidency it seemed as if the Republican goal might be to flip back the calendar pages as quickly as they could be turned. The administration had been in office only a few days when

Humphrey, working with the Federal Reserve, announced the first of a series of moves to lift interest rates and tighten credit.

"Conservative" spokesmen hailed the action as a "historic" return to "hard money" principles, reversing the trend of the previous twenty years, which had been "committing the government to underwriting the prosperity of everyone."

But the reaction of the money market showed no signs of such confidence. The sale of new Treasury bonds, bearing 3¼ per cent interest, abruptly dropped the value of all outstanding government bonds, which bore lower interest rates. Inside of eight weeks more than $2 billion in the market value of outstanding government bonds had been lost.

Part of the trouble lay in the fact that the Treasury had misjudged the bond market. More important perhaps was that Humphrey and his aides had not yet learned how drastically different "normalcy" in the 1950's was from Harding's day.

The telephone calls from bankers, whose bond holdings had lost value, were still jingling into Washington when certain economic indices began to slump. In the office of the McGraw-Hill publishing company Elliott Bell, who had been Thomas Dewey's fiscal adviser, studied these indices and broke into an editorial fuss. Early in January, Bell had published an editorial in *Business Week* which welcomed the hike in interest rates as a "milestone" in government fiscal policy. But in its May 9 issue, *Business Week* contended it was "Time to Ease the Money Squeeze." Sermonized the editorial, "We are glad to know the brakes work but we don't want to go through the windshield."

By early summer the credit pumps were operating again, with the Federal Reserve and Humphrey in full retreat away from "hard money."

This mid-1953 shift in monetary policy could be termed

the economic turning point of the Eisenhower Presidency. Some administration leaders have contended that the credit tightening never was intended to be more than temporary. Whether true or not, it took the reversal of this tight-money policy to prove that the Republicans realized that the Mellon twenties were indeed beyond recall. And with that action the economic issue which had agitated the country during the latter New Deal years began to fade as a new issue slowly moved into the ascendancy.

Through all of the New Deal years, the Republicans had campaigned as if the choice in economic policy lay between thrift and waste, economy and spending, the free market against government paternalism. It was primarily in those terms that the two parties took on meaning for the voters, with the Republicans standing for both economy and hard times, while the Democrats symbolized both inflation and prosperity.

The new emerging economic issue, however, is a clash of two rival schools of spending. Both parties today seem committed to the philosophy that maintaining prosperity requires a sustained volume of spending. If any difference divides the parties, it is that the Democrats seem somewhat more willing to contemplate spending by the government, while the Republicans would like to prove that private business can outspend any government.

How far the Eisenhower Presidency has traveled from the old Coolidge motto of "eat it up, wear it out, make it do" can be seen almost daily in the statements of business and administration leaders. The reports of the President's Economic Advisers credit the upturn from 1954 and the successful economic transition from the Korean War to the fact that as defense outlays were cut the spending of business, consumers and local governments rose even more rapidly. Virtually every prediction of a continuation of the boom is justified by pointing to the plans of business to increase its spending on new plant investment and by the reassuring "confidence" demonstrated by consumers in buying things they do not particularly need.

Actually, of course, one must doubt whether businessmen were ever so hostile to spending as they were advertised to be. Nearly every Chamber of Commerce justifies its place on the commercial map with elastic statistics of local purchasing power. The boom of the 1920's was financed largely by cheap credit.

The big change from the 1920's will be found in the conscious belief of so many business leaders that they cannot stop spending if they are to keep political and economic control in the country. Implicit in the preachings of men like Herbert Hoover was the thought that periodic depressions were almost unavoidable and should be accepted stoically as part of the price of economic freedom.

But the Eisenhower leaders have operated on the belief that a drastic interruption of spending had to be avoided if the Republicans were to continue to hold power.

The examples of TVA and the Rural Electrification Administration have strengthened this feeling that if business fails to spend enough to maintain full employment the public will turn to government spending.

Here perhaps lies the real significance of the so-called Keynesian philosophy. Its popularity is less a reflection of the soundness of Keynes' economic ideas than that his ideas dramatize what so many believe is the basic choice of action confronting our generation—that governments will step in to make work and investment where private angels fear to tread.

In any case, business, in effect, has entered upon a political contest to demonstrate how much more lavish and rewarding a spender it is than any government can be. One such battle is being fought over the expansion of electrical power facilities. Gabriel Hauge, Eisenhower's economic adviser, has argued cogently that with taxes so high, Congress will not appropriate large sums of public money for expanding power facilities. Private power companies, Hauge maintains, can raise all the funds that may be needed.

A similar line of reasoning has been used to justify the gifts to universities and colleges from the larger corporations. Some business leaders have declared that they want colleges and universities to look to business, not government, for financial support to care for expanding student enrollments in the face of mounting expenses.

During 1954, charitable donations of business corporations ran to $375 million, *Fortune* Magazine estimated, more than ten times as high as 1936. In the 1920's national advertising never rose above $3.4 billion in any year. This ceiling was pierced in 1947. By 1954 advertising had soared over $8 billion. Even the Korean War, when there was less to sell, did not check this rising trend of advertising expenditures.

The central economic accomplishment of the Eisenhower Presidency must be sought in its success in enabling business to continue this huge volume of spending for plant investment, advertising and related purposes. This goal can be described as the underlying rationale behind the administration's economic philosophy.

Business confidence in the administration has been important. But the stimulants to spending have not been solely inspirational. The Federal government's own spending has been running around $65 billion a year. The building of new plant facilities has been encouraged by liberal tax allowances for depreciation and by quick amortization. The buying of homes and automobiles—two mainstays of the business boom—has been stimulated by the loosest credit policies developed to date.

When Eisenhower was inaugurated someone purchasing a new automobile had to pay a third down and the balance in eighteen to twenty-four months. By the summer of 1955 many companies and banks were extending payment over thirty-six months, which was almost like renting out the car. In some of the more generous cases, the car's value could depreciate so much that the "owner" of the car would find it cheaper to let the car be repossessed and to buy a brand-new one.

Early in 1953 only 6 per cent of the home-purchase loans being made by the Veterans Administration were without down payments. By mid-1955 nearly two-fifths of the VA loans were without down payments. The proportion of all home mortgages being written that were guaranteed by various government agencies rose from 25 per cent in 1952 to 33 per cent in 1955.

Clearly the old issue of the "free market" against "artificial government stimulants" has lost most, if not all, of its meaning. Where the powers of government could contribute to strengthening the capacity of business to spend they have been invoked freely. To finance its proposed road-building program, for example, the administration advocated creating a separate corporation outside of the national debt—a device which Republicans criticized bitterly when practiced by the New Dealers.

As a matter of fact, the net effect of the Eisenhower Presidency has been to enlarge rather than reduce popular expectations of what the government can do in the economic field. When Henry Wallace talked of a postwar economy of "60 million jobs" he thought of full employment as a goal worth striving for, even if it might not be attained. In taking political credit for "peace and prosperity" the Republicans have gone the New Dealers one promise higher by contending that they have a special magic which soon will produce a $500-billion-a-year economy. In the face of such boasts any dispute over whether the government should be held responsible for maintaining prosperity becomes pointless.

The issue, in short, is no longer whether we are to have a "free" or "managed" economy. The dominant elements in both the Republican and Democratic parties are committed to a managed economy. Realistically, perhaps, no other choice is possible. With a national debt of $280 billion and when from a sixth to a fourth of the national product moves through the Treasury, as in recent years, the government cannot avoid affecting the economy in its actions—or inactions.

One might sum up the new politics of spending in terms of these issues: First, who is to sit at the managerial levers of the wonderful credit machine and how competently are those levers manipulated? Second, what balance is to be struck between the varied forms of public and private spending?

What is the truly conservative position in this conflict? Today the "liberal" tag is applied to those businessmen and politicians who are most ready to accept some degree of public spending while the "conservative" label is claimed by those who are most resolute in opposing public spending. But these definitions do not really fit the new choices before us.

True conservatism requires a balance between public and private spending which will meet the national needs of the 1960's rather than the 1920's. Before one can decide who are the real "conservatives" among American businessmen one must examine two things in greater detail—the implications of trying to maintain a perpetual technological boom and the raging conflict between business as usual and our national security.

2. By the Taxes We Watch

Not long after Eisenhower took office the *Saturday Evening Post* assigned me to do an article on the National Security Council. Set up in 1947 as part of the merger of the armed services into a single Defense Department, the NSC was intended to serve as the central policy-making agency over every aspect of national security. In the 1952 campaign, Eisenhower had attacked the workings of the NSC under President Truman, and "revitalizing the agency" was one of the first tasks the administration set for itself.

During several weeks of research I must have asked more than a dozen officials what tangible evidence they could cite of the NSC's new effectiveness. The most frequent response was, "You should have heard George Humphrey at the first NSC meetings and how he has changed his views since he has sat there."

That the NSC should have become a veritable school for the re-education of Secretary Humphrey is, of course, a tribute to his importance as the "strong man" of Eisenhower's Cabinet. But it also indicates the extent to which the issues of national security have become a running battle with business.

Since nearly 40 per cent of all Federal taxes are collected from corporations, it is not surprising that business should be serving as the spearhead for the drive to cut defense spending so taxes can be lowered. But the conflict runs much deeper than taxes alone.

Basically, the businessman's dilemma stems from the fact that for several decades technology has been steadily widening the cleavage between the nature of modern warfare and what is traditionally pictured as "the American Way of Life." As the managers of our economy, businessmen have become the most sensitive single carrier of the clashing forces involved in this Jekyll-Hyde conflict.

On the constructive side, the competitive vigor of American business has contributed enormously to the astonishing productivity which enabled the United States to produce as much munitions as the rest of the world during World War II.

The very bigness of American corporations, whatever its other effects, is a vital defense asset. The same drive toward trusts and mergers which brought integrated economic complexes under unified management also forged the economic organization which assures the uninterrupted flow of resources and skills needed to turn out huge quantities of tanks, planes and other weapons.

To put the atomic bomb into quantity production, for example, David Lilienthal had to hunt out a company with a high order of both industrial and scientific experience. He found it in the American Telephone and Telegraph Company, which the Justice Department was trying to break up with an antitrust suit.

But this astonishing productive strength has been accompanied by two weaknesses, both made more acute by the cold war.

First, to shift our productive resources from peaceful to war uses takes precious time and the imposition of controls over prices, wages and profits which are the exact opposite of the "free" economic ways that business cherishes.

As long as we could count on having time to mobilize, we could run the risk of maintaining only a small military establishment, although even that was proven unwise by World War II. But as the weapons at an enemy's disposal become ever more destructive, this time lag in mobilizing for defense becomes ever more perilous. It becomes increasingly urgent to maintain sufficient military forces so no enemy can hope to overwhelm us in the time that would be required to shift our productive resources from peace to war.

In short, our very determination to preserve "free" economic ways, so unlike the ways of war, requires an ever heavier expenditure on defense. The taxes which so many business spokesmen fight have become "the ramparts we watch" in guarding the very freedoms business cherishes.

The second contradiction revolves around how our economic strength is to be used on behalf of peace in the absence of actual war. The traditional attitude of business is that if it is freed to search out new opportunities for trade and investment all over the world, the economic ills of other nations will be corrected, to the extent that they can be corrected.

But our strategic interests do not necessarily match the profit-making interests of business. Trade with the Iron Curtain countries, for example, while profitable in dollars and cents could be extremely costly in terms of our national security. Again, in many parts of the world our strategic concern in promoting economic stability far outweighs any possibilities of trade and investment that can be developed.

Much of the struggle over foreign aid reflects this conflict between those who think normal trade relations will suffice and those who feel that, after all trade possibilities are exhausted, a "strategic gap" is left which must be filled in other ways.

In short, both in foreign economic policy and national defense, the interests of business *can* conflict seriously with our national security. Obviously, it is the task of government to reconcile this conflict. Yet, the still accepted "philosophy" of business regards government as a virtual enemy.

Or, put another way, the instinctive reflexes of the business community have been conditioned to protect its profit making, which, in itself, is a laudable motive. But for business to become a truly conservative force, it must learn to reconcile this desire to be "left alone" to pursue its private profit with our larger strategic interests.

That, in brief, is the basic contradiction in the character of American business which the cold war has laid bare. This contradiction has generated perhaps the most profound torment of the whole Eisenhower Presidency and will continue to torment future Presidents as well, regardless of their party affiliation.

Obviously, it is not that businessmen are unpatriotic or even that their views differ from those of the rest of us. It is simply that the decisive role they play in the economy makes them the strongest protagonists of the forces which would put our normal domestic pursuits above the interests of world security.

Can business be re-educated to resolve this conflict in its own character?

Humphrey's stewardship of the Treasury Department has been one long test of that question. In many ways he is ideally cast for the trial. While no one man can be considered typical of all American businessmen, Humphrey does manage to combine, in his own career and person, both the basic strengths and weaknesses of our business community.

3. "A Midwestern Businessman"

Born in 1890—the same year as Eisenhower and Charles Wilson—Humphrey is peculiarly a product of that age of certainty which preceded this age of total war and which Hoover once described nostalgically as "the happiest period in man's history." Always possessed of good health and economic advantage, Humphrey's life has been singularly untroubled by either great problems or crises.

His father, Watts Humphrey, who ran unsuccessfully for Congress the year George was born, was one of the more successful lawyers in Saginaw, Michigan. On his death in 1916 he left an estate of $150,000. Among his clients were the Michigan Central and Grand Trunk railways. During Theodore Roosevelt's Bull Moose insurgency, he was the leader of the Taft forces in Saginaw.

Asked once what kind of person his father was, George

Humphrey replied, pounding a fist into the palm of his hand for emphasis, "He was the most forceful, dynamic, positive man I ever knew!"

There were other paternal qualities which George took on. Believing that children should learn to exercise responsibility, Watts Humphrey taught his eleven-year-old son to carve the meat at dinner. While George was in high school he and his father were partners in raising and selling ponies. Fond of hunting and fishing, Humphrey's father did not bother with either religion or books—traits which hold true for his son today.

Saginaw itself was relatively free of social disturbances in those days. In the early 1890's the city did become something of a stronghold of the anti-Catholic American Protective Association. In fact, one advocate of the A.P.A. from nearby Bay City, "Professor" Walter Simms, tried to deliver an anti-Catholic speech in Senator McCarthy's home county in Wisconsin, where he was almost mobbed.

By the time George had entered school, this anti-Catholic "crusade" had died out. The big political agitation that rocked Saginaw in his youth was whether to do away with the town pumps and purify the water supply. Wilbur Brucker, Assistant Secretary of Defense and a native of Saginaw, recalls attending one meeting as a youngster at which a speaker held up two glasses, one clear and the other murky, and asked, "Which do you want for your children, pure water or sludge?"

To Brucker there seemed little question which was more desirable but someone in the audience rose and cried out, "Hold on there! How much will it cost?"

In those "essentially simple days," as Eisenhower once described his own youth, when "war" was discussed it was the Civil War that people had in mind. Through the entire period from 1890 to 1915 our defense expenditures averaged only about $165 million a year. Even the Spanish

American War lifted military spending to only $220 million, or less than 2 per cent of the national income.

So reluctant were Americans of that age to think of this country as a world power that the first ships of our fleet were pushed through Congress described as "seagoing *coastline* battleships." In those days, as well, it cost only $7 million to build a battleship. The *Missouri* which was completed in 1944 cost $144 million, the *Forrestal* over $200 million.

World War I first blared the warning of how sharp was the conflict between the evolving nature of war and the American way of life. But this lesson was quickly forgotten as we turned our backs on Europe and promoted disarmament, largely to reduce taxes. At the peak of World War I roughly 15 per cent of the national income was devoted to war and during World War II nearly 40 per cent. But from 1923 through 1929 the richest nation in the world was not sufficiently troubled about the threat of war to spend as much as 1 per cent of its gross national product on defense.

It was in the dozen years of Harding, Coolidge and Hoover—the last years of Republican power before Eisenhower—that Humphrey matured into—to use his own label —"a typical Midwestern businessman."

In 1917 he had left his father's law firm to join the Hanna Company in Cleveland. The postwar collapse of coal prices almost wrecked the company, of which Humphrey had become vice-president. With tough, unemotional efficiency, Humphrey wrote off inventories, junked unprofitable mines and shook up the management. He then set about merging Hanna's remaining assets of ore mines, ships and ore-purifying furnaces into a new integrated steel combine. So skillfully was the combine put together that it showed a profit through the whole depression.

This experience with the National Steel Company taught Humphrey one big lesson—that the competitive struggle favored integrated companies which had effective control over their costs. The $120,000,000 business "empire" which Humphrey had managed to amass by 1952 reflected that lesson. In the main it was built around related uses of interconnected products—of iron ore, shipping, steel, coal, rayon, natural gas, plastics and banking.

Humphrey's business career, in sum, was a dramatic example of that competitive drive which brought into existence the productive strength that enabled us to tilt the balance in both world wars. But Humphrey also shared the defect typical of so many American businessmen—in being blind to how this economic strength connected up with the problems of peace and war.

This blind spot was really a congenital defect in the vision with which businessmen looked out upon the world. In the main they scanned the foreign horizons through the eyes of their *specific business interests* rather than through the frame of any strategic whole. Both Coolidge and even more so Hoover had been eager to promote exports and to expand American investment abroad. Where such opportunities for profit developed, the American businessman could become quite "internationalist" in his viewpoint. But those parts of the world which did not provide such opportunities remained little more than blobs on the map.

In Humphrey's case, for example, as long as the Mesabi Range along the shores of Lake Michigan was our major source of iron ore, he displayed little interest in the St. Lawrence Seaway. When the depletion of the Mesabi's ores forced Humphrey to develop the ore deposits of Labrador, he became an ardent champion of both the Seaway and Canadian-American friendship.

In this instance Humphrey's economic motivations and the nation's strategic interest came together in one neat package. But virtually none of Humphrey's other business interests operated to prod him into a similar awareness of our strategic concern over other parts of the world.

It was largely for men of Humphrey's vision that Bob Taft spoke economically. To them vague talk of global responsibilities or of the need to improve living conditions all over the world seemed like sheer sentimentalism.

Nor were they sufficiently attuned to the global scale of modern war to sense the harsh realism that underlay the desire to enlist the preponderance of the world's resources on our side.

Their concept of foreign policy was one which would be limited as far as possible to areas where foreign commitments could be weighed against economic interest. One of Humphrey's first actions in Washington was to insist that any new proposal brought before the National Security Council be accompanied by an estimate of what it would cost.

If this emphasis on the specific and calculable was much too narrow a focus for waging a globe-flung cold war, still it made for a pragmatic flexibility which would adjust to actual experience.

This seeming paradox is worth underscoring since it is a revealing clue to why the American businessman baffles both the world and himself.

The mistake is often made of thinking that American businessmen believe what they say, when really they believe what they do.

American businessmen have always been functional rather than philosophical in their temperament. The drive of men like Humphrey has been powered primarily by sheer energy and the desire to get things done—well. Despite their talk of abstract principles like "free enterprise" and "rugged individualism," businessmen usually operate on a case-by-case basis.

When Humphrey was appointed Secretary of the Treasury, much was made of the fact that he had never made a public speech. This silence was fortunate. Had Humphrey's political and economic views been recorded prior to his coming to Washington they would have sounded like Frank Sullivan reciting all the anti-New Deal clichés he could collect. Anyone listening to them would have thought Humphrey a rigid, doctrinaire person.

Yet in his own business operations Humphrey was anything but doctrinaire. Asked once about the Hanna Company's plans for the future, he replied, "We have no fixed, long-time policy but stand ready to take advantage of situations that develop." He had refused to draw an organization chart of the Hanna Company for fear it might "destroy our sense of freedom to do things any way we want." Those who have worked with him agree "he is a stickler for getting the facts and facing up to them no matter how unpleasant they may be."

In Cleveland Humphrey may have thought that he really believed all the intemperate things he said about the New Deal and how easy it would be to cut spending, chop taxes, balance the budget, slash the national debt and still step up the cold war. Once in Washington he soon found that the "facts" which came across his desk permitted no such easy choice.

One of his early moves, for example, was to bring the Export-Import Bank under Treasury control with a view to tightening, if not suspending, our loans to South America. But Humphrey soon learned that our political and strategic interests below the Rio Grande required an agency which could lend money by softer standards than those which might govern a banker concerned solely with being repaid.

In talking with some businessmen friends, Eisenhower once remarked, "All of us have learned a lot since we came into office. I guess no one has changed more than Humphrey, which shows how big a man he is."

Since Humphrey has continued to use the same stock phrases in his speeches it is not easy to score the exact degree to which he has been re-educated. Still, if one were to try to rate him on a few of the more important aspects of national security, the Humphrey report card might look like this:

Foreign Aid	Good
Mobilization	
Readiness	Zero
Defense Spending	Passing

In Cleveland Humphrey had seen little justification for continuing foreign aid. To friends he often contended that the Marshall Plan was badly carried out since "you can't spend all that money wisely and well. Some countries are too ignorant to be helped."

Some of this hostility lingers, as when he cracks, "Every time a country catches cold it comes running to us for cough syrup and a quarter." Humphrey also is inclined to justify foreign aid as "good business" by pointing out how much cheaper it is to arm and equip a Turkish than an American soldier. Still, he confesses, "Before coming in here I had no idea of the extent to which our own security was involved in whatever happens in the world."

On the whole, Humphrey has come a considerable way from the viewpoint that our foreign economic policy need be nothing more than a projection of domestic business interests.

On another security test, however, Humphrey has flunked out completely—the proposal to enact stand-by-mobilization legislation in advance of actual war. Both world wars and the Korean War showed how tragically high was the cost in inflation and delayed production because of the dragging slowness with which mobilization controls were imposed over prices, wages, profits and the use of materials. As Bernard M. Báruch has pointed out so often, this neglect can be avoided by placing the necessary legislation on the statute books, ready to go into effect on the proclamation of a national emergency by the President and Congress.

A considerable part of the business community has fought this proposal, though. Characteristically, Humphrey has argued, "Wait and see what the emergency is like," ignoring the fact that mobilization for war must follow certain unchanging principles.

Other businessmen seem to fear that stand-by legislation might set a precedent for invoking such controls during peacetime. In their campaign assaults the Republicans loosely jumbled the New Deal's reforms with wartime controls, and some Republican businessmen may actually believe this propaganda. On the other hand, much of such talk is merely a cover for a greedy desire to be left "free" to profiteer from war.

On the third item in Humphrey's report card—the defense budget—how he is rated will vary with different examiners, depending on their estimate of the risks embedded in our defense program. One difficulty is that there is no way of determining exactly what our defense needs are. Since it takes three to four years to translate military appropriations into actual weapons, the defense budget must be based upon estimates of the risks which we will face several years in the future.

This three-year time lag leaves considerable room for conflicting judgments, which explains why equally patriotic men can differ with one another in complete sincerity on how best to defend the country. But this time lag also exposes both the people and their political leaders to all the temptations of wishful thinking, political expediency or simple drift. If domestic political pressures for any course of action become overly strong, it is all too easy for politicians to bend, reassuring themselves that "no one knows what the next three or four years will bring."

Only too often the gambles thus taken are veiled from the public in varied ways including that deceptive phrase, "a calculated risk." This phrase gives the impression that our military planners have carefully scaled our defense budget by some specific yardstick of danger. If that were true, as the risk abroad changed our defense program would also change.

But the record shows that on several occasions the Soviet military potential increased appreciably without any offsetting adjustment on our own part. When the first atomic explosion took place in Russia in 1949, our own defense timetable was left unchanged until Korea. Similarly, only after a long delay and even then rather feebly have we adjusted to the unexpected progress the Soviets have shown in developing the hydrogen bomb, long-range bombers and the intercontinental guided missile.

It would be more accurate to say that we have taken known but uncalculated risks. Our defense program has been shaped less by detached, objective estimates of the Soviet danger than by the needs of domestic conciliation.

Mainly, the framing of the defense budget has been a battle between two conflicting viewpoints. One school has had its eye primarily on our domestic economy and has sought to limit our commitments abroad to the "surplus" that can be spared without too much disturbance to our normal ways, even if it means incurring greater security risks.

The opposite viewpoint has believed that we should face up to whatever the struggle for peace may require, readjusting our domestic economy and our lives so these needs can be met.

In the struggle over the defense budget the advocates of each of these viewpoints muster their strongest arguments and fight it out. One side stresses the risks abroad; the other the costs at home. The balance that is struck is an uneasy compromise which only sets the arena for the next round in the contest.

Two dangers in this process should be noted. First, the compromise arrived at does not bind a foreign enemy. Second, to the extent that preserving our domestic ways is given precedence, it operates to leave the initiative in the cold war with the enemy. Before the "domestic firsters" can be aroused to agree to a more strenuous effort, the enemy must commit some overt act which will make our peril as clear as the afternoon's headlines.

This "habit of reacting rather than acting," as Walter Lippmann has phrased it, may be inherent in the pragmatism of the American character. If we are too practical a people to ignore completely changing world realities, we still tend to wait until trouble has broken out before acting.

And so in rating the business community on its attitude to national defense—and its attitude is typical of the whole country—one must give credit to the general willingness to support a larger defense effort than ever before. But there still is no evidence that business—or the rest of us—has reorganized its thinking to be capable of doing more than react to what the enemy does.

Like human beings, nations will go to extraordinary lengths to avoid having to change their thinking. Currently technology is serving us as a substitute for rearranging our brain cells. For a time our superiority in nuclear weapons and airplanes may enable us to maintain an effective deterrent against all-out war without having to match the Soviets —to use a Humphrey phrase—"body for body and weapon for weapon." But for the long run our reliance on technology is only likely to sharpen the dilemma from which Humphrey and so many other Americans are seeking to escape.

As a destructiveness of modern weapons increases, the strategic importance of our enormous productive capacity declines and it becomes more urgent that we expand the forces we have in instant readiness, regardless of the dollar cost. Some strategists, in fact, think we already have reached the point where the next war will be fought primarily with weapons in existence before the war starts. Nuclear weapons will prove so swiftly destructive, they reason, that no nation will have time to shift its productive potential from peace to war.

In short, the more hectic the pace of technological advance, the less tolerable it will become to cling to a philosophy that puts domestic interests above the needs of peace abroad.

It is also worth noting that in gambling our hopes for peace on our technological skills, we are not necessarily being smarter than the Soviets. We are, in fact, following what is the line of least resistance for ourselves, given the character of our society, much as the Soviet reliance on a superiority in manpower is shaped by the character of Russian society.

Nor is it in strategic policy alone that our national character is being swept along by obedience to that technological impulse.

4. The Man-saving Shark

One can do anything with bayonets, so the saying runs, but sit on them. That remark could be paraphrased and applied to technology. Our laboratories and scientists enable us to perform veritable miracles daily. But the net effect of technology, as Elizabeth Hoyt has observed, seems always to require still more technology. The one thing you apparently cannot do is sit on it.

And yet it is on this continuing technological revolution

that the whole Republican gamble of re-establishing itself as the party of effective conservatism is being based.

Not only have our hopes for peace been tied to staying ahead of the Soviets in the race to develop the intercontinental ballistics missile and other futuristic weapons, but it is to this same technological steeplechase that we are looking for the new products to keep business investment and consumer buying racing along.

Technology is even serving to mediate the classic cleavage between capital and labor.

Take the agreement which was negotiated between Walter Reuther's United Automobile Workers and the automobile giants over the so-called guaranteed annual wage. Soon after the agreement was signed, the major auto companies announced new programs to expand and modernize their manufacturing facilities. In considerable part, these expansion programs were the riposte to Reuther's wage thrust. The net effect of the Reuther agreement was to barter a fair-sized wage increase in exchange for three years of industrial peace during which the auto companies would be able to introduce new labor-saving machinery to offset the higher labor costs.

Through the whole postwar period higher wages and the introduction of new labor-saving machinery have been running a race, each stimulating the other. Almost, in fact, our economy has become a veritable man-saving shark, effecting labor economies to meet higher wages which in turn are devoured in new labor economies. One judgment given me is that roughly half of the $225 billion spent on new plant investment in the first nine postwar years went to reduce labor costs while the other half of this investment went into expanding capacity to meet the heavier demand of a larger, more affluent population.

Politically the net effect has been to reduce the antagonism toward business among even ardent trade unionists.

During the 1952 campaign I often ran into union workers who declared, "If the Republicans win they'll try to smash our unions." But the Eisenhower years have passed with less labor trouble than any comparable period in recent years. Real wages have been lifted to new heights; while pension and welfare funds have expanded spectacularly.

Some of this can be credited to a greater readiness by business to accept organized labor as here to stay. But, in the main, the industrial peace of recent years has been made possible by a structure of prices, taxes and techno- logical change which has enabled business to pass on to the consumer the costs of higher wages. As a general rule, net profits after taxes of the major companies have soared higher than ever.

As long as the boom continues, the prestige of business can be expected to continue to rise—and with it the Repub- lican political strength. Nor will the merger of the A. F. of L. and the C.I.O. into "one big union" reverse this trend. The election returns since 1936 show conclusively that the political feelings of the rank-and-file workers shift with economic conditions. The strength of labor's organizing effort is a secondary influence.

With each added year of prosperity, an ever larger part of the population is likely to identify its hopes of economic improvement with the cause of business.

During the depression years, for example, many college graduates learned to look to government for the employ- ment opportunities that private industry seemed unable to provide. Today it is to the industrial star that most college graduates are hitching their dreams of stationwagons.

But can the prosperity, which already has lasted longer than any previous boom, be kept going?

When I put that question to one key official of the Federal Reserve Board in Washington, he replied honestly, "No one knows. In theory there is no reason why prosperity cannot be maintained indefinitely if we have the good sense to maintain the quality of our credit system and to let things dip every so often while we make adjustments.

"The population is rising," he went on. "Immense funds are being spent on research. We can expect a constant stream of new things for people to buy and new technological developments to make old factories obsolete. Our big problem will be to know when to act to see that danger spots are brought under control before too late, and yet not take action so drastic it could upset everything."

But effective restraints are not easily maintained in an economy where price and wage rises can be readily passed on to the public. From mid-1951 to the summer of 1955 the price level held remarkably stable. The fall of 1955 brought a wave of industrial price jumps which would have cut the net purchasing power of the consumer's dollar if they had not been offset by the drop in farm prices. As it was, price and wage rises forced the military agencies to pay more for planes and other weapons, necessitating an increase in the defense budget.

Even if today's effort to manage the economy by manipulating the wonderful credit machine does fail, it is difficult to see how it could lead to anything but an attempt to build a new and bigger credit machine. It is not a question of what may be wise or desirable. The fact is that the technological drive of business has been operating to make our economy more and more of a make-spend operation, dependent upon ever looser credit arrangements.

Eisenhower's father, who had a horror of debt, never would buy anything unless he could pay cash for it. Just before tighter credit controls were imposed in the fall of 1955, installment debt had soared to $27 billion, nearly ten times the peak level of the 1920's. Installment buying has been extended to such varied items as redecorating homes, industrial stocks, college tuition, airline trips and funerals.

Currently most businessmen profess to think that this effort to turn our economy into a perpetual spending machine need not require any greater degree of government intervention than "indirect" credit controls. For a time the distractions of the technological steeplechase may encourage this belief. Since the start of the industrial revolution, however, the inexorable effects of technological change have been to make us all ever more vulnerably interdependent and therefore more needful of government.

This trend toward interdependence is not going unchallenged. Throughout the economy one can see all sorts of efforts to achieve some degree of economic independence. This trend is evident in the hectic pace of industrial and banking mergers through which companies are seeking to strengthen their market positions; in the drive of organized labor for pension and welfare funds; in the unprecedentedly large proportion of farmers who have remained free from debt; also in the curious phenomenon of a simultaneous rise in both the volume of personal savings and personal indebtedness.

At this stage one can only guess at the full significance of this search for economic independence even while we move toward a managed economy. My own judgment is that it shows how strong the fear of another economic collapse still is, even though that fear has declined in recent years.

Translated into political terms this would lead to the judgment that although the boom has strengthened the Republicans on economic issues, the methods being used to keep the boom going create enough uncertainty to deter many people from embracing the G.O.P. wholeheartedly.

Until the implications of a managed economy become a good deal clearer than they are today, the feeling of "neutralism" between the parties is likely to remain strong.

Right now, for example, no one can say how violent will

be the clash between the quest for security and what "needs to be done" to keep the boom going. Some economists, for example, contend the boom can be sustained only by increasing the volume of credit and money sufficiently to bring about a gradual rise in the general price level. Any such persistent inflationary trend would precipitate a serious political conflict between that part of the population whose savings would depreciate in value against the more indebted elements in the country.

Such an inflationary development would also throw a heavy burden on the whole pension and insurance system that has been built up in recent years. The expansion of the pension system has been used to ease out older workers and to make room for the advancement of younger workers. Once a person has lost his earning position—and the proportion of aged in the population is increasing—he becomes more acutely dependent on the maintenance of a stable value for the dollar.

Another example of how the uncertainties of technological change stimulate the yearning for security can be seen in the popularity of the liberalization of the social security laws. In my interviewing I found this the most popular single action of the Eisenhower Presidency, apart from ending the Korean War. There is a growing pressure to lower the age at which social security pensions begin. As one worker remarked, "I'm fifty-five now. If I lose my job I'll never get re-employed again. Yet I'll have to wait ten years for my pension."

To sum up, historically the businessman has been the Great American Revolutionist rather than the arch-conservative he fancies himself as being. While poets and philosophers talked dreamily of "making America over," the businessman actually did, as can be seen in the incredible changes that have taken place since the ascendancy of business after the Civil War. The curious contradiction that has plagued the thinking of businessmen for so long is that they seem to have assumed this "permanent revolution" could be spread throughout the world without being accompanied by the disciplines of government.

If Humphrey can be taken as a fair specimen, American businessmen have not yet acquired a realistic "philosophy for our time." Too many of them still are inclined to look out on the world through the eyes of their specific business interests—and this applies to many so-called "internationalists" as well as protectionists. Too many of them still are inclined to regard taxes as a burden inflicted by a hostile government, ignoring that no economic system is worth saving if it does not yield enough taxes to defend itself against a foreign foe.

And yet the lesson that conservatism can be enforced only through government is being learned. Even while the business community and the Eisenhower administration have employed the rhetoric of "free enterprise" in their speeches, they have been moving steadily toward the acceptance of a managed economy—managed to balance strategic and economic needs, foreign and domestic requirements.

Of course, the transition is far from complete. A sizable part of the Republican party resents what it describes as the existence of "two New Deal parties" and is determined to fight to reverse this trend. Also the fact that ours has become a managed economy is no insurance either that the management will be effective or that we will readily agree among ourselves as to the proper role of government.

As what the people expect of government grows, we are likely to find ourselves battling all the more intensely among ourselves over how to adjust the conflicting claims of various parts of the economy. The revolt in the farm belt, for example, is evidence of how a "managed economy" can create its own headaches.

SEVEN

Divided We Plow

1. The Big Squeeze

Tippy, the dog, was barking with excitement as the blue-and-white Greyhound bus rolled up with a caravan of sixteen cars in its trail. Out tumbled so many cameramen and newspaper reporters that for several moments the waiting farmers had trouble spotting the dozen members of the Soviet delegation.

As they were shown around the 160-acre farm of Richard Alleman, the visiting Russians peppered their host with questions: How many hours does it take to produce a bushel of corn? What profit do you make? How much taxes do you pay?

Crawling under a cornstalk cutter, one Russian lay there, lost in rapt scrutiny. Another gaped at the well-stocked refrigerator in the kitchen. But what impressed these men from Red Mars most was that Alleman, with an imposing variety of machines, was able to operate the entire farm by himself. As one Soviet expert exclaimed, "By you one man—by us a hundred!"

The newspaper accounts of this inspection tour of the Midwest read as if what the Russians saw has long been characteristic of American farming. Actually, the Soviet farm experts were witnessing evidence of a technological revolution which has remade American farming during the last decade. Since 1946 the investment in machinery on the nation's farms has tripled. Not until 1954, in fact, did the number of tractors exceed for the first time the number of horses and mules on farms.

In productivity this technological revolution has given each farmer the growing power of two. Where in 1920 the average farm worker produced enough food and fiber for eight persons, by 1954 each worker left on the farms was averaging an output large enough for eighteen persons.

Politically, however, this technological revolution has made the farmer perhaps the most shifting voting element in the whole country. In 1948 roughly 175 rural counties which voted Republican in 1944 swung for Harry Truman. Four years later Eisenhower overturned all but four, along with nearly a hundred other predominantly rural counties which had been Democratic through the whole New Deal era.

By 1954, though, nearly one-half of these counties had swung back to the Democrats. As the strategists of both parties laid their plans for 1956, the farm belt loomed as the arena which would be most hotly contested.

Why has the farmer, traditionally a bulwark of stability, become so restless politically?

Strangely enough, it is the farmer's well-being and conservatism, rather than any poverty or radicalism, which stir behind the agitation in the farm belt.

The drop in farm income since 1951 has inflicted serious hardships on some farmers. Generally, though, rural living standards have continued to rise steadily.

In Iowa, for example, there is one community of slightly

more than two thousand population—Guthrie Center—which I have visited every two years since 1948. The depression hit this town so hard that schoolteachers had to buy toothbrushes for the children to teach them to care for their teeth. As late as 1950 there still was no marked outward change to indicate that the depression pall had lifted.

Since then, though, each visit has noted fresh evidences of prosperity. The two-story hotel, so old-fashioned that it relied on a rope for a fire escape, has a new motel addition, with a bath in every room. The leading café has been air-conditioned. New ranch-style houses, an oil station, restaurant and Dairy Queen fringe the outskirts of town. The local REA co-operative, which was begun with $10 membership deposits of three hundred farmers, has erected an impressive $130,000 building, with meeting rooms, demonstration kitchens and a split-level garage.

In 1950 only 120 television sets were owned by the farmer members of the co-operative. But TV ownership has become so routine that the new measure of competitive consumption is how big a deep-freeze locker one owns.

Still, in mid-November of 1955, more than five hundred farmers crowded into the Guthrie Center sales barn to protest against falling hog prices and to hear demands for support prices at 100 per cent parity.

What has been troubling these and other farmers is not the price drop alone but the fact that this decline comes at a time when the technological revolution has been forcing them into an ever more agonizing dependence on the cash market.

Since 1940 the cash cost of fuel and repairs for farm machinery has quadrupled, soaring from $656 million to $2.8 billion.

Another billion-plus dollars is being spent annually on fertilizer, four times as much as in 1940.

All operating expenses for the nation's farms have more than tripled since World War II began.

As farm income falls it tightens the grip of this Big Technological Squeeze. To reduce costs, farmers have been expanding their holdings so they can make more efficient use of machinery and other technological aids. This, in turn, has meant still heavier capital investments and an even sharpened vulnerability to cash income, which intensify further the pressures to reduce costs through the application of still more technology.

In the face of this competitive whirl, the plight of many farmers has become much like that of the small storekeeper who is trying to keep pace with the chain or big department store. Outright bankruptcy worries him less than the ceaseless pressures which cut his profit margins even while forcing up his overhead costs as he struggles to keep modernized and efficient, with limited capital resources.

In Guthrie County falling hog prices have brought no foreclosures. But some of the smaller farmers have had to sell out to their more successful neighbors and have moved into the cities or to California, always a favorite exodus goal of Iowans. Other Guthrie farmers have taken jobs in Des Moines to earn enough cash to hold onto their land or have gone into debt, buying even farm machinery on the installment plan.

Still another trend which is being spurred by the technological revolution is the creation of veritable family hierarchies on the land. The case of young Alleman, whose farm was visited by the Soviets, typifies this trend. Still under thirty and a veteran, Alleman actually was renting land owned by his father, who operated another farm a few miles away. Alleman's brother and uncle also have farms nearby, which enable them to share their machinery and to supplement one another's labors at harvest time.

Numerous other economies are made possible by this

new kind of "family farming." In one Iowa county, where a single family controls more than twenty-five farms, it has proven cheaper for the family to lose a set of buildings a year by fire than to pay insurance on all the farms.

Forty per cent of all farm purchases in the wheat areas and a third of all farm purchases in the corn belt have been going to enlarge existing farms. Younger farmers, without family connections, who are being pushed off into the poorer land areas, complain, "You have to inherit a farm or marry one these days."

The dominant farm trend, in short, is one of entrenchment, of a strengthened grip on the land by fewer, more productive farmers. But if this evolving pattern of land tenure is obviously a conservative one, it reflects a curiously uneasy conservatism.

For as agriculture becomes more commercialized its problems of adjustment are aggravated rather than eased. This difficulty, in fact, is perhaps the crux of the whole farm problem.

The farmer's pressing need, of course, is to bring his productive capacity into balance with available markets. But this adjustment is made more difficult by the fact that the individual farmer lacks the means of controlling production and prices that are available to industry.

"A factory owner can produce more one month and less the next," complain many farmers, "but we have to plant all we can and take whatever the market price is." Nor in the face of dieting and less strenuous living can the demand for food products be raised easily. Expanding production in other countries has also cut down potential sales abroad.

Some economists have contended that high American farm prices stimulate foreign production. While true in part, this is much too simple an explanation. The decline in our cotton exports, for example, seems part of the world-wide economic revolution which shifted textile production from Britain, which imports all its cotton, to countries like India, which grow a good part of their own cotton.

Nearly all of the many agrarian revolts in our history have been directed at overcoming this peculiar vulnerability from which agriculture suffers in trying to keep pace with changing markets and prices. Just as the labor movement has centered around efforts to better wages and hours, so the farmer movement, as Carl Taylor has pointed out, has revolved around efforts to give the farmer better prices than the "free market" will bring. At times, in fact, the farmer, like the worker, has resorted to violence. Robert Penn Warren has told the story of how at the turn of the century "night riders" in Kentucky burned the barns of farmers who would not keep their tobacco from the market. In 1933 the Farmer's Holiday Association spilled milk onto the roads to keep it from reaching town.

Ezra Benson's unpopularity with farmers can be attributed largely to his failure to display any sympathy for these special handicaps that farmers labor under in adjusting to a commercial economy.

In pressing for lower price supports Benson talked as if he believed that a return to the "free market" would eliminate agricultural surpluses. In theory, of course, lower prices are supposed to drive out marginal producers, reducing total output. But this theory was tested during the 1920's and proved unrealistic.

Through much of the 1920's farm prices fell steadily, in some years below the cost of production, yet the total farm output actually rose. By the 1950's the acreage planted in cotton, wheat and corn was one-fifth lower than in 1920. But improved yields kept the production of all three crops higher than in 1920.

Some farm experts, like Lowry Nelson, estimate that farm production can be increased another 20 to 50 per cent on the present acreage through a more effective use of current-day technology. In the face of this astonishing productive potential, to try to balance supply and demand through the price system *alone* seems almost like using a tin cup to bail out a flooded cellar.

When the flexible support program was being debated in Congress, some legislators seemed to believe that lower supports could take the place of direct controls over production. But our experience since the 1920's indicates that *whatever the level of prices,* additional controls are needed if farm productivity is to be balanced with available markets. Certainly that is how the bulk of farmers feel today. Even stalwart Republican farmers have told me, "I don't like to be sewed up in a government program but there is no other way. You can't make a living by letting supply and demand alone."

The basic weakness in the original Eisenhower farm policy, in short, was not its failure to compete with the Democrats over how high a subsidy was to be paid farmers. It was that the administration undertook to operate a managed economy for the industrial side of the nation but did not develop a frame of effective management for agriculture.

Through varied devices, from liberal credit to tax incentives, the administration has managed to prevent any appreciable drop in the industrial price and wage level, which, of course, increased the farmer's costs even while his own prices were sliding. The same news columns which reported Benson's sermonizings about a "free market" also headlined "Corporate Profits at Record Peak" and "Workers Take-Home Pay Hits New High."

The resentment in the farm belt is summed up in two oft-repeated remarks, "The farmer always gets it in the neck first" and "We want a friend in Washington."

And yet, despite all this resentment, there still is no agreement among either farmers or their leaders on what should be done. Far from uniting the farmers, the Big Technological Squeeze has operated to divide them.

2. Farming Both Parties

Of the members of the Eisenhower Cabinet Ezra Taft Benson provides one of the more fascinating case studies in politics. One of the twelve apostles of the Mormon Church, Benson is a devoutly religious man, who neither smokes nor drinks. At the few Washington cocktail parties he attends, he often refuses to go through the pretense of holding a glass of ginger ale, preferring to stand in empty-handed, if awkward, conscientiousness.

Within the Eisenhower administration, as well, Benson has acquired a reputation for uncompromising righteousness. Even within the White House inner circle, few persons have been so bold as to be willing to suggest to Benson directly that he bend principle to political expediency.

Yet, in many ways, Benson and his flexible price support program stand out as perhaps the prime example of divide and rule politics in the whole Eisenhower Presidency.

When the flexible price support bill first was passed in 1954, it was maneuvered through Congress by shrewdly dividing the farm bloc. In the Senate, where the bill passed by five votes, the support of several Rocky Mountain Senators was won through a separate measure which guaranteed wool growers a price return close to 110 per cent of parity.

Similarly, in its actual operations, the flexible support program has tended to bring to the surface all the many conflicts of economic interest which divide varying groups of farmers.

For the net effect of the Big Technological Squeeze, as we have seen, has been to touch off a Darwinian struggle for survival among the nation's farmers. Virtually all the farmers one talks with feel that "the big shrinking down" is under way and that "some farmers are going to be squeezed

out—that's for sure." This feeling of competitive crowding
has turned the struggle over the level of price supports into
a battle of different producers to shift the burden of disloca-
tion onto other farmers.

In the 1955 cotton referendum, for example, farmers in
South Carolina, Mississippi, Missouri and Arkansas voted
95 per cent in favor of acreage control against only 88 per
cent in California and Arizona.

The larger cotton farms in the newer irrigated lands of
California, Arizona and west Texas use more fertilizer and
machinery than those in the old South; their yields per acre
are two and three times as high and their costs per pound
considerably less.

Moreover, while cotton production has been declining
in the South since boll weevil days, it has been expanding
prodigiously in the West. Between 1919 and 1952 California's cotton acreage increased from 85,000 to nearly
1,400,000 acres, while South Carolina's plantings were
sheared from 2,600,000 to 1,100,000 acres. Since cotton al-
lotments are based on the average acreage grown over the
five previous years, the government program tends to
penalize the newer areas in favor of the older producing
areas.

In short, high, rigid price supports serve as a competitive
shield for the less efficient Southern farmer, against the
more efficient producers in the West. Lower, flexible supports, in turn, tend to shift more of the economic squeeze
onto the older cotton areas.

The 1955 referendum bared even wider variances among
wheat farmers. In the Dakotas and western Minnesota
more than 90 per cent of the wheat growers voted for
government control. But in Pennsylvania, Ohio and New
York a majority of the farmers voted against it. In these
Eastern states where the wheat that is grown is fed to livestock, lower feed prices are to the farmer's interest.

A comparison of the referendum votes over recent years shows that these divergences among types of farming areas has widened considerably since 1953, as demand dropped after the Korean War and as the Technological Squeeze has intensified.

Actually, of course, there is no easy way for most farmers to determine what will profit them most. No single formula can meet the many varied contingencies that may develop. "I buy corn to feed my hogs so I want low corn prices," comments one farmer. His neighbor, though, will argue, "I don't mind high corn prices if meat prices are right. When feed gets too low everyone raises livestock and it knocks the bottom out of meat prices."

Again, farmers will complain profusely over "having to keep high-priced land idle." Then they speculate what would happen if all production controls were lifted? If the acreage now held out of production were to be diverted to any particular crop, the resulting surplus could ruin efficient and inefficient producers alike.

As one talks with farmers, one gets the feeling that farming has become the real $64,000 question in the country, with most of the farm population engaged in a gigantic guessing game as to what combination of price supports and market controls will yield them the highest returns.

As long as the answer to this riddle remains so elusive the political loyalty of the farm belt is likely to remain equally elusive. If farm prices drop far enough, as during 1955, the conflict of interests among farmers tends to disappear in a general demand for government action. But if economic conditions improve to where the price squeeze is moderate, farmers can be expected to divide anew, according to the crops they raise and their own individual competitive position.

In other words, whichever way the farmer swings in one election will be no sign that he can be counted on to stay put politically in the election that follows. The basic fact is that farmers today are much too divided in their own economic interests to be able to cast their political lot decisively with either party.

This "new look" in farmer voting represents a revolutionary change from the last period of Republican rule. During the 1920's the bulk of the farmers remained loyal to the Republican party through nearly twelve years of falling prices. How much more fickle and volatile the farmer has become can be seen in an incident which occurred during the 1954 campaign.

While traveling through southern Iowa, I stopped one farmer along the road. When he heard that I was touring the country to find out the "why" of people's voting, he asked, "Do you know who I am?"

I shook my head.

"I'm the Republican chairman of this county," he said. "If you won't use my name I'll tell you how I feel."

Assured of my discretion he went on, "Farmers have been too Republican for their own good. We need a farm program and we ought to work on both parties to get it. I'm for Eisenhower but I'm voting Democratic for the Senate."

In virtually every farm county, I ran into this same expressed determination of farmers to make both parties compete for the farmer's favor. Typical of the comments voiced were:

"If we keep Congress divided, each side will make the other do what's right."

"I like Eisenhower, but I want some Democrats around in case farm prices drop too far."

The fact that both parties have responded so vigorously in bidding for the farmer's ballot is likely to encourage this tactic of playing one party off against the other.

The farmer can hardly be blamed for trying to take advantage of the even balance between the two parties to protect his own economic interest. Primarily he is trying to prevent any repetition of the 1920's when agriculture was forgotten while the rest of the economy boomed along.

Still, this new preference for two evenly competing parties is likely to slow the pace of party realignment and prolong the current period of transition during which neither party will have a decisive majority in the country.

The competition of both parties for the farm vote will also have repercussions on the rest of the economy and on our foreign policy. Early in 1955 I happened to remark to one Republican leader that the Republicans faced a loss of much of their voting strength in farm areas in 1956. Nodding his head, he exclaimed, "We've just got to get rid of our surpluses even if it means dumping them abroad!"

In the fall of 1955 Secretary Benson stepped up the sales abroad of surplus farm products by undercutting the market price, which brought complaints from some of our allies that their normal trade outlets were being cut off. Despite these protests, this "solution" of the farm problem can be expected to gain considerable support among Democrats and Republicans alike. If farmers are given higher price supports the pressures will grow for some means of relieving taxpayers of this burden, whatever the effect may be upon the economies of our allies.

As long as the farm problem remains unsolved, in short, it is likely to remain a source not only of continued indecision in domestic politics but of weakness in the cold war.

The very fact that the "farm crisis" has been a constant problem since the 1920's indicates there is no painless solution. Some part of the excess agricultural capacity that was developed during the war, while Europe and much of Asia were overrun militarily, must be taken out of production. The broad issue is how this adjustment is to be effected.

The more extreme advocates of a "free economy" would

leave the adjustment to open competition, letting the fittest farmers survive. Opposed to that view are those who would use the power of government to share the burden of adjustment among farmers generally. Currently at least, this latter school seems stronger politically.

Whatever course is taken this seems clear—some years of trial and error lie ahead before we will know what degree of government management is needed to bring the technological revolution into balance. In view of this prospect of prolonged transition it may be well to see where the main trends of political cleavage in the farm belt are pointed.

3. Fathers Against Sons

"I'm a Republican and I'm going to vote for Eisenhower but I'd feel better if he lost."

It was so strangely contradictory a remark that I pressed the farmer for an explanation. A young veteran, he explained that he had bought his land only a few years before and still owed a good deal on it. "If prices start dropping," he commented, "I could be wiped out."

In sharp contrast was the reaction expressed by another farmer in Shawano County, Wisconsin. He and his brothers had been staunch Roosevelt supporters, but they were swinging for Eisenhower because "we must stop piling up this debt." In 1948, this farmer admitted, his family had stuck with Truman because they had not been quite ready to take their chances on a price drop.

"But we've got the mortgage all paid off," he pointed out. "We've bought all the machinery we need. We even have a welder so we can make our own repairs. Whatever happens we will be able to take care of ourselves."

The conflicting feelings of these two farmers—one debt free and the other heavily in debt—comes close to capsuling the new political divider among farmers today. In the main it is how hard-pressed or well-off individual farmers are.

The economic standing—and voting—of different farmers seems primarily the product of two factors, the farmer's own economic position and how much or how little of a price drop there has been in the crops on which he specializes. As these two factors change the farm vote can be expected to shift in the years to come.

Still another characteristic of farmer voting should be emphasized—a growing tendency of farmers to vote along much the same lines as do people in the cities. In 1954, for example, I found most urban voters balancing their gratitude to Eisenhower for ending the Korean War against how much of an economic adjustment they had suffered since 1952. This same pattern held through the whole farm belt.

Where the adjustment was moderate, farmers were inclined to go along with the administration's program, feeling, as one Iowan remarked, "It's not what Eisenhower promised but I don't know that there is any other way of dealing with the problem." Such expressions of patience vanished, however, when one moved into farming areas which were suffering real hardship.

In southern Illinois drought had ruined the crop of many farmers for the third successive year. Tanker trucks were rumbling along the roads carrying water from rivers for ten and fifteen miles around at $10 to $15 a load. In one county with strong kinship groups I hunted out the patriarchal head of a family known to have swung for Eisenhower. He was not too communicative at first and I tried to coax him into talking by saying this was his chance to voice any feelings he had.

"I wish you had that fellow Benson with you," the farmer replied. "I'd like to tell him something."

"Tell me instead," I urged. "Maybe Benson will read it."

Looking at me coldly the farmer retorted, "You couldn't print what I have to say."

Similarly in western Wisconsin one farmer stormed, "I

went to the fair and they charged me fifteen cents for a glass of milk! Do you know what I get for the milk I sell? Less than two cents. Who gets the other thirteen cents?"

Pointing to a new barn, he went on, "When I put that up milk was bringing $4 a hundred. Now it's $3 a hundred but I'm still paying off what I borrowed to put up that barn."

In both Minnesota and Wisconsin the basis of Republican supremacy was hammered out in 1938, when, as we saw in tracing through Senator McCarthy's career, the old Progressive and Farmer-Labor parties were torn apart. Eisenhower had carried all but three Wisconsin counties in 1952 and all but fifteen in Minnesota. The drop in milk prices by 1954 was nowhere near as heavy as the price declines farmers suffered during the 1920's. Yet in Minnesota in 1954 the Democrats were able to elect a governor for the first time since 1938, while in Wisconsin they came within thirty-four thousand votes of electing a governor. The Republican vote for Congress in Wisconsin dropped 10 per cent from 1952 to the lowest level since 1944.

During the campaign, crossing from Wisconsin and Minnesota into the corn-hog belt in Iowa and northern Illinois was like moving out of a storm into a calm. In five Iowa counties not a farmer I interviewed was losing money. The general refrain ran, "As long as hogs are selling over $18 a hundred we're not in trouble." So many different farmers volunteered this same $18 figure as their breaking point that in one campaign article I ventured the judgment that if hogs held above $18, Democratic Senator Guy Gillette might be beaten. During election week hogs brought $18.75 a hundred and Gillette lost.

By the fall of 1955, however, hog prices had dropped to $12 and Iowa farmers were talking as Minnesota farmers had the year before. Since Eisenhower swept every county in Iowa, 1956 was almost certain to bring some drop in the Republican strength. The question which faced the G.O.P.

strategists was whether hog prices could be lifted sufficiently by 1956 so Iowa could still be won.

Throughout the farm belt in 1954 the variations in voting
reflected quite closely how different farming areas were
faring economically. Within the same counties I found that
most of the complaining—and political shifting—centered
among farmers who were in debt as against those who
owned their farms mortgage free.

In Pierce County, Wisconsin, for example, one farmer
had shifted to Eisenhower with misgivings. "I have a boy
in the service and I want him out," he explained. "But
whenever I think of the debt on this farm I wonder whether
I should take a chance on a change."

When I saw this farmer again in 1954 he exclaimed pro-
fanely, "I'll never vote for a Republican again. This price
drop is terrible."

Similarly, in Dubuque County, Iowa, Elmer Greiner also
felt he had made a mistake in voting for Eisenhower. A
young farmer, Greiner had suffered more than his share of
hard luck. His barn had caught fire in his first year and he
had lost a lot of equipment.

"With expenses going up the way they are I can barely
hold on now," he complained. "We don't dare let farm
prices get much lower. We've got to keep what we have."

In large part this voting division reflects a clash of two
generations, even of fathers and sons. Generally those free
of debt are the older farmers who used their high earnings
of the war and postwar years to put themselves in a financial position to survive the "economic shakedown" which
they felt was coming. During the war years mortgages were
paid off at such a rate that by 1946 mortgage indebtedness
in the country was down to its lowest level since 1913. Farm
tenancy was cut from 42 per cent of all farmers in 1935 to
26 per cent in 1950. Seventy per cent of all farm owners
held their farms clear of debt by 1952.

In many counties I have come across farmers who voted for Truman in 1948 because they were still in debt but who shifted Republican in 1952 because in the meantime they had paid off their debt. As their economic situation changed, they would explain they felt "this spending has to be stopped before things go too far." One evidence of the increased sensitivity of farmers to government spending will be found in their holdings of cash deposits and savings bonds, which would be depreciated rapidly by inflation. Whereas in 1940 these cash holdings were about $4 billion, they have been running around $19 billion through the postwar years.

In contrast the younger farmers, most of whom started farming after the war's end, did not share in the bonanza earnings of the war years. Lacking these cash reserves, they borrowed heavily to buy their farms and machinery. The technological squeeze has been hitting these younger farmers harder than their more financially rooted neighbors. Being in debt the younger farmers have higher operating expenses. With farm prices falling, it also becomes difficult to pay off one's debts. The younger farmers also have less capital to work with.

In some instances this cleavage between the younger and older farmers is being cushioned by family ties. But in other cases it actually is splitting families politically. In one Iowa county a farmer and his son were having their midday meal when I called upon them. Asked how they felt about conditions, the farmer replied, "Things are fine. We're in pretty good shape."

The son exploded, "Things are so bad I'm going to quit!"

The son, who was working the farm on a share arrangement, found he could net little profit with expenses rising and prices slipping. The father, however, who owned the farm, was pleased that rising land values were improving his equity and that the fall in prices "isn't anything as bad as we expected."

Again, in Blue Earth, Minnesota, one farmer lamented, "I was a founder of the Farm Bureau in this county. We're all going along with the President's program. My son, though, has joined that radical Farmer's Union. He likes their talk of getting farmers 100 per cent parity prices."

Between 1952 and 1955, the Farmer's Union membership in Minnesota more than doubled.

Sharpening these differences in economic standing between the two generations are conflicting standards of living and different experiences. The prime concern of the older farmers is security for their remaining years, which partly explains their desire to remain free of debt. The younger farmers, however, have so many more needs to fill, not only on the farm but in better living at home. If to the younger farmers their parents seem smug and parsimonious, to the older farmers the new generation seems reckless, with little idea of the value of money and with no experience of the harsh times of the past. As one Minnesota banker remarked, "The older farmers remember ten-cent corn. Their sons think $1.50 corn is normal."

And yet one wonders whether the cleavage is as deep as it seems or how much choice either generation has. Occasionally one encounters a well-heeled farmer who will blurt out, "A depression would be a good thing. It would make a dollar worth a dollar again and push out some of these people who have no business farming." One also hears hard-pressed farmers grumble, "The rich farmers are waiting to see us squeezed out so they can buy up our land."

Generally, however, the bulk of farmers are striving for much the same thing, to dig in and hold onto their land. If the younger farmers want higher price supports than the older farmers, it is not because one generation is more conservative than the other. Lacking capital reserves, the younger farmers must borrow more heavily. Being in debt they are more inclined to look to government aid, if only to forestall drastic price drops until they have had time to work down their debts and make their equity more secure. The older farmers, with a better capital base, feel somewhat more independent and more willing to gamble on less government.

Still, even among these older farmers there is no strong disposition to do without any government program. The clash between the two generations, in other words, reflects a search for conservatism by different ways; their conflict is really one of degree over how much government management is needed.

One further aspect of this tendency of farmers to divide politically according to economic status is worth noting—the spread of part-time factory employment.

Nearly a fourth of the farm operators enumerated in the 1950 census worked off their farms for at least one hundred days of the year. In 1929 only 11 per cent did so. Partly this trend reflects the decentralization of industry, which, in expanding beyond the cities, has brought factory jobs closer to farmers. Also, where in past decades one had to move to the city to work in a factory, improved roads and automobiles now enable people to live on the farm while working in town.

The less-advantaged farmers seem to be the ones drawn into factory work. In Michigan, for example, a confidential survey by the Department of Agriculture of the changes in farm population brought such comments as these from farmers in eight scattered counties:

"Low income and high expenses are forcing farmers and their wives to seek employment in town. This is not reducing acreage in crops as has been said would take place, but increasing work to bring a decent income."

"The only way to make the farm pay even a living today

is to have the family work the farm and then get a job in a factory."

"Virtually all who are young enough to get outside employment do so. The average family-size farm here will no longer furnish acceptable living standards for a family."

Some farm leaders have contended that farm surpluses could be eliminated if submarginal, part-time farmers were pushed out of the picture. What actually seems to be happening, though, is that many farmers are turning to industrial employment as a means of holding on to their farms.

This trend still is too new for its full implications to be clear, but it could have important political effects. For one thing, being employed in factories does have an ideological impact on farmers. In the spring of 1955 *Wallace's Farmer* polled a cross-section of Iowa farmers on how they felt about legalizing the union shop. Among those who had never done anything but farm, only 39 per cent favored the union shop. Among farmers who had worked in town sometime or other, 69 per cent were in favor.

More important, unemployment can no longer be considered a strictly urban affair. The 1954 economic downturn showed that in many states a decline in industrial employment will now be felt even in rural areas. In Bedford County, Pennsylvania, I stopped at the home of one man who was living on his grandfather's farm. Over the years the land had been parceled out to so many heirs that only a few acres were left and this man had gone to work for an oil company.

"I was with them fourteen years, when they fired me," he complained. "Do you know when? Two o'clock on election day."

"Had you already voted?" I asked.

"I didn't vote until that evening," he replied. "It was the first straight Democratic ticket I ever voted."

The impact of decentralized industry upon rural areas also contributed to the defeat of Senator Homer Ferguson in Michigan. Ferguson's loss generally has been attributed to his bad showing in Detroit. What has been overlooked is how poorly he fared in upstate Michigan.

In staunchly Republican Isabella County, for example, Ferguson dropped 9 per cent below his 1948 vote. I searched out several precincts where the turn to the Democrats was particularly heavy. Among the farmers who shifted were a number who had been forced to take jobs in nearby cities to make ends meet. "You can't make a living on farming alone these days," complained one man. "Just before election I bought a new tractor. The price was the same as four years ago. But four years ago you could sell a cow for $200. Now it brings $100."

In contrast every full-time farmer I talked with in the Isabella County had stuck with the Republicans.

Should this trend gain momentum it could exert a considerable effect on the national political balance. Michigan, for example, has been perhaps the most consistently close state in its voting in the whole county. This division in voting has reflected a sharp rural-urban cleavage. If the spread of part-time factory employment among farm families upsets this old rural-urban balance, Michigan could be transformed into a normally Democratic state.

Almost it seems that farm politics are tending to become urbanized. Farmers generally are being split into two economic classes, each of which appears to be moving toward political alliance with similarly situated urban elements. While the more well-to-do farmers are aligning themselves with the middle-class elements in the cities and suburbs, the less well-off farmers seem to be aligning with the Democratic income elements in the cities.

In conclusion, the net impact of the technological revolution upon agriculture has clearly been to make for a more intimate pattern of interdependence between farm and cities. A better balance between land and people is being brought about through the introduction of machinery and migration from the land, which has been heaviest from the poorest areas. The gap between urban and rural living standards has narrowed. Geographical isolation is breaking down.

But if the physical basis for a new pattern of unity has been brought into existence, the immediate political impact of this technological revolution has been to divide the farmers. In part this division follows traditional sectional and agricultural lines, reflecting the crops involved. More significant, the division is tending to fall along much the same lines as in the cities—on the basis of economic status and over what the role of government should be.

One might say that the technological revolution appears to be substituting a new class division for the old sectional division. Today's "man with the tractor" is less a farmer than a businessman or a worker. Since conflicting trends are always at work in this country, it is too soon to say that we are witnessing the end of the farmer as a sectional political force. Yet the dominant trends seem to be making farmers ever more sensitive to the same forces that are reshaping urban voting.

The fact that the technological revolution is transforming the basis of farm politics suggests it is time to turn to the South and see how that fortress of sectionalism is holding up.

EIGHT

The Three-Party South

1. Of Time and Two Rivers

Like so much of the South the Savannah today is a river in transition. More than a century ago, when Augusta was our second-largest inland cotton port, as many as fifteen ships plied its muddy waters and Georgia historians still like to claim that it was in the Savannah that the first American attempt at a steamboat ran aground.

Today, however, cotton moves out by rail and the river traffic is down to three barges which haul bricks and oil. But with the completion of the Clark Hill dam just above Augusta, the Savannah is finding new economic life as the source of electric power for a growing number of industries, including the atomic energy plant at Aiken, South Carolina. And here, midway on the Savannah, where the Piedmont plateau meets the coastal plain and nuclear scientists still send their children to segregated schools, is an ideal spot for examining the conflicting currents remaking Dixie politically.

Historically, this middle Savannah Valley has always

exerted an importance far beyond any census weight of its population or resources. Four miles below Augusta was where Eli Whitney invented his cotton gin, which riveted the South to the deadly combination of cotton growing and slavery. In later years the Savannah earned the label of "the Mediterranean of the Confederacy" because so many of its leaders lived along its banks—John C. Calhoun, Alexander Stephens, who was vice-president under Jefferson Davis, and Robert Toombs, who, when Abraham Lincoln was elected, announced that "Georgia is on the warpath" and that he was quitting the Senate. (For all his anger Toombs did not overlook going to the Treasury to collect his Senate salary and mileage back to Georgia before leaving Washington.)

After "The War Between the States" the thirty-mile area around Augusta spawned the two most prominent demagogues of the Reconstruction South—red-haired Tom Watson on the Georgia side of the river and Ben Tillman on the South Carolina side. Both men coupled agrarian revolts against the "aristocracy" in their states with public defenses of lynching and a hate-rousing technique of campaigning which, a generation after their deaths, still was being imitated by Theodore Bilbo, Cotton Ed Smith and the Talmadges, both father and son.

Tillman, for example, evoked whoops of delight from his "wool hat" followers when he swore he would stick a pitchfork into President Grover Cleveland's "fat old ribs"—a bit of the oratory which won Tillman the nickname of "Pitchfork Ben." Watson's virulent campaigns helped incite the tragic Atlanta race riot of 1906, forced one Georgia governor to flee from the state and led to Watson's newspaper being barred from the mails during World War I.

By 1952, however, this middle Savannah country had become an ardent Eisenhower stronghold. In all of Georgia, Eisenhower's heaviest gains over the 1948 Republican

showing came in Augusta and the nearby counties of
Columbia, Burke and McDuffie, where Watson lived. Similarly, Edgefield, where Tillman kept a gold-pronged pitchfork on exhibit in his living room, was one of the six South
Carolina counties which gave Eisenhower more than two-
thirds of its vote.

What curious processes of political evolution explain how
the South that broke so heavily for Eisenhower grew out of
the South of Tillman and Watson, Stephens and Calhoun?
This intriguing riddle would be worth exploring if only for
the light it may shed on how social and economic changes
find expression in our political leaders. But history is also
a river which rises in the past and empties into the future.
And a time-machine exploration of this Augusta-Edgefield
area is one of the better ways of fathoming the enduring
changes in Southern politics.

At their October, 1955, conference all of the Southern
governors were quoted as feeling that "no Republican but
Eisenhower could carry a single Southern state in 1956."
But, if immediate Republican prospects seem to have
dimmed, that does not mean the South will lapse back to
the past, as if 1952 had never happened. True, much of the
Eisenhower vote reflected a hostility to Truman and an "I
like Ike" hero worship. Still, if one separates where Eisenhower was strongest from where he was weakest, county by
county and ward by ward in each of the eleven Southern
states, the striking fact that emerges is how distinctly the
vote stratifies along impersonal economic and racial lines.

So sharp is this stratification that it is plain that Eisenhower's candidacy, like the blasting of a dike, served to
release forces which had long been building up behind the
dam of one-party rule. For reasons developed later, it is my
judgment that the South is moving toward neither a two-
party system nor a return to unchallenged one-party rule,
but to something more tantalizing—a three-party South.

But, even apart from this judgment, the forces which the Eisenhower election unloosed will continue to dominate Southern politics for at least this generation.

The main elements which will be battling for political supremacy are etched plainly in the 1952 election returns. That vote showed three chief sources of Republican strength:

First, there were the traditionally Republican Appalachian counties, stretching from northern Alabama to southwestern Virginia, which opposed secession and have remained virtually unchanged politically since.

Eisenhower did not do particularly well among these mountain Republicans. Of eighty counties which Dewey won by a clear majority in 1948, Eisenhower gained more than the state average in only two. He ran behind Dewey percentage-wise in five, including Alabama's Winston County, which proclaimed itself a "free state" during the Civil War.

What swelled the Eisenhower vote to a flooding crest was the junction of two new rivers of protest—of racial and economic anger. In the 157 "black belt" counties which are most sensitive to the racial issue—where Negroes outnumber the whites but are not permitted to vote—Eisenhower jumped the Republican tally to eight times over 1948, against a threefold rise in the whole South. He gained more than the state average in 106 of these counties. In contrast, among the 152 most heavily white counties in the same states, Eisenhower gained more than the state average in only 42.

Even more spectacular was the Republican outpouring in the Southern cities, which was where the economic protest centered. Casting 32 per cent of the total vote in their states, 47 major cities provided 37 per cent of Eisenhower's gain over 1948 in the South. Except for Virginia, whose voting displayed a surprising uniformity through the whole state, these urban gains furnished the margin of victory in the four states Eisenhower won.

Victory Margin Where Eisenhower Won

State	Republican Plurality in State	Republican Gain Over 1948 in Urban Counties [1]
Florida	99,086	169,400
Tennessee	2,437	120,600
Texas	132,750	271,800
Virginia	80,360	32,000

[1] Includes Miami, Jacksonville, Tampa, St. Petersburg, Nashville, Memphis, Chattanooga, San Antonio, Dallas, Houston, Fort Worth, Richmond, Norfolk, Roanoke and Portsmouth.

Still more marked was the urban concentration of Eisenhower's following in some of the states he lost. The counties containing Georgia's three largest cities—Augusta, Atlanta and Savannah—cast only 21 per cent of the state's vote, but supplied 31 per cent of Eisenhower's gains over 1948. Jefferson (which includes Birmingham), Mobile and Montgomery counties, casting 27 per cent of Alabama's ballots, furnished 40 per cent of Eisenhower's gain.

With many Southerners, of course, racial and economic grievances against the Truman administration swirled together so intimately that the force of one is not easily distinguished from the other. But that these two rivers of protest are fed by differing and even conflicting emotions is clear from their varying impact among the Southern states.

In states like Mississippi and South Carolina racial angers dominated the 1952 voting. In other states, like Texas and North Carolina the main carrier of Eisenhower strength was economic.

This divergence between the economic and racial currents can also be seen in the voting on school segregation. Five states, South Carolina, Georgia, Louisiana, Mississippi and Virginia have held referendums to permit scrapping the public-school system to preserve segregation. The leading urban counties in these states, as the table below shows, voted from 12 to 24 per cent less in favor of school segregation than did the counties with the densest Negro population. In Georgia, the cities of Atlanta, Augusta and Savannah cast a majority against the segregation amendment.

Per Cent Favoring School Segregation

State	Urban Counties [1]	Counties 50% or More Negro	Whole State
Georgia	44	65	54
Virginia	60	81	66
South Carolina	70	83	67
Mississippi	66	90	69
Louisiana	78	90	82

[1] See Appendix for list of urban counties used.

In short, Eisenhower's 1952 showing can be attributed to the skill with which the Southern leaders who supported him merged these racial and economic grievances. But will these two rivers of insurgency continue to flow together—or will they veer off into different channels?

The answer to that question will determine the shape being given to the new party structure in the South and, perhaps, to the course of political realignment in the whole country.

2. The Cities Join the Union

Essentially, the conflict between these two streams of voter feeling is a clash between the forces of separatism and unification. Economically, the vast changes remaking the South in recent years have been pressuring for political unity with the rest of the country on a two-party basis. The dominant racial pressures, however, still are tugging hard to keep the South separate and solid from the rest of the nation. It is this portentous conflict which makes the Augusta-Edgefield area so rewarding to explore. In Augusta one can examine the economic drive of the expanding middle class, which is common to all Southern cities. Only a few miles away, Edgefield reflects the racial feelings common to all "black belt" counties.

Where in Edgefield 92 per cent of the voters favored ending public schools to avoid desegregation in Augusta only 32 per cent did.

Part of Augusta's showing can be credited to the fact that Negroes, who make up 40 per cent of the population, cast about a fifth of the city's vote. Still, the school amendment won a majority in only one non-Negro ward in the city—the fifth, which has the heaviest concentration of textile workers and was one ward that Tom Watson carried regularly. The strongest Eisenhower ward—the seventh—voted four to one against the amendment.

Known as the "Hill," this seventh ward is Augusta's wealthiest residential area. In it will be found the Augusta Country Club and all of the homes on the itinerary of the annual garden club tour. Although one street, known locally as "Millionaire's Road," is lined with palatial estates, most of the homes range in value between $20,000 to $30,000 and look no different from their counterparts in similar residential sections in the North.

Not only the upper middle class but every segment of Augusta's voting population exhibits this same tendency to stratify on identical lines with similarly situated voters in Northern cities. One can drive through Augusta and tell how different neighborhoods voted in 1952 simply by looking at the houses.

By far the heaviest Democratic majorities came along such Negro streets—so picturesque in the names they bear but in nothing else—as Thank God Alley, Electric Light

Alley or Tin Cup Alley. Although the average income of Augusta's Negroes has risen appreciably since 1940, most of the side streets in the Negro neighborhoods still are unpaved. On one block I saw something I hadn't seen since childhood—a dead dog lying in the gutter.

The next heaviest Democratic vote was recorded among white textile workers. "This is a rough part of town," commented my guide as we drove along. On the streets nearest the mills every house was alike, even to being exactly the same shade of weatherbeaten brown. Generally, even in the poorest neighborhoods some homes will be newly painted, reflecting the pride or individuality of the owners. But these were company-owned houses, always painted at the same time and left exposed to the weather with the same anonymous conformity.

The break-even point in Augusta's voting fell in the oldest part of the city, once known as "the Gold Coast" but now given over largely to boardinghouses. Like so many "break-even" precincts in Northern cities, it has become a "transition" neighborhood in which lower-income workers live side by side with the older "better-class" families who have not climbed out to the upper residential stretches.

Augustans like to explain Eisenhower's popularity in their city by the fact that he was a frequent visitor to the Augusta National Golf Club even before his election. But the faithfulness with which the vote scales on economic lines indicates that social class was the decisive political divider in 1952.

Nor does Augusta's voting differ appreciably from that of twelve other large Southern cities whose returns I have analyzed. A sampling of precincts in these thirteen cities shows that Eisenhower drew only about 12 per cent of the Negro vote, roughly 40 per cent in the labor areas and better than 70 per cent in the upper-income precincts. This close identity of voting and economic status revealed in the table which follows leaves little doubt that as far as the cities of the South are concerned the battle stations are already manned for two-party politics, mirroring the same economic cleavages which prevail in the rest of the country.

Per Cent for Eisenhower by Economic Class

City	Negro Precincts	Labor Precincts	Silk Stocking Precincts
Mobile, Ala.	11	34	72
Jacksonville, Fla.	13	28	79
Miami, Fla.	24	56	78
Tampa, Fla.	23	49	62
Atlanta, Ga.	25	28	67
Augusta, Ga.	23	40	75
New Orleans, La.	10	56	73
Baton Rouge, La.	5	36	64
Greensboro, N.C.	7	44	64
Charlotte, N.C.	7	39	82
Houston, Tex.	5	37	87
Dallas, Tex.	10	44	85
Richmond, Va.	15	43	75
13-City Average	12	39	75

Two other points stand out from this table. First, it goes far to demolish the widely held belief that voting in the South still is dominated by the Civil War. The South's allegiance to the Democratic party generally has been credited to tradition. But the sharp economic stratification in these election returns suggests that if the Southern worker remained loyal to the Democratic party, while his employers were turning Republican, it was primarily because he felt the same as workers did all over the country. The optical illusion created by the one-party system probably has led us to overestimate the importance of tradition in Southern voting and to underestimate the degree to which the South already has realigned to the issues of our day.

Second, the fact that Eisenhower drew between two-thirds and four-fifths of the upper-income vote in such varied cities as Richmond and Dallas, Miami and New Orleans is further evidence of what has been stressed earlier —the astonishing degree to which Eisenhower has unified the vote of the American middle class.

In fact, if we turn back to the table on page 113, showing the voting change in Northern cities and suburbs since 1936, we get a vivid picture of the role that economic class conflict has been playing in nationalizing the basis of American politics.

In the earlier New Deal years the laboring and lower-income elements were the carriers of the trends which worked to wipe out the old sectional and religious differences in voting. Today, the unifying surge is coming from the middle class, which is asserting its economic solidarity through the whole country, almost as a counter-thrust to the earlier solidarity of the New Deal elements.

This upsurge of the Southern middle class was not effected in a single election. In Houston, for example, I was able to obtain a sampling of nearly fifty voting precincts which corresponded closely to census tracts and therefore could be scaled readily economically. These precincts show a clear economic division in voting even in the peak Democratic year of 1936.

The consistency in voting revealed in the table below is astonishing. With each successive income rung, the Democratic strength declines. With each successive election, the lines of economic conflict sharpen at every income level.

Where in 1936 the Democrats won a majority in all these precincts, by 1940 the break-even voting line fell around the $19,000 level in home valuation. By 1944 the $15,000

rung had become the breaking point; by 1948 it was down
to $9,000 and in 1952 to $7,000.

Democratic Per Cent for President in Houston Precincts
Ranked by Average Home Valuation

Average Valuation	1952	1948	1944	1940	1936
Over $30,000	6	7	18	29	57
$19,000	13	29	35	47	71
$15,000	22	25	50	58	81
$13,000	22	23	52	60	79
$10,000	26	33	64	74	86
$ 9,000	33	40	68	80	90
$ 8,000	50	61	79	85	93
$ 7,000	49	57	78	88	93
$ 5,000	60	66	84	89	94
Under $5,000	60	72	87	89	91

So strong had the sentiment for a "break" become in 1952
that some Houstonians I interviewed during the campaign
confessed they were voting for Eisenhower because "everyone else is doing it."

Houston happens to be a prime example of a city whose
voting is dominated almost entirely by economics. In
Augusta, where race and economics have always been in
sharp conflict, the revolt against the Democrats was slower
in coming to a boil. As late as 1940 Roosevelt drew 90 per
cent of Augusta's vote, while in 1944 he simmered along
with 86 per cent.

Even during these years, however, the Republican temperature among the upper-income elements rose steadily.
In 1936 the swanky Hill ward gave the Republicans only
14 per cent of its vote. By 1940 the G.O.P. had risen to 23
per cent and by 1944 to 30 per cent. In 1948 the Dixiecrats
swept nearly two-thirds of the ward; Eisenhower pulled
three-fourths of its vote.

Behind this steady rise in Republican feeling stirred a minor economic revolution. In 1938 a WPA guide pictured Augusta as "a leisurely Southern city" which went in for two-hour siestas on hot afternoons and which showed little sympathy for those to whom "progress means bustling activity."

Today Augusta is clearly a city on the make. Its hyperactive Chamber of Commerce is constantly working up new statistics that are intended to convey the impression that Augusta is rapidly becoming a formidable trade rival of Atlanta. In the editorial columns of the Augusta *Chronicle* the acme of praise is no longer a comparison with the Old South, but the new adjective "progressive."

Among the thirty local members of the Augusta National Golf Club will be found at least nine millionaires, several of whom made the bulk of their fortunes since 1940. In the 1930's Augusta's wealth still was drawn primarily from the cotton trade. The newer fortunes—and this is symptomatic of a change in the whole South—have been made mainly in construction and fields which rely on mass purchasing power, like candy, food and furniture. In place of the earlier emphasis of combining natural resources and cheap labor, Augusta's economy has been shifting steadily to one based upon more abundant spending.

This change seems to have begun to take form during World War II. Higher farm prices gave the farmers in the surrounding counties new purchasing power. The reopening of Camp Gordon, at which thirty thousand troops were stationed, supplied another injection of spending power. But the really big shot in the arm was the construction of the $1.5 billion atomic-energy plant at Aiken, fifteen miles away.

In little short of two years, according to local estimates, Augusta's population jumped by one-fifth, retail sales by 11 per cent, building permits by 50 per cent. One furniture dealer, Grover Maxwell, reputed to be the richest man in Augusta, saw his business leap 50 per cent. Typical of the boom in realty values was the experience of one Augustan who had paid about $3,000 for the old Presbyterian manse in which Woodrow Wilson once lived. At the height of the boom he was offered $30,000 for the house but refused to sell.

As Augusta's bank deposits grew, so did the political militancy of its expanding middle class. Augusta's business leaders were no different from businessmen elsewhere in opposing Democratic policies in Washington. But, as one Augusta merchant commented, "In a one-party, Democratic state our votes were thrown away. We were paying all these taxes. We wanted to reverse the trend in Washington. The only way we could make our anger felt was to vote for a Republican President."

That comment nutshells the dilemma of the better-income elements in all the Southern cities. To protect their economic interests they feel they must make their weight felt in the scales of national politics. But they cannot do so effectively as long as the South has only one party.

Their quarrel, of course, is not with the Democratic party locally but with what it has become outside of the South. This, in turn, points to the crucial difference between the splitting of the South in 1952 and in 1920 and 1928. In those earlier years the makeup of the Democratic party nationally posed no such challenging conflict of economic interest between the Northern Democratic voters and the business-minded elements in the South.

The rise in Republican strength in the Southern cities, in sum, cannot be viewed as a mere passing phenomenon. While a Republican is in the White House, the need to counter the economic orientation of the Democratic party nationally may be subdued temporarily. But it is likely to flare up anew with a Democratic Presidential victory, as long as the Democratic party remains what it is like now in the North.

Perhaps the chief political weakness of this new Republicanism lies in the fact that the South still is so predominantly rural. Although the 1930–50 decades brought a dramatic urban expansion, in no Southern state, except possibly Florida, are the cities strong enough to dominate. To carry the electoral vote of their states, the urban middle class must find some basis of political alliance with those racially sensitive black belt counties like Edgefield.

But the desegregation battle is giving racial sectionalism a far different drive from that of the unifying economic surge in the cities.

3. A Test of Polite Society

From Augusta to Edgefield is only a forty-five-minute run by bus but it is like passing into a different social world. Where Augusta is so stridently in the mainstream of economic change, Edgefield seems to languish in a sluggish back current.

In Edgefield my bus pulled up at Timmerman's drugstore on Main Street. Nat Gray, a young Negro, took off the freight, a bundle of newspapers, two reels of film and some auto parts. He carried my bag around the corner to the local hotel. Erected in 1920, the year before the boll weevil reached Edgefield and cut its cotton crop by two-thirds, the hotel seemed almost on its last stilts.

When I asked the clerk at the desk if he had a telephone that I could use, he shook his head. "We've just taken over this hotel and they asked a $100 deposit," he apologized. "That's pretty steep for me."

I had picked Edgefield County to explore because, as the home of Pitchfork Ben Tillman, it seemed so historically logical a place to visit to gauge the political implications of the Supreme Court's decision outlawing segregation.

For it was Edgefield which gave birth to the famed "red-shirt" movement, which swept so many Southern states during the reconstruction period and which eventually forced the enactment of the segregation laws.

These "redshirts"—they took the name in defiance of the tactic of the Northern Republicans in waving the "bloody shirt"—were secret military companies which undertook to establish white supremacy by terrorizing the Negroes. Re-calling his exploits as a leader of one of these companies, Tillman once boasted on the floor of the U.S. Senate, "We took the government; we stuffed the ballot boxes; we bull-dozed the niggers and we shot 'em. And we are not ashamed of it."

Would the desegregation battle revive Tillmanism with all its bloody violence and racial strife? Or had the South changed sufficiently in the nearly forty years since Tillman's death so that acceptance could be won for a gradual relaxation of segregation barriers?

Hoping to gain some insight into what the future might bring, I set about to determine how much of Pitchfork Ben still lived on in Edgefield and how much of him had been outgrown. My trail of inquiry soon led to another historical puzzle—what was the continuity of social development between Tillman and another native of Edgefield, Strom Thurmond, who was the Dixiecrat candidate for President in 1948?

At first, from talks with Edgefield residents, the two men seemed to have nothing in common. Tillman, who had lost one eye through disease, was invariably pictured as a crude, lusty frontier spirit whose left-handed eccentricities were still amusing to recall.

During one gubernatorial campaign, his opponent, a man of aristocratic bearing, was sitting on the platform while Tillman was speaking. Halfway through his speech, Till-man halted, walked over to his opponent and knocked him out of his chair. To the delighted crowd he explained, "I just couldn't stand how he looks."

Another Edgefield old-timer recalled how Tillman made a practice of requiring the clerks in his Senate office to labor on the Tillman farm during Congressional recesses. An ardent physical culturist, Tillman was constantly developing new health fads, which he was ever ready to demonstrate to his neighbors in Edgefield or to his Senate colleagues in Washington.

One favorite set of exercises called for kicking his feet in the air and twisting his body in seventeen intricate movements, which were calculated to bend every joint and muscle. Periodically as well, Tillman would go on an onion diet, eating nothing but raw onions, tomatoes, bread and buttermilk. Whenever he spent a night at someone's home, a quart of milk had to be left at his bedside to be drunk before retiring.

In contrast, Thurmond was talked of in Edgefield as having a "fine" character, being polite and genteel, "a devout churchgoer," and "not liked by the liquor crowd."

These personality differences took on more meaning when examined against the political forces each man embodied. Where Tillman personified the revolt of the crude, not too literate farmer, Thurmond mirrors the revival of respectability which succeeded Tillmanism. The raging segregation battle can be viewed as a trial of the meaning of this transition, whether it has brought a fundamental change in the character of the South or merely in its external manners.

Tillman's age was one of violence and agrarian recoil. His father, who died when Ben was two, had killed a man. Three of Ben's brothers were killed in quarrels, while a fourth, after killing a mechanic in a drunken brawl over a game of faro, fled to South America, where he joined a revolutionary expedition.

This frontier tradition of shooting it out had not been overcome when it was given renewed vitality, first by the terrorism employed to establish white supremacy after reconstruction, and then by the agrarian revolt which Tillman led.

From almost a dollar a pound at the end of the Civil War, the price of cotton fell steadily to twenty cents in the 1880's and to nine cents in the 1890's. The bitter hardships suffered by the farmers swept Tillman into the governor's office after a stormy campaign against the "aristocracy." The passions aroused by this economic struggle, which raged in every Southern state, became all the more inflamed by racial agitation. It was no accident that lynchings in the South reached their peak in 1892, at the height of the Populist agitation.

Even the august surroundings of the U.S. Senate failed to tame Pitchfork Ben's temper. When John L. McLaurin, his fellow Senator from South Carolina, with whom Tillman was feuding over patronage, charged that a Tillman criticism was a lie, Tillman assaulted McLaurin on the Senate floor. Tillman and McLaurin were both censured by the Senate, setting the precedent on which the censure of McCarthy, fifty-two years later, was based.

Curiously, the most famous previous case of physical assault in Congress also involved an Edgefield man, Preston Brooks, who on the eve of the Civil War beat Charles Sumner unconscious with a cane on the floor of the House of Representatives. Brooks resigned so the people of Edgefield could send him back to Congress unanimously.

But every age breeds its own reformation and Thurmond can be said to typify the triumph of "polite society," which rose in protest against all this violence. Family remorse may have been one influence. Before Strom was born, his father, John William, had killed a man in a quarrel. But killing was no longer something to be proud of by the time

Strom was growing up. The family rarely talked of it. Strom was repeatedly instructed, "Defend yourself if you have to but obey the law."

More important was the fact that Strom's childhood coincided with a revival of prosperity and the rise of the town to social and political dominance. After 1910 the price of cotton climbed steadily until it was over thirty-five cents a pound after World War I. Coincident with this prosperity, many of the planters began to move into town, where they could give their sons and daughters the kind of education which would prepare them for college.

The Thurmond family was one of those which made this move, Strom's father being the attorney for the Southern Railway. In 1890 when Tillmanism was at its strongest, South Carolina was still more than four-fifths rural and Edgefield village had only 493 people. By 1902, when Strom was born, Edgefield's population had more than tripled, growing to 1,865 in 1920 and to 2,132 in 1930.

It was in these years that the "Bible belt," with its fundamentalist opposition to the teaching of evolution, became something of a laughingstock in the country. But the struggle for conformity on Main Street, South, had its heroic side as well. If it was laced with bigotry, it was also a struggle to forge new social disciplines for a people whose tempers and emotions had gone unchecked for too long.

In Edgefield, for example, the prohibition crusade was tied intimately with a drive to end local killings. One of the town's leading drys was the wife of a storekeeper who liked to tell his customers that he could point out eighteen different spots on the main square where someone had been killed. The husband of another dry leader had a habit of seizing their daughter and threatening to throw the child down a well, unless he was given money for liquor. Thurmond's mother was a charter member of the Edgefield WCTU, while his father neither smoked nor drank—habits

which Strom has emulated. In the 1915 prohibition referendum Edgefield went dry ten to one.

As Walton Mims, the editor of the Edgefield *Advertiser*,
recalls, "In the prohibition fight respectability climbed on
top. The most high-minded people were the drys."

The expanding town life was also the carrier for other
social traits which operated to bring forward a new type of
political leader—better education, more literacy, improved
roads, the new status of women, and, by no means least important, more varied forms of entertainment.

In Tillman's day a politician was expected to double as
an entertainer. Thurmond's father, who was Tillman's campaign manager, often took Strom to hear Tillman speak.
"He was the greatest stump speaker ever known," Strom
recalls. "He had only one good eye and it would grow
larger and glow like a coal of fire. The effect was almost
hypnotic. His voice sounded like the raging of a wild beast.
His speeches were highly inflammatory. He would set
people rolling in the aisles in emotional frenzy!"

In Georgia, Tom Watson had much the same ability to
inflame his listeners. Eugene Talmadge confessed that he
once walked ten miles to hear Watson speak. In Mississippi,
James K. Vardaman dramatized his championship of white
supremacy by garbing himself in white from hat to shoes,
riding through the towns and villages in a wagon drawn by
white oxen. Theodore Bilbo, who succeeded to Vardaman's
demagogic estate, memorized many of Watson's and Tillman's speeches, often opening his stump meetings with
"Hallelujahs."

But by the time Thurmond entered politics, the enter-
tainer-politician was a vanishing species. Better education,
the movies and the radio had set the stage for the emergence of a smoother, town-type leader.

In 1954 Thurmond was elected Senator by a write-in
vote. No such campaign would even have been possible a

generation before. As late as 1914 a fifth of South Carolina's voters could not even write their own names but had to sign the primary rolls with a mark. In 1919 when Thurmond went off to Clemson College he was the only boy of fifty with whom he started school who managed to finish high school.

By 1955 the Edgefield graduating class numbered fifty boys.

Equally impressive was the growing influence of women. In Tillman's time politics was a stag party and this accent on the male animal was reflected in his use of barnyard language. In the towns, however, the women led in the drive for respectability. They were the principal church workers, the founders of the local historical societies, the crusaders for moral reform. In short, they were the carriers of all the qualities of "polite society" which Thurmond came to embody.

This contrast between Thurmond and Tillman, and the ages they grew out of, can also be seen in their attitudes toward the Negro. Brutally outspoken in declaring the Negro "no better than a monkey," Tillman opposed education for Negroes, contending it was "idiotic" to disenfranchise the Negro and then "turn right around and provide the means to undo our work."

Thurmond, as governor, expanded appropriations for Negro schools in hope of providing a school system that would be "separate but equal" to the white school system—something which was pushed even more strongly by James F. Byrnes, who succeeded him. Both Byrnes and Thurmond threw their influence against any revival of Ku Klux Klan activity. When a young Negro, who had robbed and killed a white taxicab driver was lynched by a mob of other cab drivers, Thurmond had the lynchers arrested.

Where Tillman openly proclaimed the South's determination to preserve white supremacy, Thurmond, in his 1948 campaign for President, sought to camouflage the racial issue under the banner of "states' rights."

The rise of the town, reflecting this transition from Tillman to Thurmond has unquestionably brought some ebbing of racial prejudice in the South. The crucial questions that will be at test in the immediate years ahead are, how strongly rooted is this progress and will it be advanced or be snuffed out?

As far as Edgefield itself is concerned, there seems no evident danger of a resurgence of violence. That part of Pitchfork Ben's heritage appears outgrown, possibly because Edgefield has lost much of its economic vigor since the boll weevil cut through the county.

A few years ago Edgefield missed out on a chance to get a new industry because of its restrictions against employing Negro labor. Only recently the local water system was improved in hopes of attracting industry, and the general desire is to avoid racial strife.

On the other hand, the Supreme Court's desegregation decision is resented as an effort of "the North to tell us what to do." The local editor, Walton Mims, who is a passionate defender of Tillman as a champion of "violence for right," has been urging that the segregation problem be "solved" by turning over white schools to the whites and Negro schools to the Negroes, letting each apply for state and Federal funds. Still, even Mims does not seem to feel that segregation can be maintained indefinitely.

Edgefield appeared sufficiently torn by conflicting pressures so that a wise leadership, given time, probably could move it to the side of tolerance. Actually, though, the dominant political leadership in the deep South seems determined to force all such hesistant communities into irreconcilable opposition to the Supreme Court.

The strategy behind the Supreme Court's decision aimed at breaking the solidarity of the South on segregation. By entrusting the enforcement of its ruling to the individual district courts, the Supreme Court left room for differing rates of compliance within the same states. Localities with few Negroes were expected to take advantage of the opportunity to relieve themselves of the financial burden of maintaining two separate school systems, while areas with the heaviest proportions of Negro schoolchildren would have more time for adjustment.

This strategy has borne fruit in all of the border states, as well as in Texas and Arkansas, where some mixing of races started with the 1955 school term. But particularly in Mississippi, South Carolina and Georgia the foes of desegregation have mobilized to prevent any crack in the racial solidarity of their states. Local school boards have been threatened with the denial of state funds if they try to break out of the state mold. White citizens' councils have been organized not only to frighten Negroes from filing local school suits but to silence potential dissenters among the white population as well.

In effect what these white-supremacy councils are trying to do is kill off hopes of gradual, evolutionary change by hammering Southern opinion into an embattled, unified state of feeling which will brook no compromise. What happens next in the Deep Southern states will hinge on whether these extremists win this battle for the mind of the deep South.

So far the evidence indicates they will.

4. Thermostat of Insurgency

In 1895 when South Carolina, under Tillman's leadership, amended its constitution to disfranchise Negroes, Tom Watson, who liked to boast that he had the finest library in the South, wrote an indignant editorial. But the burden of defending the Negro proved too heavy. To gain support for his economic agitations Watson soon turned to demanding that Negroes be disfranchised and walled off in every aspect of Georgia life.

Watson's experience may be worth recalling in view of the crucial battle for Southern opinion now under way. For one thing, it suggests that the race issue in the South has a peculiarly totalitarian quality which is too easily overlooked.

For years, liberals in both the North and South have consoled themselves with the belief that the race problem would tend to lighten with time. Racial attitudes would be liberalized, it was felt, as the general educational level in the South improved and as the proportion of Negroes in the population was thinned by migration to the North.

This theory could have validity only in an atmosphere which left room for the dissents of individual Southerners. But something about the dynamics of racial prejudice operates to sweep individualistic shadings of gray into a monolithic black or white.

Between 1900 and 1950 in the deep South states of South Carolina, Georgia, Louisiana and Mississippi the proportion of Negroes in the population dropped from 52 to 36 per cent. But the counties in these states with the biggest declines in the number of Negroes show up no less strongly opposed to desegregation than the counties with the smallest Negro losses.

In the cotton-tobacco belt in these four states are forty counties where the Negro population dropped at least a fifth since 1900. Twenty-five of these counties voted 80 per cent or better to preserve segregation by abolishing the public school system if necessary. Another nineteen counties show a gain in Negro population. Thirteen of these voted at least 80 per cent in favor of segregation in the school referendum.

Or, turning back to 1900, there were fifty-seven counties whose population was at least 70 per cent Negro. More than half of these counties cast at least four-fifths of their ballots for school segregation. Yet these counties vary from 1 to 44 per cent in their loss of Negro population since 1900.

What does differentiate the counties in their voting on the school issue?

Two main dividers emerge:

First, a fairly sharp rural-urban cleavage. In Georgia, for example, there were thirty-three counties where at least 75 per cent of the voters favored ending public schools rather than permit desegregation. All but two of these counties are more than half rural. Of thirty-one counties where the school amendment was defeated, only thirteen show up as more than half rural. In all but two, Negroes make up less than 10 per cent of the schoolchildren.

The second main division in the school voting is remarkable in how closely it parallels the political cleavages that divided these states before the Civil War.

In Mississippi, for more than a century the plantation owners of the rich Delta lands along the Mississippi River have been pitted against the so-called "rednecks" in the northern hills and in the piney-woods country near the Gulf coast. It is along these lines that the school vote divides. The fifteen Mississippi counties which voted to keep the public-school system cluster in the hill and piney-woods country. The heavily Negro Delta counties voted 81 per cent for the amendment.

In South Carolina, as well, the school voting follows the century-old cleavage in the state between the agricultural low country, where the bulk of the state's Negroes live, and the heavily industrialized "upcountry," which has only a scanty Negro population. All five counties voting against segregation along with the four additional counties voting less than 60 per cent for the amendment are in the upcountry. In the low country every county voted at least two-thirds in favor of the amendment.

As the maps on the next page show this low country–upcountry cleavage divides South Carolina almost into two separate states. The counties which Eisenhower lost in 1952 are in the main the counties most heavily opposed to the school amendment. They also are largely the same counties which led the fight to establish the direct primary in 1886. Heaviest in manufacturing and strongholds of prohibition sentiment, they are the areas which supported Senator Olin Johnston in his 1950 race against Strom Thurmond.

In both South Carolina and Mississippi the pre-Civil War struggle was largely one of the slaveowner in the rich black belt against the yeoman farmer who tilled his upland farm without the aid of slave labor. That the antagonisms of that conflict should persist into our atomic age is evidence of how inextricably interwoven racial attitudes are in the very warp and woof of the South's social and economic fabric.

It also provides a clue to understanding why the black belt counties have striven to impose their racial views on other parts of their states. Racial feeling seems almost a form of nationalism which, when under attack, is driven to stamp out every competitive allegiance, including that of tolerance.

As long as this struggle continues and the South remains a nation apart racially, no clean-cut political realignment on a two-party basis is likely. And yet a return to the old one-party rule no longer meets the needs of these racial sectionalists either.

On the one horn of their dilemma, the Southerners who feel most strongly about the race issue cannot bolt the Democratic party locally since only through control of their state governments can they hope to impose and hold a solid racial front. But if they settle back to where the South's allegiance to the Democratic party can be taken for granted, they have no means of countering the influence of the Northern Negro in Presidential voting.

1952 Presidential Vote

■ Won by Eisenhower

□ Won by Stevenson

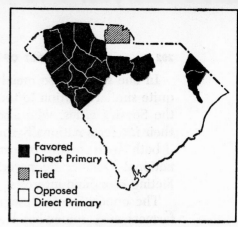

1886 Vote to Establish Direct Primary

■ Favored Direct Primary

▨ Tied

□ Opposed Direct Primary

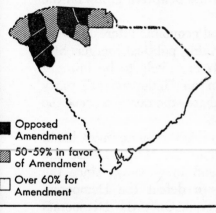

School Segregation Amendment, 1952

■ Opposed Amendment

▨ 50-59% in favor of Amendment

□ Over 60% for Amendment

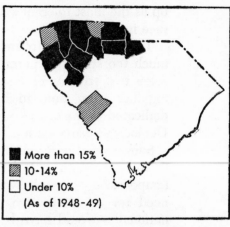

Per Cent Employed in Manufacturing

■ More than 15%

▨ 10-14%

□ Under 10% (As of 1948-49)

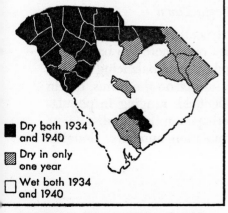

Prohibition Votes, 1934 and 1940

■ Dry both 1934 and 1940

▨ Dry in only one year

□ Wet both 1934 and 1940

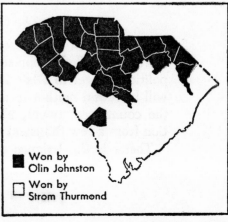

Johnston-Thurmond Senate Contest, 1950

■ Won by Olin Johnston

□ Won by Strom Thurmond

In one sense these racial insurgents find themselves in a quite similar position to the rising middle-class elements in the South's cities, who also feel that they cannot protect their interests nationally through the one-party system. But if both these streams of insurgency are in revolt against the national Democratic party, they remain divided by conflicting economic interests.

The opposition to desegregation is strongest among the farmers and, somewhat less so, among the workers, both of whom are drawn to the Democratic party economically. In contrast, the better-income elements in the cities show up as the most tolerant single white Southern group on the race issue.

This cross-conflict of racial and economic interests seems much too strong to permit a lasting political merger. Still these two streams of insurgents are likely to be brought together from time to time in an "independent" party dedicated to the one aim both share—the desire to beat the Democratic party nationally.

Such a third-party mechanism might operate much like a thermostat. With a Republican in the White House the temperature of revolt would tend to go down since the need for an alternative party—to defeat the Democrats nationally—would have been served. Once the Democrats won the Presidency, though, the thermostat of insurgency would start up again.

5. *The One-Party Town*

This forecast of a three-party rather than a two-party South is fortified if one searches out where the balance of political power in Dixie lies today. This balancing margin will be found neither in the cities nor on the farms, but in the county-seat towns, like Edgefield, ranging in population from a few thousand to perhaps ten thousand.

Theirs is the balance of population numbers. Roughly

half of the South's population today is urban, divided between middle class and worker elements. Another 25 per cent are farmers, while the remaining fourth is rural non-farm, chiefly townspeople.

In voting as well, the towns approximate the median for their states, balancing between the better-off urban elements at one extreme and the farmer and factory worker at the other.

From various sources I have managed to collect detailed precinct breakdowns for nearly two hundred predominantly rural counties in five Southern states. The county-seat towns voted consistently more strongly for Eisenhower than the surrounding countryside. The difference ranges from 5 per cent in Texas to between 10 and 15 per cent in Mississippi, South Carolina, Louisiana and Georgia.

On school segregation, a sampling of fifty-eight Georgia counties shows the county-seat towns voting 11 per cent more heavily against the segregation amendment than the rest of the county. These same county seats voted 10 per cent more for Eisenhower than the nearby farmer precincts.

In Mississippi the county-seat towns are slightly more opposed to segregation than the surrounding countryside in the Delta counties. But in the most heavily white counties in the hill country the towns vote more strongly for segregation than do the rural precincts.

At least in the deep South, the middle-class townspeople constitute the decisive political battleground today. Somewhat more tolerant racially than the rest of the rural South, they would have to lead the way in racial change. Economically as well, they are more likely to vote Republican than the farming areas they serve.

How individual towns will shift during the years to come will vary, of course, with their own racial and economic composition. Still, as a group, the towns seem likely to slow rather than quicken the processes of party realignment.

For the very structure of the small town seems to require a one-party monopoly in local politics. This was first impressed on me during the 1952 campaign in sampling a number of Southern counties. I found most townspeople strong for Eisenhower but equally adamant against building a local Republican party. To defeat the Democratic party nationally was one aim many shared but none of those interviewed wanted two-party competition locally.

As I talked with them it became clear why they felt as they did. Most small towns are run by what is loosely termed "Main Street," meaning the leading merchants and other property holders working in harmony with the courthouse ring. To these merchants local political control is indispensable. Many extend considerable credit to farmers and Negroes for miles around and the local officials are, in effect, their collection agents. Since these merchants, as the heaviest taxpayers, would also bear the brunt of the cost of local improvements, they want to keep control of county spending.

Similarly, a one-party monopoly helps ease many problems of local business competition. The publisher of the county-seat newspaper finds it easier to hold onto the contract for official printing if he has to deal with only one party. The leading undertaker, who generally doubles as the coroner, doesn't want his hold on that post subject to the uncertainties of a real political contest for the office.

Nor does local political factionalism help a county get more effective representation in the state legislature or in the distribution of state funds for highways, hospitals, roads, schools and other purposes. Usually the benefit of doubt in state spending goes to the county which delivers solid support for whoever is running the state.

This affinity of the small town for a one-party system is not confined to the South. Few county-seat towns in any Northern state have more than one effective political party locally. In Iowa, for example, the Democrats carried many counties in every Presidential election from 1932 through 1948, without jarring the hold of the local Republican courthouse ring. In some Midwestern counties I have run into Republican town chairmen who confided that they had voted consistently for Democratic Presidents since the New Deal.

The primary system, although not designed for this purpose, has worked out as almost the answer to Main Street's prayer. Townspeople generally cast a higher proportion of the primary vote than the rest of the county, which facilitates their control of who is to run on the majority ticket in the general election.

In the South the fear of party competition is sharpened by the relatively low voting participation. In one Southern county seat a majority of the people I stopped around the courthouse square told me they never bothered to vote. Later, walking up and down the few blocks which constituted Main Street, I made a rough guess of how many votes the business community could muster. It was readily apparent why these merchants would be frightened by the prospect of any abrupt increase in the size of the electorate, as might come through letting Negroes vote.

"We're in the minority here," was how one small-town Texas merchant put it, and that seemed the general feeling. It was difficult to see these merchants leaving the Democratic party for good as long as they felt themselves so insecure politically. To forsake the Democratic party locally would be to risk others' coming in and taking dominance over Main Street.

If local solidarity is as important as sketched here, then the townspeople would seem to have two alternatives. One would be to change parties en masse, as a virtual bloc, so as not to imperil their control locally. The other would be to develop an "independent" party mechanism through which they could register any protest on national issues, without endangering their one-party dominance.

To sum up, on economic issues the South today shows much the same voting divisions as those which prevail in the rest of the country. Republican prospects loom best in those states where economic considerations dominate. But where the racial conflict is strongest, as in the deeper South, the insurgencies that develop in the future are more likely to take the form of third-party movements as in both 1948 and 1952.

Such a three-party politics obviously is a symptom of transition. But that does not mean that it could not persist for a considerable period. In Wisconsin and Minnesota, the Progressive and Farmer-Labor parties served as a halfway house between the Democrats and Republicans for a full generation. It took the emotional conflicts stirred by both the New Deal and World War II to realign the followings of these third parties.

Until the racial issue finds some resolution, the South, like the farm belt, will probably remain a force for continuing the present uneasy party balance in the country. The very closeness of the national voting in the rest of the country can be expected to encourage Southern politicians in developing their own techniques for playing one party off against the other.

This situation may please many conservative-minded people who see the South's attachment to racial separatism as a barrier to further "centralization" of government. Still, there is an enormous difference between balance and stalemate, between gaining time for orderly, unifying adjustment and letting time aggravate all the tensions that make for disunity.

Which of these two courses are we likely to follow? Since the influence of a "separate and solid" South is felt most strongly in Congress, much will depend on our understanding the new relationship being forced upon the President and Congress by the absence of a decisive party majority.

NINE

The Anatomy of Congress

1. How People Vote for Congress

Next to the Vice-Presidency Congress has probably been the butt of more jokes than any other aspect of our political life. Fred Allen had his windy Senator Claghorn; while the late Will Rogers could always count on a laugh when he recalled visiting the House gallery and feeling, "An ordinary comedian like me would have no chance there. I was the most unfunny man in the entire building."

On the more serious side Congress has often been attacked as a veritable "house of misrepresentatives." Its members are widely portrayed as being concerned primarily with local interests or with obstructing whoever happens to be President. Because of the over-representation of rural areas and the seniority system through which committee chairmen are selected, it is often contended that the workings of Congress as a whole fail to reflect the true will of the people.

With this commonly held view I would like to register a

fairly strong dissent. Congress is what it is primarily because that is what the American people are like.

This holds true not only in the sense that individual Congressmen are typical of the average run of our citizenry. Beyond that, it is really our own weaknesses and strengths, extremism and moderation, which give shape to Congressional decision and indecision. A seat-by-seat study of the makeup of Congress which I have completed for this book shows that in recent years at least Congress has become far more sensitive to national issues, despite gerrymandering, than most people realize.

Similarly, although Congress and the Presidency have played deadlock with one another since 1938, today's struggle between the White House and Capitol Hill is a drastically different affair from the old stalemate of Roosevelt's time.

One reason why these changes have gone unrecognized, I suspect, is that the dynamics of voting for Congress have not received anything like the attention that has been given Presidential voting. For my own part I never fully appreciated how vastly different the two voting processes were until the 1954 campaign when I tried to penetrate into how people picked their Congressmen. The results of my talks with several thousand voters were something of a revelation.

As might be expected, I found that most people do not even know the names of their Congressional candidates. What is intriguing is how they get around this blank spot.

To overcome this lack of knowledge about the men running for Congress, two conflicting habits of voting have developed.

Most people, including many who protest stoutly that they always "go for the best man," simply vote the party label to which they are predisposed, and it is through such party voting that the predominant political trends in the country get registered. But many other persons fight against following a blind party line. Some try hard to form considered judgments on the candidates. Others assert their independence by clutching at even the smallest straw of identification, which makes them feel they "know" one of the candidates.

"He once gave me a shopping bag," was how a Dayton, Ohio, worker explained his support of Congressman Paul F. Schenck. Other persons justified their preference for a particular candidate with remarks like these:

"He sent me a questionnaire which asked my opinion on the farm bill."

"I shook hands with him at an American Legion meeting."

"I wrote him a letter and he answered me so nice."

"He sent me a booklet on infant care."

"I've seen his name on more billboards. I never even heard of the man running against him."

"The other man is a city feller."

Some of these comments may seem amusing, even senseless. But they are largely evidences of how strong is the urge to break party lines in voting. They also help explain the antics which some of our politicians perform, from strumming guitars to sporting coonskin caps, to get themselves remembered.

Other things being equal the Congressman in office enjoys a considerable advantage in that he usually is better known than his opponent. Often, in fact, "maverick" legislators appear whose following cuts across both parties and who get re-elected repeatedly regardless of the trend in the country.

Some of these mavericks rely on personal charm. At other times a man may run under one party label and then defy everything ordinarily associated with that party. The late Fiorello La Guardia was such a Republican and his example has been copied in recent years by Jacob Javits, who, although a Republican, voted identically with New York Democrats on most issues. When Javits stepped out of Congress to run for Attorney-General in New York State, his district voted 67 per cent Democratic.

Still, although these mavericks make colorful copy, the bulk of the voting for Congress is governed by the party trend. And that brings us to what makes present-day relations between Congress and the President so unusual—and disturbing.

For since the end of World War II there really has been no dominant or sustained trend in favor of either the Democrats or Republicans.

One effect, of course, was seen in the 1954 election, which gave the Democrats control of Congress while a Republican tenanted the White House. Herbert Hoover, after 1930, and Woodrow Wilson, after 1918, also had to grapple with hostile legislatures. In both these instances, though, unified party control of the Presidency and Congress was re-established at the next election to continue for a considerable time. In recent years, party control of Congress was lost not only by Eisenhower but Truman, after 1946.

Twice before in our history we have undergone the ordeal of prolonged periods of divided government. For the twenty years preceding the Civil War and again for the twenty-two years from 1874 to 1896, no President had the support of a Congress of his own party through his complete term.

Both these periods were remarkably like our own in one respect—they were years during which political loyalties were being reshuffled and neither party held a decisive majority. Once the forces of realignment had completed their task and one party emerged as the undisputed majority in the country it had no trouble commanding both approaches to Pennsylvania Avenue. But while the voters tossed in restless transition, control of the government remained divided and shifted from election to election.

This historical pattern suggests that a new third dimension needs to be added to our thinking about what governs the balance of power between the White House and Capitol Hill.

Most students of history agree that this balance is determined primarily by how "strong" a character the President is or by how critical are the times. But our history has been marked by the alternation of not only strong and weak Presidents, times of crisis and relaxation, but divided and united government, reflecting the absence or presence of a clear-cut party majority.

In the light of this, the usual solutions which are trotted out when the going in Washington gets tough will hardly meet our need. Some persons will continue to cry "we must have a strong man in the White House" or "Congress needs reorganizing" to reflect the will of the public. And yet the root fault will lie with the people themselves, in why they refuse to choose decisively between the parties.

Nor, as earlier chapters have shown, is a dominant majority likely to emerge soon for either party. At least two broad segments of the population—the farmers and racial extremists in the South—are consciously developing a technique of working both sides of the political street. This spirit of "neutralism" between the parties runs strong among other groups of the population as well.

What would have to be done politically for either the Democrats or Republicans to achieve a decisive majority? And until that is brought about how are we to judge the inevitable battling between Congress and the President that is bound to develop in the years ahead?

Largely to answer these two questions I have tried a novel experiment in dissecting the anatomy of Congress by examining how every seat in the House of Representatives has shifted or held since 1932. At first this probing into the Congressional "innards" yielded what seemed like a strange contradiction—the same trends of social and economic change were making one part of Congress more rigid in its party loyalty and other districts more volatile and uncertain.

Explored more fully, though, this contradiction proved to be a reflection of the struggle between extremism and moderation—of the past against the future—which constitutes the political crisis of our generation.

It is in the rigidly held seats that the feuds of the past are most jealously locked, while the newer emerging issues of our times are making themselves felt through the more closely contested Congressional districts. The stand-off stalemate that prevails in Congress today reduces itself to the paradox that the moderate political elements in the country dominate the shifting seats which determine which party controls Congress, but the "sure" seats remain the strongholds of the extremists in both parties.

2. Cracking the Democratic Party

In sheer numbers it is surprising how few truly contested seats there are.

Following through each district as best one can despite redistricting changes, we find that 220 seats, or more than half of the entire House, never have changed parties since 1932.

Another 64 seats have swung so rarely—only once or twice and prior to 1940—that they also can be classed as virtually unchanging.

This means that during most of the years since the New Deal the party struggle for Congress has been fought out through roughly a third of the seats.

Even this estimate overstates the number of seats which

can be considered as really contested. Within the "fluctuating third" of the House will be found 39 more seats where the winner got at least 60 per cent of the vote in 1954.

The Democrats show up with a considerably higher proportion of rigid districts than do the Republicans. Of 232 seats held by the Democrats in 1954, as many as 155 never have gone Republican since at least 1932. Another six were won by the Republicans once or twice prior to 1940 but have been Democratic since.

Those figures pretty much tell the story of how heavy run the odds against the Republicans' regaining their old standing as the nation's majority party. The 161 seats which have been Democratic since 1940 represent 37 per cent of the whole House membership. In another 23 seats—5 per cent more of the House membership—the Democrats won in 1954 with at least 60 per cent of the vote. This leaves hardly ten per cent of the House seats for the Republicans to work on.

A clean sweep of the contested seats would give the Republicans a sizable majority but it would be a majority subject to quick overturning by a counter-swing in relatively few districts. To obtain a firm hold on Congress, one which can be counted on for election after election, the Republicans must crack some of the rigidly held Democratic seats.

The largest proportion of these "sure" Democratic seats are in the South, of course. Less generally realized is the fact that the second largest bloc of such seats is in those Northern cities where the Negro vote has been becoming steadily more important.

Of the 161 seats which have been Democratic since at least 1940, 98 lie in the South, while 45 are concentrated in Northern cities or nearby industrial areas. Thirty-four of the Northern districts cluster in ten of the larger cities.

Between 1940 and 1950 the Negro population in these

ten cities leaped more than two-thirds while the white population increased less than 4 per cent. In these cities Negroes now account for roughly 12 per cent of the population. Moreover, as their numbers have increased so has their Democratic party loyalty. Negroes, in fact, have been the one voting element in the country which has grown more Democratic with every election since 1936. Truman got a heavier proportion of the Negro vote than did Roosevelt, while Stevenson did even better among the Negroes than Truman.

Given this composition of "sure" seats the conflicts of race and economic class are clearly conflicts from which the Democrats cannot escape. These conflicts can be said to constitute the *very character* of the Democratic party. The real Democratic choice lies between developing some means for reconciling these issues and permitting them to tear the party apart.

Time seems to be sharpening this conflict. The migration of Negroes from the South is working inexorably to increase the number of rigidly Democratic seats in the North which are particularly sensitive to racial problems. In Philadelphia, for example, only one Congressional district was as much as 20 per cent Negro in 1932 while two more were over 15 per cent Negro. By 1952 two of the city's six districts were over a fifth Negro—one being as high as 44 per cent—and two more were more than 15 per cent Negro. In 1952 Negroes represented 16 per cent of the registered voters in Philadelphia.

In Detroit the number of Negroes soared from 4 per cent of the population in 1920 to 16 per cent in 1950. There were 97 census tracts without any Negroes in 1940. By 1950 the increased Negro population had spread so widely through the city that there were only 17 census tracts without Negroes. Detroit in 1954 elected its first Negro Congressman, bringing to three the number of Negroes in the House.

The migrations of population may also be sharpening the economic conflict between the two wings of "sure" Democratic seats. Except for New Orleans, no Southern city is large enough to lie in more than one Congressional district. This, of course, means that the economic solidarity of the urban districts in the South is thinned by the wide range of income elements embraced in the district. In many of the larger Northern cities, though, the flight to the suburbs has left behind whole districts with a preponderant concentration of low-income voters.

In some of these cities during the last few years, the Republican Congressional strength has been virtually wiped out by the combined effects of the exodus to the suburbs and the growing solidarity of the Negro. In 1954 the Republicans lost the last of Detroit's six seats—Michigan District 17—mainly because of the reshuffling of population through the city. In Chicago the Republicans have been pressed back to the outskirts of the city, holding three partially suburban districts.

In Philadelphia, Boston and Manhattan the remaining Republicans are making their last stand veritably on the one-yard line. In each of these three urban centers the last Republican seat was won in 1954 by a fraction of 1 per cent of the vote. The Boston district, which embraces aristocratic Beacon Hill, would have gone Democratic in 1952 and 1954 if it had not been gerrymandered to include nearby suburbs.

The most heavily Democratic districts in the North, in short, are becoming those which are poorest economically and which have the largest Negro populations—two characteristics which tend to pull the representatives of these districts back to the old appeals of the New Deal. If this trend continues, as seems likely, the Congressmen from these districts will find themselves in sharpening conflict with the Southern districts, both with the anti-Negro sentiments, so strong in the rural South, and the economic conservatism of the rising middle-class elements in the Southern cities.

The impressive show of party harmony which the Democrats in Congress have mustered since 1952 is certain to pass off. It seems primarily a change in political manners, brought about by the chastisement of defeat, rather than any change in political character. Far from being outgrown, the old inner Democratic conflicts have been gathering new strength.

The underlying tensions between these two wings of "sure" Democratic seats are sufficiently intense so that the cracking apart of the Democratic party must be rated as a possibility. Still, two conflicting considerations should be borne in mind.

First, there is the astonishing ability of American political parties to reconcile the conflicts which threaten to tear them apart. The hidden strength of the American political party, as I have pointed out, lies in the fact that it serves as an arena for hostile political elements. The need to reconcile these clashing elements compels each party to bring to the surface unifying compromises, without which neither the Democrats nor the Republicans could have survived this long.

Second, the very intensity of this North-South conflict makes it difficult for the Republicans to appeal to either faction in truly dramatic fashion—since any open appeal to one side might solidify the other in the Democratic ranks.

Some Republican strategists have argued that since the Negro vote is so strongly Democratic it should be written off as lost. Other G.O.P. leaders are hopeful that the Republicans may profit politically from the fact that the desegregation decision was handed down by a Republican

Chief Justice, Earl Warren. My own studies of Negro voting indicate that the Negro attachment to the Democratic party has been as much economic as racial in motivation. As the lowest-paid worker in our industrial society, the Negro is both class and race conscious.

The referendum in Ohio in 1955 to liberalize the basis of unemployment compensation affords one graphic illustration of how sensitive Negroes are to economic issues. Throughout Ohio the amendment won only 37 per cent of the vote, and even in the major cities only 39 per cent. Fourteen Negro wards in five cities—Cincinnati, Cleveland, Columbus, Toledo and Canton—voted roughly 78 per cent for the amendment.

Republican prospects of cracking the Negro vote seem no better, and perhaps somewhat worse, than their chances of gaining votes among other workers.

Still, it does not follow that "writing off the Negro vote" would help the Republicans in their fight for control of Congress. The areas of the South which are most sensitive to the race issue are precisely the areas which are most insistent upon maintaining a one-party system locally and a solid Democratic delegation in Congress. The surge of racial sectionalism, it should not be forgotten, is to keep the South separate and solid from the rest of the nation. Among the racial extremists there is no real drive for political competition except in terms of Presidential voting.

Significantly none of the seven Southern seats the Republicans held in 1954 are districts where racial issues dominate. Three cover areas of traditional mountain Republican strength; the other four seats are urban or suburban.

Throughout the South in 1952 Eisenhower carried thirty-eight Congressional districts in the voting for President. Only seven or eight of these districts are ones where racial feelings were paramount.

The main Republican hope for further gains in the South, in short, would seem to lie in an economic appeal, which, as it turns out, is also the strongest force reshaping the Republican party in the rest of the country as well.

3. The Republican Conflict

If, as we have seen, the tensions of race and economic class are lodged in the very skeletal bones of the Democratic party, farm and foreign policy seem the main conflicts embedded in the "sure" Republican seats.

Of 123 districts which have been unwaveringly Republican since 1940, only 6 are completely urban, 30 are either suburban or a mixture of suburbs and cities, while almost 70 are more than 40 per cent rural. Nearly three-fourths of the urban or suburban seats are in the East or West Coast, while about two-thirds of the rural seats are in the Midwest.

The Republican party battle has always followed sectional lines, of course. Most historians trace this back to the bitter economic struggle between the industrial East and the agricultural Midwest that accompanied our rise to world economic power in the 1890's. For thirty years after the Civil War, farm prices, which were exposed to world competition, dropped steadily, while the profit margins of tariff-protected industry rose. The Populist uprising has often been pictured as a semi-colonial revolt against the "international money power" and its agents in Wall Street.

Although some of this old economic hostility may be revived by the current drop in farm prices, the sectional Republican cleavage in recent years developed mainly out of our involvement in World War II. In 1936, when the Democrats swept all but eighty-nine seats, the Eastern Republicans held more districts than did their Midwestern cousins. But in the elections which followed, the G.O.P. gained much more heavily in the Midwest. During the war

years the spread between the East and Midwest widened
to more than twenty seats, the largest difference since 1918.

Since the war's end, though, a new pattern of Congressional realignment has been at work. Perhaps the outstanding feature of this new realignment has been the progress
that the Republicans have made in establishing themselves
as a *national party*, with strength in every section of the
country.

This change in the Congressional battle map can be seen
in the table which follows, showing the number of seats
held by the Republicans in different regions since 1936.
Compared with 1938, when the anti-Roosevelt coalition
first came into control of the House, the G.O.P. has lost
four seats in the East and picked up four in the Midwest.
The impressive Republican gains have come on the Pacific
Coast, in the South and in the mountain states.

One result which already has registered has been a shift
of the balance of power within the Republican party. Since
1946 the Pacific Coast has accounted for more Republican
seats than the difference between the Eastern and Midwestern Republican strength. California, today, comes
close to wielding the balance of votes in any sectional conflict within the Republican party.

Rise and Fall of G.O.P. Strength
Number of Seats Held [1]

	1936	1938	1940	1942	1944	1946	1948	1950	1952	1954
East	46	72	60	74	69	90	64	70	75	68
Midwest	34	79	81	95	88	102	75	90	90	83
Pacific	5	10	11	18	13	23	21	21	29	28
Border	2	3	5	15	12	20	5	10	12	8
Mountain & Southwest	0	3	3	5	6	9	4	6	9	9
South	2	2	2	2	2	2	2	2	6	7
Total	89	169	162	209	190	246	171	199	221	203

[1] The states grouped in each of these regions are listed in the Appendix.

That the means through which the Republicans are seeking to nationalize their following are primarily economic is evident from the districts which they held in 1954 but which they never won during the war. Outside the West Coast, there are thirteen such seats. Four are in Nevada, Utah, Montana and Arizona, while five are in the South, four of these being predominantly urban or suburban. The other districts picked up by the G.O.P. since the war's end include the traditionally pro-Southern Eastern Shore of Maryland, another largely suburban Maryland seat, Louisville and its suburbs and Indianapolis.

The transformation the Republican party is going through might be summed up as an effort to hold its anti-war, rural following in the Midwest, even while reducing its influence by gaining new economic strength in the South, on the West Coast and in the Mountain states.

The two spots of sorest vulnerability for the Republicans are in some of the Eastern industrial centers, where population shifts are threatening districts which have never gone Democratic, and in the Midwest, where the Republicans suffered their heaviest losses in 1948.

The 1948 election, as a matter of fact, provides a rough but revealing outline of what the Democrats would have to do to regain their old New Deal ascendancy. In that vote nearly all of the wartime Republican gains were wiped out and enough rural seats were won by the Democrats to drop the G.O.P. strength in the Midwest below its 1938 level. At the same time the Democrats also won back most, though not all, of the urban seats which they lost in 1946.

All of these factors are not likely to reappear unless there is a considerable economic downturn. Even if the Democrats were swept back into power they would face formidable difficulties both in holding that majority and in achieving sufficient internal cohesion among its elements to be able to function. On the one hand a Democratic victory could be expected to start up the thermostat of Southern insurgency and conflict with the Northern urban elements.

Then, an economic revival would soon push the Democrats back against the ceiling of their economic appeal among the more moderate conservative elements—the threat of inflation.

In short, because of their backlog of Southern seats the Democrats can muster a large numerical majority in Congress far more readily than can the Republicans. But having done so the Democrats find themselves torn by all the problems of racial and religious tolerance, foreign policy and preservation of the gains of varied economic elements who range from the slums to the new spreading middle class.

How delicate is the political balance between these economic elements is evident in the most closely contested districts. Fifteen seats have shifted at least twice between 1948 and 1954, four being won in 1954 by less than 1 per cent, while thirteen more seats break almost exactly even between the parties.

Two-thirds of these seats are hybrid districts, part urban and suburban, or part farm and city, or a mixture of farm, city and suburbs. Any appreciable shift in the economic balance that affects some one of the major voting elements in these districts is apt to shift the seat.

In Indiana's eighth district, for example, the Republicans in 1954 actually held a slight edge in Evansville, which ordinarily would have insured their victory. But the G.O.P. loss in the surrounding farm and coal-mining counties swung the seat to the Democrats.

Across the country there are enough such hybrid districts to tilt the balance of control in Congress.

In other words, the narrow party balance in Congress is a surprisingly sensitive reflection of the same divisions of economic interest and concern over maintaining the post-depression gains which have led so many voters to develop political insomnia when trying to choose between the parties. Both in the fluctuations of the hybrid seats and in the rigidity of its unchanging seats Congress has become a mirror for the conflicting forces that are in transition through the whole country.

The evils of gerrymandering should not be brushed aside. Some districts, in fact, are so closely balanced that they tempt legislators to try to shift the seat by a skilled snipping here and there. The Wisconsin legislature, for example, has undertaken to make the fifth district a Republican seat. A hybrid district, the fifth includes suburbs north of Milwaukee, which regularly turn in a Republican plurality of eight to ten thousand votes. This has been enough to swing the district if several worker wards in Milwaukee defected. When the worker wards have solidified the Democrats have won the seat. By adding additional suburbs to the district, the Republican leaders have figured the district can be made to yield a consistent, if narrow edge.

One incidental effect of such gerrymandering seems to be to intensify the rigidity of the Congressional alignment. To make a Republican seat "safe," state legislatures usually must make other seats safer for the Democrats. Both San Francisco and Pittsburgh, for example, have been divided so that neither the Republican nor Democratic districts are seriously threatened.

Despite such actions we should not overlook the new sensitiveness of Congress to national issues, reflecting the many forces operating to nationalize the basis of American politics. There will continue to be Congressmen who think exclusively in terms of some single sectional interest like cotton or silver. But such changes as the spread of industry through the country, the upgrading in economic standing of most Americans and the impact of technology upon the farm belt have tended to draw much the same conflicts of economic class across the whole country.

Up to now these changes have brought an equilibrium but not real unity, which is perhaps the fundamental weakness in what we have termed the "revolt of the moderates." These moderate political elements represent the margin of victory in the voting for both the President and Congress, but if theirs is the balance of political power they still have not been able to remake either party.

As far as Congress is concerned, it is doubtful that the rigidities of the past can be shaken loose by a tactic of balancing one party against the other. How people vote for Congress, as was pointed out earlier, revolves around the choice of "the man" or "the party." In the absence of a strong party trend the pace of change in Congress tends to be slow. The men already in office are more easily re-elected. Many seemingly "sure" seats are not even contested. Only through a strong party trend can the grip of the past be really shaken loose.

In denying either party a majority, the moderate elements risk defeating themselves. Their "revolt" must be put down as a transitional movement rather than as a solution of our political crisis. The battle against extremism and the past cannot be won so long as the moderates remain "above both parties." To carry the country they must cast their lot decisively with one or the other parties, completing the struggle for realignment.

One further possibility should not be overlooked—an extremist attempt to realign the parties. The most likely form such a thrust for power would take would be to seek to establish a new anti-foreign, states rights coalition, embracing both the racial revolt in the Democratic South and the disillusionments over foreign policy within the Republican ranks.

This possibility must be taken seriously. Particularly in the deep South, the extremists are sweeping into political rule, and when emotions of such violence are unloosed there is no telling how far they may sweep. Spreading industrialization has also weakened the South's traditional allegiance to lower tariffs, building a growing protectionist sentiment. The South's support for foreign aid, as we have noted, has also declined dramatically in recent years.

It may indeed be an omen of things to come that when Herman Talmadge began his campaign to unseat Senator Walter George the issue he drummed away on through the winter of 1955–56 was foreign aid. Talmadge's attacks had enough effect so that Senator George was driven to oppose Eisenhower's request for a long-range extension of the foreign-aid program.

If such a "states rights" coalition ever did sweep into power in this country it would be a reproduction of the tragedy now engulfing South Africa. While this danger that we will crack apart as a nation cannot be precluded entirely, both our history and political character indicate that in this country the forces of unification will win out in the end, however long the torment.

Still, how do deadlocks of such intensity and complexity as the one we now face get broken? It may be helpful to examine briefly the long stalemate that prevailed the last time this country had two evenly competing parties and how it was finally ended.

4. Breaking the Deadlock

During the panic of 1873 the Kansas legislature, casting about for means of reducing expenditures, decided to dispense with the services of a chaplain—an economy which saved the state $3 a day. The following summer a plague of locusts swept the wheatfields. Hastily making amends, in their next budget, the guilt-stricken legislators provided for the services of two chaplains.

The hard times of 1873 and 1874 did more than prod the consciences of the Kansas legislators. It also ushered in the closest and most indecisive political period this country has ever known. In the 1874 elections the Democrats won the

House of Representatives for the first time since the start of the Civil War. Not for twenty-two years were the Republicans able to re-establish sustained control of the Presidency and both houses of Congress.

When the election returns for these years are studied they reveal an almost unbelievable rigidity in party allegiances.

Who won the Presidency was settled from one election to the next by the shifting of a finger count of states, chiefly Indiana, New York and Connecticut.

Even within the "doubtful" states the rigidity of voting was amazing. In Ohio, for example, the voting for Congress was so close that it led to McKinley's being gerrymandered into the Presidency. Each time the Ohio legislature changed party control it redistricted the Congressional seats, paying special attention to McKinley's district. Five times between 1876 and 1890 his district was revamped in an effort to defeat him. In 1882 McKinley squeezed through by eight votes but a Democratic Congress refused to seat him. Not until 1890 was a gerrymandering hit upon that finally beat him.

The indignation aroused by this "outrageous gerrymander," records Joseph P. Smith, an Ohio historian, and McKinley's "magnificent fight . . . for re-election against overwhelming odds, led the press of the state . . . to declare for him for Governor of the state. . . ." McKinley's election as governor in 1891 and re-election in 1893 made him the G.O.P. nominee for President in 1896.

In Indiana, thirty-two counties were unwaveringly Republican through the 1876–92 period; another thirty-nine counties were equally strongly Democratic, while only twenty-one counties did any shifting between elections.

Each of these three blocs of counties cast roughly a third of the state's vote. As the following table shows, neither the Democratic nor Republican counties varied by more than

3 per cent in their voting until 1892, when the Populists cut in on both parties. The ups and downs which swung Indiana every four years from one party column to the other came in the shifting counties. Not until 1896 could either party get an actual majority of the vote in these shifting counties or in the state as a whole.

Per Cent Republican—1876–1896

	32 Staunch Republican Counties	39 Staunch Democratic Counties	21 Shifting Counties	Whole State (92 Counties)
1876	56	40	48	48
1880	57	42	49	49 [1]
1884	59	41	45	48
1888	56	43	49	49 [1]
1892	53	40	46	46
1896	56	45	51	50.8

[1] Republicans carried state with less than a majority of the vote.

Mainly this rigidity in voting reflected the strength of the political chains which had been forged even prior to the Civil War and which were hammered harder by that bloody struggle. Of the thirty-two unwavering Republican counties all but six were carried by John Frémont in 1856. These counties were settled primarily by New Englanders.

The rigid Democratic counties were chiefly in the Southern half of the state and around Fort Wayne. One group of counties had been settled by Southerners; the other by Germans. Two-thirds of these counties had been Democratic from 1844 on.

Among the twenty-one shifting Indiana counties, only one had been consistently Democratic before the Civil War and none consistently Whig or Republican. Most of them had swung between the Whigs and Democrats before 1860 and they remained the swing counties after the war.

That these loyalties can have remained so inflexible for

so long becomes all the more remarkable considering how mighty was the sweep of events during the years after the Civil War.

Between 1860 and 1900 our population doubled, a third of the 44,000,000 increase representing the arrival of new immigrants from abroad. Virtually every phase of American living was transformed by a succession of inventions—the harvester and thresher, electric lighting, the typewriter, telephone and telegraph; also the endless variety of machines which replaced manual labor, from the linotype to the shoe stitcher.

Ida Tarbell wrote of the era as one marked by the "nationalizing of business." Not only business but virtually everything else was being nationalized. In that fact, I believe, will be found the key to the politics of the period.

At the start of this era, neither the physical, social nor economic basis for a truly national political coalition existed. This whole age can be said to have been devoted to bringing into being the basis for such a coalition.

It was an age of mergers and "trusts" in politics as well as in business. In Philadelphia, for example, each individual ward leader had acted like a minor, feudal baron until Boies Penrose came along. Penrose had been elected to the state legislature by reform elements who were trying vainly to wrest political power from the aldermen by centralizing the management of the city in a mayor. Penrose persuaded Matt Quay, the state boss, to have the necessary law passed, although the argument Penrose used would hardly have pleased the reformers.

"You can control one man," he told Quay, "but a dozen ignorant saloonkeepers can raise hell."

Assisting this process of political consolidation was the expansion of the power of state governments. In Cincinnati, George Cox was still only one of many ward bosses until he allied with Governor Joseph Foraker. Through the State

Board of Public Works, Foraker turned over to Cox the patronage power over two thousand jobs. The next year Foraker carried Hamilton County for the first time in three tries. Cox soon became the undisputed boss in Cincinnati.

Economically, as well, the basis for a more nationalized politics was being built up steadily. Between 1866 and 1890 railroad mileage increased fivefold, from 35,000 to 163,562 miles of track, as both ends of the continent were linked. The number of Federal employees was six times as high in 1900 as in 1861. The steady commercialization of agriculture was evidenced by a nearly tenfold increase in the use of fertilizers, although the number of farms did not quite triple.

But the truly watershed event of the age was the emergence of the United States as a world economic power. In 1874 our foreign trade accounts showed an export surplus for the first time. Before the Civil War half of our imports consisted of finished manufactures. By 1900 manufactured goods made up only a fourth of the things we bought from abroad. It was at the turn of the century that the value of manufactures we exported first exceeded the value of manufactured products we imported.

This transformation from an agricultural to an industrial nation left its lasting stamp on both the American political character and that of other nations as well. From the 1890's on, Britain, which had enjoyed a virtual industrial monopoly in the 1870's, faced the constant problem of readjusting her economy to meet the intensifying competition of other industrial nations. Even today, in Bevanism, we can see the effects upon her political character of that long and only partially successful adjustment.

Within this country, as well, we never have outgrown fully the political impress left by the economic squeeze of those years. In the South those hardships erupted through Tillman and Watson. The Populist agitation, which swept the Midwest, helped force a number of reforms such as the income tax and the direct election of Senators.

Through this whole period of deadlock, numerous efforts were made to realign the country. But somehow the political pieces for an effective coalition defied being put together.

The trouble was that the pieces did not belong to the same puzzle. If some groups were stirred to protest by the squeeze that acompanied the economic transformation of the country, others continued to vote "as they had shot" in the Civil War. The different third parties tried to break free of the Democratic and Republican bonds but these "crusades" had a strange way of simultaneously splitting and solidifying the party coalitions. In Iowa, for example, the Populist revolt strengthened the Republican sentiments of the German-Americans, who had no use for the temperance and nativistic feelings that went along with Populism.

In retrospect it seems clear that before a decisive realignment could take place three developments were necessary: first, the vengeful memory of the Civil War had to fade; second, the sense of economic cohesiveness had to be strengthened and, third, a new generation had to come of age to serve as the carrier for these changes.

By the early 1890's these three developments had moved pretty much into place. One amusing evidence of the ebbing of the Civil War memories could be seen in the end of bearded presidents. Lincoln had been our first President with a beard and the Republicans who followed him seemed to feel that they should emulate the martyred President. Benjamin Harrison was the last of the bearded line. In 1896, for the first time since the Civil War, both parties put up smooth-shaven candidates.

With this coming of age of a new generation, old party ties loosened, a trend which the tugging of the third parties had helped bring about. In 1890 the Democrats won the governorships in Michigan and Wisconsin and, the following year, in Iowa, indicating that even Republicans no longer considered it treason to vote for a Democrat. In 1892 the Democrats went on to win both houses of Congress in an astonishing sweep that cracked even such hitherto stalwart Republican states as Massachusetts, Iowa and Michigan.

At this point, in short, not only was the attrition of stalemate moving toward a decision, but it seemed that the Democrats might emerge triumphant.

Then came the event which wrecked the Democratic hopes.

Most historians date the political turn from the McKinley-Bryan campaign. The election returns indicate that the turning event really was the panic of 1893. The long party deadlock had begun with a depression—that of 1873—and it was ended with this second depression twenty years later.

So much more severe than any previous depression, the 1893 collapse forced the closing of 642 banks in one year. The new edition of Webster's *Dictionary* which appeared that year included for the first time a definition of the word "unemployment."

Despite these hardships our rise to economic power was not slowed. In 1893 our exports of iron and steel products exceeded our iron and steel imports for the first time.

In the 1894 elections the Democrats failed to return a single member to Congress in twenty-four states—including Indiana—and returned only one Democrat in three other states. In the twelve largest cities in the country the Democratic representation in Congress dropped from twenty-nine seats in 1892 to only twelve in 1894.

These same cities, as the table which follows shows, provided almost 60 per cent of McKinley's plurality in the whole country. In 1872 when Grant scored his landslide re-election these cities furnished 9 per cent of the total vote in the country. In 1896 they cast 12 per cent of the nation's ballots.

This whole period was marked by a tremendous expansion of the urban population and this "rise of the city" has been credited with being the means through which the long political deadlock was broken. And yet, if we study how these cities voted in each election after 1872, a significant fact stands out.

The Republican strength did not mount steadily as the urban population expanded, as might be expected. In 1892 the voting trend in the cities actually seemed to favor the Democrats. What happened was that the growth of the cities brought together vast numbers of people who, by swinging together on an issue which struck a common voting nerve, produced a heavy enough shift to upset the old balance.

Pluralities in Twelve Largest Non-Southern Cities [1]

	Net 12-City Plurality	Nationwide Plurality
1872	30,700 Rep.	763,000 Rep.
1876	74,600 Dem.	264,200 Dem.[2]
1880	24,300 Dem.	9,464 Rep.
1884	26,900 Dem.	23,000 Dem.
1888	55,900 Dem.	100,400 Dem.[2]
1892	144,600 Dem.	380,800 Dem.
1896	351,900 Rep.	601,800 Rep.

[1] Includes New York, Philadelphia, St. Louis, Chicago, Baltimore, Boston, Cincinnati, San Francisco, Pittsburgh, Buffalo, Newark and Cleveland.
[2] The Republican candidate was elected with a minority of the popular vote.

This realignment might not have held if McKinley's administration had not been accompanied by the end of

the long agricultural depression and the return to prosperity. The real solidification of Republican power came
in the 1904 election. In Ohio, for example, thirty counties
which had been unwaveringly Democratic through the
entire deadlock period showed a gain of only 3 per cent
for the Republicans in 1896. In 1900 they broke another 3
per cent and in 1904 five per cent more, ten of these counties going Republican.

History always speaks in parables which lend themselves
to conflicting interpretations. Still, the way this long stalemate was broken suggests three conclusions that bear on
our present situation.

First, the tenacious strength of political loyalties should
not be underestimated. Once the emotions of people become attached to a political party, an almost catastrophic
event is required to cause many of them to change. In fact,
a whole new generation, free of these old memories, may
have to arise before a decisive change can be registered.

If this is true, that we must wait for the record births of
the postwar years to be translated into voters, the present
period of political indecision could continue into the 1960's.

Second, political realignment seems a two-stage affair.
In this 1874–96 period, at least, there was no steady,
gradual build-up of strength which finally overwhelmed
one side. There seems first to have been a preliminary
period during which old loyalties were shaken loose, while
varied new political combinations were tried, with nothing
decisive happening. Once the old ties had weakened sufficiently, the second stage of lasting change emerged
quickly.

For some years now, of course, we have been shaking
ourselves loose from old symbols and trying on new political feelings. How much more of this we must still undergo
is not clear, but the grip of the past is being pried loose,
finger by finger.

Third, apparently prodigious economic and social changes can take place in a country for a time at least, without seeming to have any decisive political effect. Yet here, as well, the seemingly slow pace of change can be deceptive. Population movements and technological changes do regroup people both in their geographical and social locations so that when they do swing the shift can be decisive.

Throughout this book I have reported new forces which are making the country ever more interdependent and knitting us closer together than ever before. In their immediate impact some of these forces seem to have a dividing effect, as in the sharpening economic cleavage in both the farm belt and the South. These divisions may seem like evidences that we are cracking apart. But I believe they really are signs of the necessary breaking down of old habits and old ways in preparation for a regrouping on a more unified and nationalized basis than ever before.

In short, there is no doubt in my mind that the unity of the country has been advanced immeasurably in recent years. The double uncertainty is how long it may take for the dawn to break for the new political sun and how we will manage our political affairs in the meantime.

During these years of transition we shall have to continue to look to whoever is President rather than to the Congress or to the parties themselves for unifying leadership. But if we are to have a President capable of rising above all the dividing influences in the country, "we the people" must also be able to rise above such influences. This, in turn, imposes a new responsibility upon all of us, particularly in determining how high a price is to be put upon domestic conciliation.

TEN

Democracy as an Arena

1. Of the Never-ending Fight

At the beginning of this book the drama of the Eisenhower Presidency was described as the testing of the American political character at perhaps its most critical juncture in history.

Having come thus far we can be more specific—as this trial takes shape it has become primarily a testing of middle-class America.

It is not that the rest of the nation does not share in this trial, the poor as well as those better off, debtors along with creditors, Democrats as well as Republicans. Politically, though, the middle class seems certain to remain the central arena of decision during the immediate years ahead.

For only the middle class can serve as the means of political unification in the country today. In sheer numbers, of course, its elements have expanded to where they hold the balance of voting between both parties. It is these same middle-class elements who stand political guard over the structure of our post-depression gains, around which both

234

parties have been compelled to reshape their appeals. Also, it is through this middle class, more broadly based than ever before in our history, that most of the dynamic nationalizing trends of our time are currently finding expression.

The key to Eisenhower's political accomplishment may well lie in the degree to which he has made the middle class a nationalizing political force. The new conservative coalition, for which he has been acting, is still torn with its own torments and has not yet cemented itself. However, Eisenhower has done what no Republican President before him was able to do—he has opened to the G.O.P. the opportunity of becoming a truly national political party for the first time in over a hundred years.

The backbone of "Eisenhower conservatives" stretches across the whole country, arching over sectional and occupational differences—in the suburbs voting identically in every part of the nation, in small-town merchants along Main Street, South and North, in the better-off farmers consolidating their hold on the land, in the factory workers for whom the memory of the depression has been fading.

For the Republican party the task ahead remains that of completing what Eisenhower started, of utilizing this middle-class following as the means for easing the hostility between business and labor, of reuniting the farmers, both those in debt and those debt-free, even perhaps of bringing at least part of the South back into the Union politically.

The G.O.P. problem, in short, is one of reconciling two historical streams, the older Republicans, who moved into the middle class in the 1920's or earlier, and the newer elements who climbed into the middle class out of the depression depths and from a Democratic background.

Even with the Democrats back in power, this struggle for unification through the middle class would not stop. The Democrats cannot regain—and hold—their Rooseveltian ascendancy by going back to either the New Deal or the Fair Deal. They must move forward and make themselves enough of a middle-class party to regain the one-time supporters of Franklin Roosevelt, whose own economic status has bettered so dramatically in recent years.

And yet, as an instrument of national unification, the middle class suffers from its own congenital excess—an overfondness for contentment and quiet.

Inherent in the makeup of the middle class is a tendency to overvalue the importance of material prosperity. In the past the booming prosperity of the economy as a whole was often allowed to obscure the difficulties being experienced by less-advantaged segments of society. But the cold war has rigged an even more treacherous ambush.

However high the indices of wealth and prosperity are pushed *inside* this country, we will remain under siege by a war-menacing foe. The constant danger ahead is that the evidences of material prosperity all around us will lead us into thinking that our problems are working themselves out —and waste the time which can never be recovered.

Nor are quiet and conciliation necessarily the best means of achieving political unity at home. Bitter conflict accompanied every decisive realignment in the past—the emergence of Jacksonian Democracy, the rise of Republican supremacy with the Civil War, the reassertion of that supremacy in 1896, the toppling of that supremacy by the New Deal. Up to now, at least, in our history, moderation has never been an effective means for achieving basic changes in voting habits.

As our dissection of Congress has shown, there are many psychological reasons for this. For one thing, strong emotional attachments do not melt except under the heat of red-hot conflict. Of perhaps more basic significance, our whole political system—our parties, the Presidential nominating conventions, our very government itself—is set up to serve as an arena.

The continuing fight—not sweetness and light—is the hallmark of the American democracy. The hidden strength of our democracy springs from the very vigor with which we battle ourselves into unity.

That was largely how our founding fathers planned it. The government they devised was designed to be a perpetual friction machine.

This was accomplished by a *double* separation of powers. One of these divisions of the powers of government—by function—has been blurred by the complexities of modern life. Who makes a law today is often less significant than how it is administered. A host of commissions have grown up which merge the executive, legislative and judicial functions in one agency.

But the Constitution provided for another separation of powers which has not lost its vitality. It also spread the authority of government among several competing centers of power, leaving each free to act—until it collided with some other.

This distinction between the separation of powers by function and by collision is often overlooked. Yet it is basic to any understanding of the continuing battle over "what is constitutional."

Given this dispersion of power, it is inevitable that some branch of government—sometimes Congress, sometimes the Presidency, sometimes the judiciary—should always seem to be invading the province of other branches. Outcries of "That's unconstitutional" should reassure rather than alarm us. For such outcries mean that our form of government is working as our founding fathers intended it to work.

One can appreciate why there is so much agitation to "make clear what the Constitution means." But such efforts should not be confused as attempts to restore the original

intent of the Constitution. In some fields such as foreign
affairs and war, the founding fathers refused to set rigid
limits to the authority of either Congress or the Presidency.
The minutes of the Constitutional Convention also show
that the framers of the Constitution did not believe that
any words could be written that would anticipate every
contingency that might arise, or safeguard a nation's liberties. They were relying upon "power to balance power," in
Alexander Hamilton's phrase, upon the belief that the best
guarantee against usurpation was to have a rival branch of
power capable of challenging any such abuse.

Because of the existence of these competing centers of
authority, the chance to fight back in defense of one's
interests and liberties has not been lost. The talk in recent
years of "the decay of the Republic" is belied by the vigor
with which those who have been defeated in the battle for
the Presidency have taken their fight into Congress and to
the courts. Similarly, those who have lost out in the Federal
arena have carried on the battle through state governments
and vice versa.

The existence of so many seats of power makes the
political battle in the United States a never-ending one. It
is difficult, if not impossible, to defeat anything completely
and finally, which helps explain why the American political
character changes so slowly.

Some nations remain rigid in their political character
because the ruling classes maintain so autocratic a hold on
the government that the forces of change cannot make
themselves felt. But the stability of the American political
character seems to derive from an almost opposite cir-
cumstance—the political effects of change are not suppressed but they must fight their way through a succession
of governmental barriers. Veritable revolutions can take
place socially and economically with small change in our
political institutions.

At all times in our history there has been an "old guard" element which has been able to fight literally unto the grave for some "cause" which it knew to be lost.

In short, the continuing fight must be put down as the very essence of the American political character. Often the "American Way of Life" is pictured in terms of rigid adherence to some ideology, ignoring that our search for "a more perfect union" has been directed less to seeking final solutions than at establishing a tolerable balance of conflict among ourselves.

That perhaps is what makes our democracy simultaneously so frustrating and so rewarding. While none of us is able to have our own way in all things, our strivings do enable us to register some improvement in the balance of unity that is struck. The workings of this principle can be seen in all of the more important running conflicts which constitute what might be termed the "American War of Life"—in the ceaseless duels between economic and political power, war and peace, tolerance and intolerance.

2. Of Tolerance and Conformity

Early in 1955 nearly seven hundred authors, book reviewers and publishers gathered at the Hotel Commodore for the annual National Book Awards ceremony. When the principal speaker, Senator J. William Fulbright, assailed the "remorseless pressures to conform" the audience rose to give him a rousing ovation.

For several years now, of course, we have been warned that a new "age of conformity" threatens us. What with loyalty oaths and Congressional investigations of foundations, we have been told that the intellectual climate in the country is such that people are afraid to speak their minds freely.

But how reliable are these warnings as a measure of the degree to which our liberties actually are threatened? Has the cause of tolerance really been set back? Or does much of this agitation reflect a failure to appreciate the peculiar means by which progress in tolerance has always been won in this country?

Simply because civil rights are being fought over does not mean that our liberties are being lost. On the contrary, as with our battling over the Constitution it may mean our liberties are being strengthened.

Ideally, of course, it would be so much nicer if democracy in the United States functioned according to the philosophical precepts of Plato's *Republic* or even if Americans undertook to convince one another of their errors through orderly debate and patient persuasion.

But the processes of tolerance in this country have never been those of civilized indifference to what others say or do, as is true, say, of France.

Americans have always been trying to make one another over.

The "remorseless pressures for conformity" being exerted upon "liberals" today, for example, are no greater than the pressures for conformity that many of these same "liberals" exerted some years ago upon people whom they considered as sympathizers of Hitler and Mussolini. Did Owen Lattimore suffer any more cruel an ordeal of slander than Charles A. Lindbergh in the early years of the war?

There never has been a time in our history when one part of the country was not trying to make the rest of the nation conform to its ideas. This crusading zeal has often been invoked for economic purposes, at other times for religious or racial reasons. Often, the same persons who were zealous in championing one "truth" will protest violently when they become the target for the missionary zeal of some other cause.

Recently, for example, I listened to one Southern editor justify his opposition to desegregation on the ground that the government had no right to compel Negroes and whites to attend the same schools. Later in the same conversation this editor argued that prohibition had never been given a fair trial and ought to be reinstated. This editor seemed unaware of the contradiction in arguing that the government had no business "meddling" with racial relations but that it had a moral responsibility to stop a man from buying liquor.

Similarly, groups who violently opposed prohibition in the 1920's are quite eager to use the power of government to end racial or religious discrimination. Other groups who fight government regulation of child labor as an invasion of parental authority agitate that it is the government's responsibility to provide religious instruction in schools. Men and women who felt that the Sunday blue laws of the 1920's were a Fundamentalist effort to legislate the moral behavior of other religious groups now form themselves into legions to police the "morals" of movies and books.

In sum, Americans have always been intolerant of the ways of other Americans. What has kept this country so sane a place to live in has been the fact that the means were available to fight back against these reformist crusades. Progress in tolerance has come largely through the resistances which intolerance aroused.

This constant battling has made a double contribution to our unity. The reforming crusades have forced changes on different groups of Americans. The resistances to these crusades have compelled the reformers to recognize what could not be changed and had to be lived with.

The Americanization of immigrants affords a good illustration of this dual process. Every immigrant family must survive a bitter hazing before being initiated into the American fraternity. Cruel and usually unjustified discriminations are suffered. Still, these discriminations have contributed to our cultural unity by compelling immigrants to discard their old-world traits and to seek to become as much like other Americans as possible. But these discriminations have also served to strengthen our sense of individualism as well. The very pressures to conform which must be bowed to, reinforce the desire to be treated as individuals, equal before the law.

The tragedy of the "loyalty" fight has lain less in its pressures for intellectual conformity than in its disregard of the processes of law. True, one prime objective of McCarthy's investigations was to intimidate those with whom he disagreed. Still, the so-called intellectuals whose ideas were under attack had the means to defend their ideas. The real victims of McCarthyism have been the men and women who had their careers damaged by being unjustly labeled "security" risks, or who were punished for "crimes" which were defined by no law and without being given an opportunity to fight back against their accusers.

Some persons have maintained that government employment is a privilege and not a right and that therefore the accused individuals were not entitled to truly judicial hearings. Others have contended that any doubt should be decided "in the government's favor." But it is unsound principle for any Democratic government to say it is too big and busy to be just to its citizens.

One of the more dismaying aspects of the whole fight against subversion is how little progress has been made in bringing it under the process of law. To balance justice with security, we must be able to distinguish between those who were guilty of subversive activities and those who may have joined the Communist party or one of its "front" organizations some years ago for reasons which had nothing to do with subversion—because they disliked their employers, hated Hitler, were youthful exhibitionists, neurotic or just stupid.

Unfortunately, the investigations still seem to be directed

primarily toward blurring over any such distinction. Con-
spiracies, of course, are difficult to deal with. But after so
many years of investigating, some mechanisms should have
been developed for dealing with the problem through lawful means rather than through appeals to vigilante vengeance. The loyalty commission named in 1955 can be judged
largely by its success in devising a *lawful* frame for dealing
with subversion.

Not only on the "loyalty" front, but in every other aspect
of the struggle for tolerance, the one indispensable require-
ment is the chance to fight back. No form of government
may be able to ensure that the odds of combat will always be
equal. Still the opportunity to fight back even under heavy
odds remains our most effective check against intolerance.

The race tragedy in the South is largely a result of the
fact that the Negro never had this opportunity. If his
powers of resistance had been greater, nothing like the
caste system that now prevails in the South could have
developed.

White Southerners like to point to segregation practices
in the North as evidence of how well the South treats its
Negroes. But these contentions overlook the vital point—
in the North the Negro enjoys the indispensable privilege
of access to the democratic arena, of being able to come
back to carry the fight again and again and to hope that
even if he loses his children may win.

It is no accident that the sorest grievance in American
society—the status of the Negro in the South—has been the
one issue in our history which never was allowed to fight its
way into balance.

Nor have many white Southerners been willing to stand
up for racial tolerance. Consider, for example, what happened during the summer of 1955 when two Negro lads
entered the annual soap box derby sponsored by the Augusta *Chronicle*.

A "States' Rights Council" began writing the families of
the eighty white boys who had signed up for the derby,
charging that the entry of the two Negroes was part of "a
plot to undermine White civilization in the South." It is
doubtful that many Augustans took this charge seriously.
Still, the derby was scheduled to be held at Camp Gordon,
which worried several *Chronicle* editors. What if a racial
incident took place on the camp grounds? The U.S. Army
might even close the camp, costing Augusta businessmen
the camp's purchasing power.

And so the *Chronicle* circulated a questionnaire among
the white parents, asking how many would withdraw their
children from the race if the two Negro boys were left in.
Enough parents indicated withdrawal so the derby event
was canceled.

The end of the affair would do credit to O. Henry. When
the derby was canceled, the Charlotte *Observer* extended
a blanket invitation to all of the Augusta entrants, white
and colored, to participate in Charlotte's derby. One of the
boys whose parents had threatened to withdraw him from
the Augusta derby went to Charlotte. There he raced
against not two but twenty-odd Negro entrants and won
the race!

This tempest in a soapbox could be dismissed as much
ado over nothing if it did not demonstrate so graphically
how readily white Southerners allow themselves to be
intimidated on the race issue. Although there are notable
exceptions, even more liberal-minded Southerners do not
care enough about racial tolerance to fight for it as a matter
of principle. The anti-Negro extremists, however, do feel
strong enough in their intolerance to resort to violence and
even murder.

These extremists may not be typical of the South's citizenry. But they dominate the scene because they weigh so

heavily in the scales compared to those who are ready to fight for tolerance.

Outside of the South, of course, the Negro has been in a position to battle for his rights and he has made considerable progress during the last generation. Even here, though, continuation of that progress cannot be taken for granted.

The 1952 election returns convey an ominous warning. That vote showed that the two groups who are furthest apart in their voting today are Negroes and suburbanites. In every part of the country the suburbs voted from 75 to 90 per cent Republican. In every part of the country, including Southern cities, the Negroes voted from 75 to 90 per cent Democratic.

This polarization at opposite extremes may seem all the more strange since no two groups in our society live further apart. But that is precisely the problem. The Negroes have been migrating into the cities at the same time that the better-income white residents have been leaving the cities for the suburbs. As a result, they are tending to move further apart rather than closer.

If this pattern persists, with so few Negroes in the suburbs, segregation in the North could harden rather than ease.

Or, put another way, progress in racial tolerance has not kept pace with economic progress. The spectacular expansion of the middle class since the war's end has narrowed many of the economic cleavages in our society, such as that between workers and employers. But this same upsurge of the middle class may be widening the gap of racial understanding.

The pattern of suburban migration raises serious doubts whether the middle class can prove an effective vehicle for achieving further progress in tolerance. These doubts arise in relation not only to Negroes but to other ethnic and religious groups.

In the cities, as the urban masses climbed out of the slums during the 1920's and 1930's, residential segregation tended to break down. As each ethnic group rose on the economic ladder it moved into "nicer" neighborhoods where its own ethnic density was thinned by living alongside of neighbors with other ethnic backgrounds.

To some extent, however, the suburban exodus appears to have revived the old patterns of ethnic segregation. Around New York City there are suburban districts which have become as heavily Jewish, or Italian, or Irish in family ancestry as were the ghettos or "Little Italys" or "New Erins" of the Lower East Side of twenty-five years ago. The old-law tenements of the East Side have given way to ranch houses with sylvan settings and neatly cultivated lawns. Yet the walls of discrimination and intolerance still stand.

In large part, of course, the whole pattern of economic and social climbing has been a flight from the problems of racial and religious tolerance. As soon as some new ethnic group began to move into a neighborhood, the older residents would flee to some other residential area. The flight might be inspired by the fear that property values would tumble, or by an aversion to mingling with families with foreign-sounding names.

What the "better class" people who took flight may not have realized was that their refusal to live alongside of these rising ethnic elements slowed or retarded the process of Americanization. These "better class" people were also contributing to the persistence of so-called bloc voting, with all the problems that such ethnic solidarity creates in terms both of domestic unity and our foreign policy.

To sum up, neither in the North nor the South is there any assurance that better economic conditions will bring a greater degree of racial and religious tolerance. If further progress is to be gained it will not come of itself but will have to be fought for.

3. Of Political and Economic Power

In writing of any country the temptation runs strong to picture it as beset by contradictory tuggings between which the country must choose.

Yet in most such cases it probably is a wiser rule to conclude that the very refusal to make the choice is the true measure of both the country's character and of what it will do.

In the matter of tolerance, for example, the American people are often told that the issue lies between the rights of the individual and nationalistic conformity. But if these alternatives seem diametric opposites in theory, they usually are joined inseparably in real life. In the Americanization process acceptance as an individual can be achieved only as one conforms to American ways and mores. The stamp of the American character will be found in neither individualism nor conformity but in the constant struggle to balance the two.

A similar conflict dominates our economic character. "Conservative" spokesmen are warning constantly that any step in the direction of government control of the economy must lead us down the road to totalitarian serfdom. On the opposing extreme, some "liberals" contend that "political democracy requires economic democracy," that unless democratic political power takes over the economy, big business will take over the government.

But these dire ideological horoscopes from both "right" and "left" overlook one thing—the American economic character rests upon a stubborn refusal to accept either of these choices, either to merge political and economic power in any complete sense or to keep them completely divorced.

At times American opinion has moved toward a sharper separation between economic and political power; at other times the temper of feeling has favored their more intimate intermingling. But we never have been willing—or able—to resolve the issue finally.

That we should struggle endlessly over the relationship of economic and political power is inherent in the continuous arena which our democracy provides. At every stage in our history some Americans have sought economic advantage by strengthening the powers of government, while others have sought advantage by weakening the government. In this struggle different groups have been beaten down from time to time, as was the labor movement for so long, but the chance to return to the fight never was completely lost.

Today, as a matter of fact, we appear to have arrived at perhaps the most even balancing of the varied segments of our economy in our history.

In achieving this balance, both socialism and so-called "laissez faire" have been rejected. That both these doctrines should grow obsolete simultaneously is not accidental, for they were born of the same nineteenth-century optimism.

The visionary flavor of socialism has always been recognized, of course. Yet it was not much more utopian than the laissez-faire assumption that all the many complex adjustments of economic life, both inside nations and between nations, would fall into automatic balance if left free of government intervention. How romantic was this dream which World War II shattered!

It was a fruitful dream in many ways, but also a tragic one. For it left behind in the minds of many people the strange illusion that there was little or no need for government.

In recent years many scholars have speculated on why the Western democracies seem to have become a declining force. My own belief is that the root of the trouble will be found in this weird illusion that men did not have to govern themselves, which swept the Western world during the latter part of the nineteenth century and the early part of this century.

This illusion was nourished by the fact that for a time things did seem to take care of themselves. But it was in that generation span in which this "no need to govern" tradition held sway—the years in which Aneurin Bevan grew up—that the technological top which is our world spun out of control. Ever since then we have been struggling to bring it back under control.

Quite often we are told that the "sickness of the Western world" is due to some spiritual lack, that people no longer have a "faith" in which they can believe. Walter Lippmann, Russell Davenport and Russell Kirk preach eloquently of the need to discover a new public philosophy or ideological dogma or "myth" which can be championed in competition against the creed of Communism.

But a "time of troubles" is precisely not the time to abandon reason. True, the most important single talent that distinguishes the human race from animals is the ability to project themselves out of their own skins. This power of imaginative and even spiritual flight is wonderfully useful. It enables us to anticipate what we have not yet experienced, giving us the foresight to forestall threatened events. Imagination, armed with moral values, can also give us the heroic courage to stand fast against whatever the future may bring.

But this same talent exposes us to the constant temptation of using these ideological "myths" as a means of evading the taxing realities and disciplining drudgeries which must be faced.

What the Western world needs is not a formula for escapism but to learn anew the arts of government. This task is made more difficult by a historical accident. When the laissez-faire system, which transcended national frontiers, collapsed, a terrible vacuum of power was left in every country. To fill that vacuum every government was forced to exercise powers which had lain unused. In some instances, as in Germany, governments swung to the extreme of totalitarianism.

This world-wide reaction against laissez-faire also happened to coincide with both the emergence of Soviet Communism and the rise of the so-called masses all over the world. As a result, the strengthening of government and collectivism came to be identical in the minds of many people.

But effective government need not be collectivistic. As this book has shown, how people use their government depends on the kind of people they are.

The idea that government had to be wedded to some ideology developed largely out of the effort to reduce what was happening in the world to some single pattern which once fastened upon would serve as a substitute for thinking.

Perhaps my optimism is ill-founded. But it seems a good omen for the future that, in both the United States and Britain, the people appear to have turned their backs on the old ideologies, on both laissez-faire and socialism. Reflecting this change, the political parties in both countries have turned to rediscovering the arts of governing day by day and problem by problem.

For some years, of course, the war of Victorian ideologies will continue to rage around us, particularly since these ideologies remain powerful economic and military weapons. But the more quickly we complete the process of purging our minds of the old ideologies, the sooner we will be able to give full play to the saving quality of our democracy—the ability to battle things through, changing what we can change and adjusting to what cannot be changed.

4. Of War and Peace

Not long after the end of World War II, a German youth, who was working with Military Government as an interpreter, showed me around Berlin. He had been taken prisoner by our forces and I asked him what it was about American soldiers that impressed him most. The quick instinctive impressions foreigners form of us, I felt, are often more revealing of the American character than the most detailed study.

The youth hesitated and then replied, "It is that your enlisted men stay seated while talking to their officers. In Germany that could never happen. We must stand at rigid attention when an officer speaks to us. And yet your men fight very well."

Not until recently did the full significance of his reaction become clear to me. While reading William Allen White's autobiography, I was struck by his description of his tour of Germany immediately after World War I. White had put the same question as I had to many of the Germans he met and had received the same response.

"We notice always your American officers talk with the men, play games with them," one Rhineland peasant told White. "Your soldiers treat the men as though they were folks. With us, only the officers are folks. The rest are cattle. We see your men obey their officers in the drill and our soldiers tell us your men have fine discipline in battle. We do not understand this!"

Two wars, more than a quarter of a century apart, but the American character had not changed—nor had the German character.

Between 1918 and 1946 many things happened in the United States which were supposed to be softening and weakening our national fiber. There were prohibition, the jazz age and the dollar-crazed materialism of the 1920's.

There was also the New Deal, which its critics contended had subverted the Republic. But the American soldier, plucked through random conscription, remained basically unaltered.

The incident demonstrates, I believe, not only how enduring is the character of any nation but how exaggerated is the common talk that the United States is in danger of becoming either a regimented or militaristic nation. The cold war threatens to turn our society into a garrison state, so the complaint goes. Our freedoms are being imperiled by the level of taxation, too many generals have served in diplomatic posts, the military is running the country. . . .

If anything, our behavior since the war's end has demonstrated how immovable are our resistances to militarism. Despite nearly ten years of cold war, we still do not have universal military training. Although for several years we were alone in the possession of atomic weapons, and despite repeated Soviet provocations we never used these weapons or issued any ultimatums.

The alarms that have been voiced over the alleged drift toward militarism reflect two things mainly—the dread of war itself, which evokes hostility to all its symbols, and the zeal with which Americans stand ready to battle anything that seems to threaten their accustomed habits.

When World War II broke out some Americans warned that if we allowed ourselves to be drawn into the conflict we would become Fascistic ourselves. But when the war was over wartime controls were dropped quickly as we demobilized all too hastily the most powerful military machine any nation had ever put together.

Our problem is not that we will become overly militaristic. Our real danger lies in the likelihood that we will remain too set in our normal peaceful ways and fail to narrow the gap between our concept of "normalcy" and the Soviet threat.

It is in organizing for war that the Soviet Union poses the most formidable challenge to our way of life. We have shown that our economic system is infinitely superior to the Soviet system as a means of lifting living standards. The refugees coming from behind the Iron Curtain prove anew that, if able to choose, man prefers to live under conditions of freedom.

There is only one superiority that the Soviets have shown. Although the Soviet Union lay devastated at the end of World War II and could command far less economic or technological resources, it has been able to sustain a heavier arms effort than either we or our allies have been willing to manage.

This one superiority the Soviets have demonstrated reflects the difference in the structure of totalitarian and democratic power. Under the Soviet system the Kremlin takes what it wants of Russia's resources for war and defense *first*, leaving the people to subsist on what is left. In the United States and other Western democracies, economic resources lie dispersed among the people in their holdings of private property. Before those resources can be used even in defense against a foreign foe, they must be collected from the people through appropriations and taxes.

In Russia, in short, *the people have only what the government gives them.* In the Western democracies, *the government has only what the people give it.*

Almost that sums up the whole of the cold war. The constant test which we—and our allies—will face as long as the cold war lasts can be reduced to one question—can free men be led to yield to their own government what the defense of their freedoms requires or will they deny their own government the means of survival?

The test would be met readily if the dangers were plain and immediate. If we had no choice, all of us would know what to do. Our political leaders would be ready to ask for all that was needed and the people would be ready to give it.

But our trial is more subtle—and more perilous—precisely because we are given the freedom to choose. In the years ahead the dangers abroad are not likely to be so apparent that we will not be left exposed to the temptations of conflicting choices. It will always be possible to "make out a case" for reducing taxes, for demanding that our allies should do more, for reducing our own defense costs by underestimating the enemy's progress, for arguing that we must keep our government weak so we do not "jeopardize our freedoms" at home.

That, in sum, is the test that our new "middle road" conservatism will have to survive. Despite our anti-government tradition we must muster enough faith in one another —enough national unity—to yield to our government the power it needs to protect us.

It is a test which permits us no escape from ourselves, from our own character. Nor can any formula be laid down to guide our decisions unless it be this general caution—

For a people under siege complacency is the worst possible sentinel. We are less likely to slip into those tragic neglects which could destroy us if we remain alert and aroused than if we think things are taking care of themselves.

The time to worry about this country is not when we are battling among ourselves, for it is then that our democracy functions best. The time to worry is when all is "moderation."

APPENDIX

1. Acknowledgments

As with *The Future of American Politics*, this book was written with the aid of a fellowship from the John Simon Guggenheim Foundation. The workings of this Foundation represent one of the finest of American traditions. To obtain a fellowship, one submits an outline of the project, along with the names of six persons who are either specialists in the field or who know the applicant personally.

Once the fellowship is granted, the writer is left completely free in his inquiry. No attempt is made to influence his opinions even indirectly.

Strong pressures are being exerted upon foundations to make them responsible for "policing" the viewpoints of those receiving grants. In view of the cold war, one can understand why many Americans feel driven to attempt to stamp out what they consider hostile doctrine and to favor "proper opinion." But in the long run our country will be served better by encouraging the fullest freedom of inquiry, particularly in controversial fields of politics, economics and social development.

A rapidly changing world requires a constant re-examination of our thinking so our basic ideals can find the fresh applications which living demands. It is far wiser to allow new ideas to compete for our minds than to stop thinking.

Democratic government draws much of its strength from the vital principle of change through law. This principle is truly a political fountain of youth. If it is adhered to, we need never fear the truth, since we can adjust to whatever needs adjustment. The ability to face up to the truth brings into play hidden strengths which partisanship can never mobilize.

Each Guggenheim fellowship amounts to a sort of wager on an unfinished idea. In expressing my appreciation for two Guggenheim grants, I would like to add my gratitude for the courage with which Henry Allen Moe and the other Foundation Directors have continued to place their bets on the general principle of the search for truth rather than on what may be the dominant opinion of the time.

In my actual writing, I was assisted enormously by Corinne Silverman who, besides serving as chief research aide, was extremely helpful in discussing and developing numerous points.

Additional research was contributed by Mrs. Mary Mickey Simon, Eve Glassberg, William Spinrad, Howard Allen, who did fine legman's work in Senator Joseph R. McCarthy's home town, and Miss Anthea Browne-Wilkinson, who did a similar job on Aneurin Bevan's birthplace.

The manuscript was edited in various stages by Walter B. Everett of the American Press Institute at Columbia University. As with my previous books, he helped mightily with its clarity and organization. I am also indebted for editorial suggestions to Evan Thomas and John Fischer of Harper & Brothers.

My debt is particularly large to Walker Stone, Editor in Chief of the Scripps-Howard newspapers, who made possible my campaign interviews with voters all over the country in both 1952 and 1954; and to the *Saturday Evening Post* editors, particularly Martin Sommers and Ben Hibbs, for whom I did post mortems on both elections.

Several editors who ran my campaign series went out of their way to encourage me in what was a pioneer venture—of reporting a campaign by bypassing the politicians and going directly to the voters themselves. I am particularly appreciative of the confidence shown by Walter Lister of the Philadelphia *Bulletin;* Basil Walters of the Chicago *Daily News;* Lee Hills of the Detroit *Free Press;* Sevellon Brown (father and son) of the Providence *Journal and Bulletin;* Vincent Jones of the Gannett Newspapers; Alexander Jones of the Syracuse *Herald-Journal* and Bill Steven of the Minneapolis *Star,* whose wife, it was nice to learn, won the election pool among her friends by following my reports.

The chapter on the South was read in an earlier draft by Virginius Dabney of the Richmond *Times-Dispatch,* George S. Mitchell of the Southern Regional Council and Walton Mims of the Edgefield, (S.C.) *Advertiser.* Mr. Mims disagreed vehemently with much of what I wrote. Although Mr. Dabney and Mr. Mitchell were not too critical, neither can be blamed for the chapter's shortcomings.

Professor J. F. Bruce of Oxford University was kind enough to give me the reaction of an extremely well-informed Englishman to my interpretation of Bevanism. Other chapters were read by Donald R. Murphy, editor of *Wallace's Farmer and Iowa Homestead;* Ben G. Weiss, of the Barbizon Corporation, one of the better-informed, medium-sized businessmen in the country, and Bernard M. Baruch. I also profited from talks with Solomon Barkin, Research Director of the Textile Workers of America.

Ben Kaplan, formerly of the Houston *Press,* gathered the material which made possible the striking correlation of home valuation and voting in Houston. Herbert Spendlove of the Saginaw *News* was most helpful with information on Secretary Humphrey's father.

It would be impossible to list the many other persons who were so generous with their time. Among the government officials who were particularly helpful were H. Chapman Rose and Nils Lennartson of the Treasury; Franklin Thackrey, Norman Wall, Willard Lamphere and Calvin Beale, all of the Agriculture Department; H. Von Struve of the Census Bureau, and Irving Perlmeter of Internal Revenue. Ralph Young of the Federal Reserve Board checked many of the statistics used.

The election returns of recent years were gathered mainly from local officials and newspapermen. Among the election officials especially helpful were: James P. Brock at Annapolis, Maryland; Ted. W. Brown, Ohio's Secretary of State; Don Butler in Springfield, Illinois; Wendell L. Cottrell in Utah; Donald T. Nystrom of St. Paul; Paul Shanahan, Kansas Secretary of State; Frank J. Suttill, of Camden Co. and Mrs. Helen Roussel of Bergen Co., N. J.; Tom Terrell of Cleveland; Harry W. Chapman of Los Angeles; M. G. Toepel, Wisconsin Legislative Reference Service and Louis Urban of Detroit.

Among the editors and reporters who responded so graciously to my requests were: R. C. Barton, Lima *News;* Herbert Bayer, Florida *Times-Union* in Jacksonville; George Beebe, Miami *Herald;* Mace Broide and Earl Richert, Evansville *Press;* John Calpin and Burt Chardak, Phila. *Bulletin;* Hugo Frear, Bedford (Pa.) *Gazette;* Charles B. Cleveland, Chicago *Daily News;* John H. Colburn, Richmond

Times-Dispatch; George Carmack, Houston *Press;* Betty and Hodding Carter, *Delta Democrat-Times* in Greenville, Mississippi; Arthur C. Deck, Salt Lake City *Tribune;* Dawson Duncan, Dallas *Morning News;* Karl Elebash, Mobile *Press Register;* Ford Fuller, Freeport *Journal Standard;* B. S. Griffith, Charlotte *News;* George W. Healy, Jr., New Orleans *Times-Picayune;* Tom Harris, St. Petersburg (Florida) *Times;* John B. Johnson, Watertown (New York) *Times;* Walter Leckrone and Andy Olafson, Indianapolis *Times;* Kenneth MacDonald, Des Moines *Register;* Ben Maidenburg, Akron *Beacon-Journal;* Ralph McGill, Atlanta *Constitution;* Jack Meddoff, Buffalo *News;* James E. Mills, Birmingham *Post-Herald;* William Maag, Jr., and Clingan Jackson, Youngstown (Ohio) *Vindicator;* Paul Ringler, Milwaukee *Journal;* Morton Margolin, *Rocky Mountain News.*

Also J. Leo Dery, Manchester (N.H.) *Union Leader;* Frank Ford, San Francisco *News;* W. W. Forster and Bob Taylor, Pittsburgh *Press;* Dick Maher, Cleveland *Press;* Ed Heinke and Russell Bridwell, Scripps-Howard Columbus Bureau; Carl Saunders, *Kentucky Post* in Covington; Otis Sullivant, *Daily Oklahoman* in Oklahoma City; Dick Thornburg and Paul Welsh, Cincinnati *Post* and Don Weaver, Columbus *Citizen.*

Professor V. O. Key, Jr., of Harvard University made available some voting returns from his Election Statistics File. Cortez A. M. Ewing loaned me the tabulations used in his *Congressional Elections.* For 1876–96, returns were provided by the public libraries in Buffalo, Chicago, San Francisco, Baltimore and St. Louis. New York City's Room 228 was always efficiently responsive to my many queries.

Both the Republicans and Democrats were helpful through Leonard Hall, Bill Warne, Floyd E. McCaffree, and C. J. North on the G.O.P. side, and Phillip Stern on the Democratic side. Mary Goddard Zon of the CIO-PAC made available election analyses done by local labor groups, one of the best being the New Jersey study prepared by Harry Kranz.

Numerous other sources and persons to whom I am indebted are cited in my Clinical Notes.

Finally, custom decrees that an author should end his acknowledgments with an inadequate tribute to his wife. It is a wise custom, since no words can really express the tortures authors inflict upon their wives. They are indeed the "G.I.'s" who do the dirty work, while the officer-husbands collect the decorations.

Perhaps it is not inappropriate to express my appreciation of my own "G.I." with a moment of silence.

2. Some Clinical Notes and Readings

Since this book is directed to the general reader, I have tried not to burden it with footnotes or too much election data. Still, there may be some readers who share my own passion for fathoming the psychology of voting and who will be interested in the research problems that arise in writing of the American political character and how these were overcome.

Also, after my previous book was published, many students of history and political science expressed a desire to know more about the methods I have developed for determining how people vote. Others regretted my findings were not presented in more detail so interested students could build on them.

Hence, these informal and by no means complete Clinical Notes:

If I have made any contribution to political research, I suspect it lies mainly in showing how election returns can be used to re-interpret history and to penetrate to the deeper feelings of people as they adjust to social and economic change.

Many persons, of course, look on voting as an indifferent, even accidental process. Others think that once an election is over, it becomes "old stuff" to be filed and forgotten. But like old soldiers, election returns never really die. Long after the campaign committees have sold their furniture, the "lesson" of each campaign lives on in both the people and our politicians, spurring them to certain actions and blocking others.

As one revealing test, take a copy of the *Congressional Directory* and group our Congressmen and Senators by the year in which they first got elected. Then note how the issues and emotions of that year linger on in these legislators. The "Class of 1946" will exhibit a special sensitivity to issues related to Communism. Those elected in the recoil against the Korean War are likely to be less eager to intervene abroad than those who won in 1940. While many factors modify the rule, generally the alumni of any election serve as carriers of the agitations of that campaign.

Turning to the public, election returns are perhaps our best available measure of the almost instinctive predispositions that dominate most voting. In explaining past elections, most historians have relied too heavily on the "issues" stressed by campaigners and done too little with actual voting results. My talks with voters have impressed me with how much of the vote is determined by things campaigners hardly mention. Also, as with Henry Wallace in 1948, candidates often bid strenuously for one part of the electorate only to gain strength somewhere else.

In urging a more sensitive use of voting returns, perhaps I should emphasize I am not thinking simply in terms of the broader trends which can be portrayed in statistical tables or graphs. Really to use election returns, one must break down the vote into intimate units, like counties and even precincts. Then the election figures leap alive.

Through the returns one can pinpoint exactly where the decisive changes that shifted control of the government in any election took place. By studying census data and local historical material, one can determine what kind of people lived in these areas and whether their feelings corresponded to the accepted versions of what settled these elections.

Another prime tool of voting analysis is to plot the contrasts among different groups and how these change from election to election. As often as not Americans vote *against* rather than for something and how their ballots polarize bares the underlying tensions and conflicts in our history. By tracing how the voting gap between clashing elements narrows or widens, one obtains a sensitive recording of when the tensions between these groups were being eased and intensified.

In truth, voting returns are like the boundless sea—the further and deeper the net of inquiry is cast, the more revealing are the historical facts brought to the surface. And as with the sea, one soon learns that the vast expanse of election statistics is not just one body of water but really consists of many rivers, churning through submerged valleys, and of currents as distinctive as the Gulf Stream and Labrador Current, which maintain their political temperature wherever one follows them across the country.

It is this I consider *the key concept in interpreting election statistics*—that Americans have always voted less as individuals than as part of a particular voting stream, with its own marked flow.

These streams may have taken their original form from the economic contours of the country, as with the tidewater–back country cleavage in many Southern states. Or they may have been shaped by human differences in cultural outlook, religion or even between family clans. But it is these voting streams—and the barriers of prejudice and interest which channel off one from the others—which explain why our political parties have behaved as they have.

Since everything that happens to people affects their voting, each of these streams can serve as a river along which one can travel, backward or forward, into American history. Currently, for example, to learn how economic improvement effects the Americanization of some immigrant group, one can follow the group in the succession of neighborhoods through which it climbed from slums to suburbs. A comparison of several such groups will show the adjustments common to all immigrant elements and what is attributable to the special characteristics of each separate group.

Similarly, in probing the past, any stream of voters can be followed to see how their attitudes were changed by the conditions under which they lived. What effect did the type of farming have on politics in the Midwest? To get the answer the voting of identical ethnic elements can be examined in counties where a single cash crop was raised and in counties of diversified farming. By following the shifts in successive elections in some one locality, it is possible to determine how areas of insurgency were converted into strongholds of conservatism.

It is my own feeling that much of American history could be rewritten and made more accurate and more meaningful if election returns were read as "Scrolls of the Past."

This same concept, that voting returns are watermarks which reveal the flow of history, applies to the present and future as well as the past.

One main difference between my own interviewing of voters and that done by polling organizations lies in just this effort I make to measure the continuity with—and departure from—the past.

During the 1952 campaign, I managed to talk with about 3,500 families—roughly equal to the number of interviews pollsters conduct in a national sampling. My interviews, though, were spread carefully through areas which, taken together, constituted a miniature reproduction of the Roosevelt coalition.

Before going out into the country I isolated each major element in the New Deal coalition. In my itinerary, I arranged to sample each of these elements in at least three localities and at different times in the campaign. As a result, my campaign reports proved not only an accurate forecast of how the voting was going but, far more important, they caught the historic significance of what was happening

—of how the Roosevelt coalition was cracking apart and why a new era in American politics was being opened.

My technique, in other words, can best be pictured as sampling not individuals, but streams of voters, moving in continuity with the past and in the context of the communities they live in.

It is a technique which enables one to penetrate beyond a mere head count of what part of the electorate may be shifting to the deeper, historical reasons for their change. The technique is also easily adapted to measuring the political significance of any impersonal trend. To gauge the likely effects of the decentralization of industry, localities receiving the new industries can be visited. Selective interviewing will establish whether the community's traditional voting pattern is being altered or reinforced.

This technique of concentrating one's interview in definable voting areas also corresponds more closely than does random sampling to the actual dynamics of how people decide for whom to vote. Most people tend to reduce the "issues" of any election to their own personal experience, as whether they personally are better or worse off economically.

The second key to their voting is how friends or fellow workers feel. This group influence largely explains why so many persons are sure they know who is going to win an election. People generally associate with others of similar economic status or kindred cultural background and interests. It becomes easy to get the feeling, "everyone I run into is voting" for the same man.

By the same tokens, no really sharp political break is possible unless whole groups shift politically.

And so, in sampling communities or neighborhoods, my questions are directed to bring out the emotional conflicts causing the deepest divisions in the area. These are the issues which will be argued over around the dinner table and among friends. These are the issues which will determine the outcome of the election—not what the campaigners may be saying.

The group nature of voting has been studied by some social scientists, notably Paul F. Lazarsfeld, Bernard Berelson and Angus Campbell. So far, though, their studies have been confined largely to individual communities, like Erie County in Ohio and Elmira in New York. Much of the significance of neighborhood and group influences tends to be lost in ordinary nationwide samplings of voters.

By studying past elections, one can also begin interviewing with a clear picture of the political character of the particular community.

Every election bares something. Each election, in fact, sheds new light on previous elections. Truman's 1948 gains in isolationist areas, for example, explained why Roosevelt lost so heavily in these same areas in 1940. Again, the fact that Eisenhower won much more of the Dixiecrat vote in Southern cities than rural counties points up the economic differences in Thurmond's 1948 following.

By cross-checking how some community votes on varying candidates and referenda, one can separate what issues or agitations tend to solidify the community from what will divide it.

Voting is indeed a psychological action, but the psychology of voting can only be understood by analyzing the responses of individuals in the context of the inherited history that is passed on through family voting traditions and how those traditions are modified by changing times.

In sum, I am too keenly aware of the gaps in my techniques to think of terming them "scientific." Also the varieties of political experience lend themselves to a variety of tests and interpretations. Still, if the full potential of political polling is to be developed, I do think it must come to be based upon and verified against the actual voting returns.

Fine work in analyzing election results has been done by political scientists like V. O. Key, Harold Gosnell and Edward H. Litchfield. Combining their methods with polling would pose difficulties. In compensation, though, a more sensitive use of election returns as a tool of research might prove the means through which research in history, political science and social psychology could be merged and made generally more effective.

Some such merger of research disciplines is important because of the new dimension of significance given politics in this atomic age. My own writings, I hope, have shown some possibilities that await development by such a new research approach. Here and there in the notes on individual chapters which follow, I will try to cite other illustrations of what can be done.

ONE *The Conservative Ordeal*

1. The turn toward conservatism by the American people has been the subject of at least three worth-while recent studies—Russell Kirk's *The Conservative Mind;* Clinton Rossiter's *Conservatism in America;* and Gordon Harrison's *Road to the Right.* All are concerned primarily with the development of a conservative philos-

ophy in this country. My own focus on "conservatism" and "liberalism" has been upon the symbolism voters attach to these terms.

2. The members of the United Nations whose form of government has not changed since 1914 are: Australia, Canada, Great Britain, Liberia, New Zealand, Sweden, Union of South Africa, the United States and Uruguay.

3. George Washington's styling himself a citizen of humanity is quoted in *The Decline of American Liberalism* (p. 36), by Arthur A. Ekirch, Jr.

4. The trend toward having advertising agencies run campaigns has taken hold even in the South, long the habitat of "natural" political performers. In South Carolina I ran into two advertising men from Mississippi who were studying the methods used by Strom Thurmond in his successful write-in campaign. Even "Happy" Chandler in Kentucky was backstopped by Madison Avenue. So far the net effect of injecting advertising techniques into Southern politics has been to exploit the race issue more extravagantly, as was done against Claude Pepper and Frank Graham in 1950.

TWO   *Ye Compleat Political Angler*

1. My portrait of President Eisenhower is based largely on talks with twelve of his sometime aides: Sherman Adams, Robert Cutler, Leonard Hall, Gabriel Hauge, C. D. Jackson, Jack Martin, Kevin McCann, Wilton B. Persons, Maxwell Rabb, Murray Snyder, Harold Stassen and Tom Stephens. I also benefited from interviews with Herbert Brownell, Dulles, Humphrey and Nixon.

2. Eisenhower's reply to newsmen that he would do anything to beat the Germans is related by Harry C. Butcher in *My Three Years with Eisenhower* (p. 120), which remains the most revealing of the many Eisenhower books. After reading any book on Eisenhower, one should turn to Dixon Wector's *The Hero in America* and see how closely the Eisenhower stories fit the traditional hero-meets-country formulas.

3. The research prepared for Leonard Hall on campaigning by Presidents in off-years showed that Wilson in 1918 issued just one statement asking for a Democratic Congress. He also wrote letters endorsing a number of candidates and urged his Cabinet to deliver campaign speeches, but made none himself. Nor did Harding, Coolidge and Hoover undertake mid-term campaign tours.

Truman, in 1946, although traveling by train to vote in Missouri, did not make a single rear-platform speech. In 1950 he delivered one talk, on election eve.

Roosevelt made a "non-political" tour of the West in 1934. In 1938 he was quite active in trying to purge Democrats he did not like. But in no mid-term election did his campaigning approach the number of speeches Eisenhower made in 1954.

4. During the 1952 campaign I kept a careful record of the main reasons why one-time Democrats were swinging Republican. Eisenhower's popularity stood about fourth in importance, far behind the angers stirred by the Korean War and by higher prices and higher taxes. The South was the one part of the country where people I interviewed talked most about corruption.

One might have thought Southerners had far higher standards of political morality than other Americans. Actually, the righteous indignation expressed over corruption was primarily a cover for less polite feelings on the racial question, about which many Southerners did not like to talk openly.

The "Communist" issue I found of considerable importance, although its effects tended to merge with angers over Korea. On the other hand, two polling interpretations of the 1952 election—*The Voter Decides* by Angus Campbell, Gerald Gurin and Warren E. Miller, and *Is There a Republican Majority?* by Louis Harris—minimize the importance of "Communism" as an issue. Alfred De Grazia's *The Western Public*, also based on polling techniques, rates the "red" issue as significant.

5. The 1952 election may well have been our most emotional campaign since the McKinley-Bryan or Hoover-Smith contests. Many people burst into profanity at the mere mention of Truman's name. Others prayed for divine guidance on how to vote. Said one elderly widow in Florida, "I've never voted for a Republican. Maybe I won't vote this time. If I do, I'm going to pray to the Lord and ask him to ignore my vote and just see the right man gets elected."

Truman has charged that Eisenhower won the election through demagoguery, referring apparently to his "I will go to Korea" promise. Although the frustrations over Korea were the most important single propellent behind Eisenhower's sweep, his actual promise to visit Korea was not too important. I was in the field talking to voters a full six weeks before the campaigning began. Even then, in every community I visited one-time Democratic supporters told me they were swinging politically because of Korea.

The popular reaction to the Korean War should puncture one

long-cherished myth about the "blameless public"—that "the people have only to be told the facts to do what is expected of them." The expression "We don't know what the War is all about" was voiced most frequently by persons with sons or husbands in Korea. Clearly, they did not lack information; but emotion had stopped their ears to all explanations of why we were fighting in Korea.

The savagery with which the public turned on Truman seems all the more ironic in view of the universal acclaim which greeted our intervention in Korea at first. When Truman's decision was read to the House of Representatives, the members rose and cheered. The conflict did not become "a useless war" until after Red China entered the struggle and turned what had promised to be an easy victory into endless attrition.

6. The description of what Eisenhower did on the Helena after his trip to Korea is drawn from Merriman Smith's *Meet Mister Eisenhower* (pp. 70–72) and from persons who were aboard.

7. For an early example of Dulles' thinking on centering our deterrent strength in this country see his speech before the American Association for the United Nations December 29, 1950. For a criticism of "massive retaliation" see Dean Acheson's *A Democrat Looks at His Party* (pp. 68–81).

8. Gen. Matthew Ridgway's letter to Secretary Wilson was published in *U.S. News and World Report,* July 29, 1955. Ridgway's memoirs, *Soldier,* reveal how impossible it has become to separate strategic decisions from political influences.

THREE   *The Politics of Revenge*

1. The parallel in the careers of Aneurin Bevan and Senator McCarthy first occurred to me while writing *The Revolution in World Trade.* My study of the changes in the structure of world trade since World War I explains much of my emphasis on the need for arriving at a new concept of the role of government—one which will break free of the obsolete nineteenth-century ideologies.

2. For a penetrating analysis of Anglo-American relations since 1946 see *Britain: Uneasy Ally* by Leon Epstein. The emotional clash within the Labour party can be sensed nicely by reading Jennie Lee's *The Great Journey* and then turning to Clement Attlee's autobiographical *As It Happened.* Where Attlee's musings are tinged by the outlook of middle-class reform, Jennie Lee's story bristles with class warfare.

3. W. H. B. Court's contrast between the new and the dying industrial centers will be found in his *Concise Economic History of Britain* (p. 295), an admirable one-volume survey of Britain's economic development.

4. The anecdotes on Senator McCarthy's childhood are drawn from *McCarthy: The Man, the Senator, the Ism* by Ronald May and Jack Anderson, and Saul Pett's articles in the Associated Press series on McCarthy.

5. The vote-getting importance of "isolationism" for Republicans is not to be measured solely in terms of predominantly German-American counties. In an excellent Master's thesis (University of Chicago) on Hamilton County, Illinois, Howard Allen shows how a relatively small German settlement held the balance of votes which swung control of the county. Democratic from 1836 to 1916, Hamilton County went Republican for the first time in 1920. The voting of Crouch township, the main German settlement, follows Grand Chute's pattern. In 1940 Roosevelt dropped 33 percentage points in Crouch; Truman in 1948 regained 22 per cent; Stevenson fell below Roosevelt's 1940 showing.

6. One clue to the violence of the German-American shifts is family structure. In Crouch two families, the Aydts and Karchers, are dominant. If one clan breaks, a fourth to a third of the voters may swing. Similarly, in Putnam County, Ohio, one farmer told me he had eighty-three cousins living in the nearby area.

The high birthrate in these communities also means there almost always are sons around to be drafted. In Plymouth County, Iowa, I called on one farmer at dinnertime. "You can see why I'm against war," he remarked, waving to five sons seated around the table. Their ages ran from sixteen to five. For at least another fifteen years one of his sons would be of draft age.

The residents of this Plymouth County township are largely descendants of families who settled at the other end of Iowa, outside Dubuque. The two areas invariably swing together:

Republican Percentage for President

	1928	1932	1936	1940	1944	1948	1952
Plymouth Townships	21	16	22	51	57	38	65
Dubuque Townships	5	3	13	63	61	45	70

7. In tracing the change in La Follette's appeal after World War I, the counties taken as typically German-American are Taylor Marathon, Green Lake, Shawano, Sheboygan, Dodge, Jefferson,

Ozaukee, Calumet, Washington, Wood and Marquette. The predominantly Scandinavian counties are Dane, Vernon, Pierce, Burnett, Polk, Price, Bayfield, Trempealeau, Douglas, Sawyer, Jackson and Washburn.

These counties show the highest percentages of Germans and Scandinavians in the *Wisconsin Blue Book* for 1899 (p. 488). The same counties were used to calculate the vote on woman suffrage of the two nationality groups.

8. How the Progressive and Farmer-Laborite parties were torn apart by the New Deal and World War II is detailed in *The Future of American Politics* (pp. 141–146). One revealing example of the realignment which followed will be found in the Second Congressional District. In 1932 Dodge County, heavily German in background, went Democratic by better than two to one while Dane County was a Republican stronghold. By 1954 Dane had become the chief source of Democratic strength, while Dodge was voting nearly two to one Republican.

9. My grass roots interviewing during 1950, 1952 and 1954 revealed two chief sources of support for Senator McCarthy. One was the frustrations that arose out of the Korean War, which often took the form of voters demanding, "Why don't we clean up these Commies at home with our boys dying in Korea?"

This indignation was not concentrated in any voting element but seemed generally spread through the country. It was far stronger in 1952 than in 1954, with the Korean War over.

The second main source of McCarthy strength came in areas which opposed our entry into the last war. Here one found the most vehement McCarthy supporters in 1954 as well as in 1952.

In New Jersey, Clifford Case almost lost the Senate race because of his attack on McCarthy. Bergen County, ordinarily good for a Republican plurality of 75,000 to 100,000, gave Case a lead of only 47,192. In some Bergen communities like Cliffside Park and Teaneck, a sixth of the normally Republican voters I interviewed declared they would stay at home rather than vote for Case.

Without exception every one of these anti-Case Republicans had favored Taft over Eisenhower for the 1952 Presidential nomination. Contrary to popular impression they were not the wealthiest families in their communities but concentrated in neighborhoods with $15,000 to $20,000 homes.

The similarity in the following of Taft and McCarthy can also be seen in Wisconsin. In the three-man 1952 Presidential primary, against Harold Stassen and Earl Warren, Taft got better than 50 per cent in twenty-two counties. These counties gave McCarthy 66 per cent in November to 41 per cent in the eleven counties where Taft fared worst.

From what common source did Taft and McCarthy draw most strongly? The table which follows shows how both men fared in three groups of strictly rural townships. In the German townships, Taft and McCarthy ran well ahead of their showing in all Wisconsin, while lagging behind the state average in the Norwegian and Polish townships—which also holds true for Eisenhower's vote.

That McCarthy ran behind Eisenhower in the German and Norwegian townships, but ahead among the Polish-Americans, indicates many Poles were sufficiently agitated over the Communist issue to break for McCarthy, even while holding to their normal Democratic allegiance.

	% Taft 1952 Primary	% McCarthy Nov., 1952	% Rep. for President			
			1952	1948	1944	1936
[1] German	46	70	76	56	77	26
[1] Norwegian	33	51	57	38	45	36
[1] Polish	28	29	24	10	9	7
State Average	40	54	61	46	50	32

[1] These townships were selected by Don Kanel, now at the University of Nebraska, whose unpublished study on Wisconsin voting is most revealing.

10. In South Dakota, where Taft and Eisenhower ran against each other in the 1952 primary, there were six counties where Roosevelt dropped at least 20 per cent between 1936 and 1940. All but one— Miner—gave Taft better than 60 per cent of their vote. Taft drew 67 per cent in the group against his state average of 50.2 per cent.

That much of this isolationist feeling reflects an anti-military tradition can be seen in Hutchinson County, where Taft did best with 78 per cent. Inhabited largely by Russian-Germans, Hutchinson voted 1,155 to 77 against creating a state militia in 1910. Hutchinson also voted 1,186 to 174 against woman suffrage; 1,082 to 204 against requiring railroads to have electric headlights; and 1,117 to 230 against a proposal that embalmers be licensed by the State. Hutchinson would seem a quite clannish community, highly suspicious of change—which typifies Russian-German communities through the country.

FOUR	Remaking the Republican Party

1. South Africa provides a vivid case history of the pathology of revenge in politics. More than fifty years have passed since the Afrikanders lost the Boer War. However, they won the war of birthrates which followed and are now, in effect, rewriting the results of the Boer War. The tragedy, one suspects, lies in the failure to utilize this fifty-year interval to make the Union of South Africa a truly unified nation.

2. The enduring significance of one's feelings about Franco Spain as a political divider reflects the fact that the Spanish Civil War raised for the first time the conflict which has troubled most Americans ever since—who was our greatest foe, Hitler's Germany or Stalin's Russia? The balance of sentiment in the nation refused to choose between the two at first, but those Americans who felt most strongly about Hitlerism and Communism did make their emotional choice at the time of the Spanish Civil War. The shifts in public opinion generally—it is worth stressing—were forced by events outside this country. Even after World War II was on, and despite our commitments to Britain, it still took the attack on Pearl Harbor to get us into the war. Similarly the reversal of our wartime friendship with the Soviets was forced by repeated Soviet aggressions to which public opinion adjusted.

3. The slow processes by which we decide the "national interest" probably contributed to the ethnic disunity which the two world wars stirred. Two years of bitter debate preceded our entry into each war. In that period one could favor either side in the war without feeling unpatriotic. Only after we entered the conflict did sympathies with Germany seem unpatriotic.

If this held true of the German-Americans during the world wars, it remains true for many who sympathized with Russia in the 1930's. Today such sympathies could be classed as indicating disloyalty, but in the 1935–40 period, it was not disloyal to look on Russia as a bulwark against Nazi Germany.

4. Only in recent years have political scientists awakened to the importance of ethnic influences in American politics. The earlier neglect probably reflected the assumption that ethnic factors were primarily a manifestation of hyphenated Americanism which would disappear as immigrants died off.

But the deeper significance of ethnic characteristics lies in their being so important in shaping those distinctive voting streams which we discussed earlier. Since the time immigrants came to this country helps fix their economic status, ethnic cleavages tend to be reinforced by economic conflict as well.

Proportionately too much emphasis has been given to the immigrant's relationship to the big-city machines, while not enough attention has been paid to how pervasive ethnic influences in American life generally have been. The Yankees have been the most important single ethnic element in our history, of course, and Roosevelt's gains in New England in 1940 are evidence of how persistent is their pro-British bias. The Scotch-Irish are credited by many historians with being one of the chief carriers of Jacksonian democracy, but there has been no follow-up study on their historical influence after the Civil War.

The one element which seems to have changed its politics least through the years is the Quakers. I have yet to find an area of Quaker settlement which has not been unswervingly Republican.

5. Eisenhower's problems in remaking the Republican party would be better appreciated if viewed in terms of the curious dynamics of coalition politics. Only twice in our history, of course, has a new majority coalition arisen to replace an old one, in the Civil War period when the Republicans succeeded the old Jacksonian coalition and with the New Deal when the Republicans were toppled from their ascendancy.

Both instances indicate that a major realignment requires the rise of new issues powerful enough to dissolve old chains of political loyalty, as with the issues of the Civil War and the Great Depression. These new issues serve as political dividers, moving certain elements into one party and opposing elements into the other party. As each rival coalition cements its following, it acquires its own orbit of prejudices. These orbits define the "norm" of people's voting until new issues arise strong enough to produce a new orbit of conflict to which the parties realign.

Eisenhower has not broken free of the orbit of conflict set by the New Deal. He has blurred many of the old cleavages and brought Republican policy into closer harmony with public opinion generally, but he has not changed the symbols which the voters attach instinctively to both parties.

My emphasis on the orbits of conflict pursued by our parties will

be recognized as an elaboration of the new theory of the nature of
our parties set forth in my earlier book.

6. The political hostility of a sizable portion of Jews and Catholics
is not confined to New York City. It has been stronger in Boston
where (pp. 211–213, *The Future of American Politics*) the Jewish
and heavily Irish wards have fluctuated in reciprocal hostility to one
another since Father Coughlin's preachings. These shiftings have
involved about 15 per cent of the vote of the two groups. This, of
course, indicates that most Catholics and Jews get along together
and have no irreconcilable political differences.

In an excellent thesis (Harvard College), *The Decline of the
Democratic Party in New York State: 1932–1952*, Milton S. Gwirtzman attributes Republican victories in New York State since 1938
to the Catholic-Jewish conflict in the Democratic party. Gwirtzman
points out how powerless Democratic leaders have been in checking
this conflict.

The 1952 campaign afforded an opportunity to test these reflexes
of hostility. Shortly after Eisenhower's nomination I sampled Jewish
areas in both Detroit and Los Angeles and found a fairly strong
shift to Eisenhower. I then went into the Southern states. By the
time I got back north, Eisenhower had made up with Taft and
McCarthy. In the next Jewish areas sampled in Philadelphia and
New York the sentiment had shifted away from Eisenhower.

I then went into heavily Catholic areas and found that people
who had been lukewarm about Eisenhower earlier in the campaign
were now for him because of his understanding with Taft and
McCarthy. This shift was the only major change of sentiment I
noted during the whole campaign. Eisenhower registered a small
gain in Jewish areas.

7. That Lemke's 1936 vote can remain so sensitive an indicator
twenty years later corroborates the "stream of voting" theory. If
Lemke's supporters had been an erratic fringe of individuals, the
areas where he was strongest would not have followed so uniform a
voting pattern in later elections. Actually, the Lemke "insurgents"
simply felt more deeply the agitations which were shared by the
communities in which they lived.

8. The different course in foreign policy taken by Eisenhower
compared to Harding becomes more significant when one considers
the parallel role that disillusionment over foreign policy played in
both the 1952 and 1920 elections.

At the 1920 Republican Presidential convention, the keynote

speech of Senator Henry Cabot Lodge—for whose sins another Lodge has done penance in the United Nations—sounded this battle cry: "We must be now and ever for Americanism and nationalism against internationalism."

But where, after 1920, the Republicans completely repudiated Woodrow Wilson's foreign policy, Eisenhower and Dulles preserved an essential continuity with the policies of Truman and Acheson.

Two main reasons why history failed to repeat itself might be cited: After 1920 it was possible for the Republicans to think they could turn their backs upon the rest of the world and concentrate on the pursuit of domestic profit. This delusion has become impossible today.

The second factor is the greater political strength of the Democratic party. The revulsion against Wilsonism left many parts of the Midwest with virtually only one major party for nearly a decade. In 1954, the Democrats were able to regain control of Congress despite the 1952 G.O.P. sweep.

9. Along with the Marshall Plan, the roll calls used to trace Republican sentiment on foreign aid were (see *Cong. Quarterly*):

> 1952, May 23: passed 246 to 109.
> 1953, June 19: passed 280 to 108.
> 1954, June 30: passed 260 to 126.
> 1955, June 30: passed 273 to 128.

Midwestern Republicans are often referred to as if they were a monolithic group. The table on the next page groups them by states —East Central, North Central and Plains. While the Plains States Congressmen have remained virtually unchanged, those from the East Central States show quite a shift.

10. These foreign aid roll calls refute the criticism voiced by Professor Ralph H. Smuckler of my thesis that the *hard core* of isolationist feeling is ethnic in nature. In the *American Political Science Review* (June, 1953) Professor Smuckler undertook to disprove this by analyzing the voting in Congress on foreign policy issues in the 1933-50 period.

When the article appeared, I wrote the *Review* and Professor Smuckler that the centers of isolationist sentiment could be spotted more accurately by using the break in Presidential voting by counties in 1940 and 1920 than through voting in Congress. A 12 to 17 per cent drop in Roosevelt's strength in 1940 in some Boston wards, for example, was not reflected in the voting of the Boston Congressmen.

Republican Voting in Congress on "Isolationist" Issues

Region[1]	Selective Svc. 1941		Lend Lease 1941		Marshall Plan 1948		Foreign Aid Bills							
							1952		1953		1954		1955	
	No	Yes	No	Yes	No	Yes	No	Yes	No	Yes	No	Yes	No	Yes
New England	7	7	9	6	0	20	2	12	2	13	3	13	3	15
Mid-Atlantic	32	9	31	12	4	62	12	31	7	43	6	45	9	35
East Central	47	0	47	0	30	26	41	12	33	17	30	20	28	19
North Central	17	1	17	2	7	17	12	4	13	5	15	3	13	6
Plains	13	0	13	0	8	6	9	3	10	2	9	1	11	2
Mountain	4	0	4	0	2	7	4	0	5	4	4	5	2	7
Pacific	6	4	8	2	1	22	4	9	5	22	5	19	5	21
Border	5	0	5	0	9	9	3	7	5	8	5	8	4	4
South	2	0	2	0	0	2	2	0	1	5	2	4	2	4
Total All Regions	133	21	136	22	61	171	89	78	81	119	79	118	77	113

[1] New England includes, Maine, N.H., Vt., R.I., Mass., Conn.; Mid-Atlantic: N.Y., N.J., Pa.; East Central: Ohio, Ill., Ind., Mich.; North Central: Iowa, Minn., Wisc.; Plains: N.D., S.D., Nebr., Kans.; Mountain: Colo., Nev., Wyo., Mont., Idaho, Utah, Ariz., N.M.; Pacific: Calif., Ore., Wash.; Border: Del., Ky., Md., Mo., Okla., W.Va.; South: Ala., Ark., Fla., Ga., La., Miss., N.C., S.C., Tenn., Tex., Va.

As it now turns out, the roll calls of Congress on foreign aid also show how strong is the "isolationist" feeling in German-American areas. Of course, as I have emphasized, other factors contribute to isolationist sentiment.

One other factual error in Professor Smuckler's article should be corrected. He writes of North Dakota as "the most isolationist of all" states and yet as relatively unpopulated by persons of German origin. This ignores the extremely heavy concentration in North Dakota of Russian-Germans, whom the census lists as of Russian nationality, but who have remained decidedly German in language and tradition—see *The Future of American Politics*, pp. 146–148.

FIVE *The Return of Two-Party Politics*

1. The comparison of families earning over $4,000 currently and in 1929 is necessarily an estimate since income statistics were computed differently in 1929. Much of the recent expansion of the middle class reflects the fact that both husbands and wives are working. *Fortune* has estimated that two-fifths of the families earning more than $4,000 a year do so because more than one person is working.

2. The Presidential vote in our twelve largest cities (New York, Chicago, Philadelphia, Pittsburgh, Detroit, Cleveland, Baltimore, St. Louis, Boston, Milwaukee, San Francisco and Los Angeles) was:

	Democratic	Republican	All-Party Total
1948	5,176,809	3,694,943	9,499,168
1952	5,702,859	4,621,334	10,423,081

3. As an example of how evenly spread were Eisenhower's gains, the table below divides Minneapolis into four income levels. Except for the most strongly Republican precincts, Eisenhower's gain is almost identical at each level.

Minneapolis Republican Percentage

by Income Fourths	1948	1952	Gain
Highest Fourth	69	76	7
Middle Income	50	60	10
Low Middle	35	45	10
Lowest Fourth	20	29	9

4. My remarks before the editorial writers in the fall of 1955 were inaccurately interpreted by some persons as implying that "any Republican could win in 1956." The full text of my talk can be found in *The Masthead*, Vol. VIII, No. 1, the organ of the National Conference of Editorial Writers.

5. How one-time Democrats who swung for Eisenhower really feel about the Republican party will not become clear until after Eisenhower is out of the political picture. Still, my own judgment is that the gap between Eisenhower's popularity and the Republican strength, while appreciable, is not as wide as generally pictured. Much of Roosevelt's following was considered "personal," but after he died it developed that the emphasis on Roosevelt's personal appeal had obscured the strength of Democratic loyalty which had developed among his followers.

Roosevelt had more than three full terms to transform his own popularity into a party loyalty. Still, I am tempted to paraphrase what I wrote of Roosevelt's following in 1941, that once Eisenhower is out of the picture, "his vote will not slip back automatically into its former slots."

6. Outside the Solid South the 1954 Congress vote was Democrats 19,169,175, Republicans 19,375,340. The other close contests were:

Won by Less Than 1%			Won by 1 to 2%		
State	Office	Winning Plurality	State	Office	Winning Plurality
Conn.	Governor	3,115 Dem.	Colo.	Senate	12,424 Rep.
Mass.	Senate	28,706 Rep.	Iowa	Governor	25,116 Rep.
Mich.	Senate	39,085 Dem.	Mass.	Governor	74,968 Rep.
Mont.	Senate	1,728 Dem.	Wis.	Governor	33,699 Rep.
N.J.	Senate	3,370 Rep.	Wyo.	Senate	3,438 Dem.
Ohio	Senate	2,970 Rep.			
Ore.	Senate	2,462 Dem.			
Wyo.	Governor	1,112 Rep.			
N.Y.	Governor	11,125 Dem.			

7. Percentage-wise the suburbs do not appear more Republican today than in the 1920's. Cook County's suburbs voted 84 per cent Republican in 1920 to 66 per cent in 1952. Nassau, Suffolk and Westchester counties, near New York, were 74 per cent Republican in 1920 and 70 per cent in 1952. The new importance of the suburbs, of course, reflects the fact that nearly a fifth of the nation's population now lives there.

Note the abrupt decline with the war's end in Democratic pluralities in Chicago, Los Angeles and New York and the equally sharp rise in G.O.P. pluralities in the suburbs outside these cities:

Party Pluralities [1]

	Chicago City	Cook County Suburbs
1932	248,807 Dem.	19,722 Rep.
1936	555,386 Dem.	3,428 Rep.
1940	297,822 Dem.	68,135 Rep.
1944	417,836 Dem.	67,128 Rep.
1948	315,507 Dem.	114,671 Rep.
1952	161,242 Dem.	177,761 Rep.

	Los Angeles City	L. A. Co. Suburbs
1932	133,374 Dem.	47,364 Dem.
1936	263,929 Dem.	136,021 Dem.
1940	168,157 Dem.	80,295 Dem.
1944	157,596 Dem.	62,215 Dem.
1948	48,800 Dem.	40,342 Rep.
1952	40,401 Rep.	236,477 Rep.

	New York City	Nearby Suburbs
1932	871,120 Dem.	37,552 Rep.
1936	1,375,396 Dem.	46,737 Rep.
1940	718,459 Dem.	178,129 Rep.
1944	774,254 Dem.	182,664 Rep.
1948	488,257 Dem.	240,603 Rep.
1952	359,439 Dem.	375,830 Rep.

[1] Los Angeles figures were computed specially by Della Daniel, Deputy Registrar of Voters; Chicago's returns come from Isaac Gershman, City News Bureau.

One or more additional Presidential votes are needed before the full political significance of the postwar flight to the suburbs will become clear. Some suburban returns I have analyzed point to a long-run trend to make the suburbs somewhat more Democratic, although not on any scale that would threaten Republican ascendancy in these communities.

8. In my writing of class conflict and class consciousness in American politics, perhaps it should be stressed that these terms are not used in the Marxian sense.

The pattern of class conflict in the United States differs from Marx's theories in at least two crucial respects. First, continued social and economic mobility makes our class lines fairly fluid—barriers to be hurdled, not unscalable walls. Second, intermingled with economics distinctions are ethnic conflicts. Often, in fact, our class distinctions are more a reflection of ethnic than economic status.

9. My term "newer middle-class elements" may also require more precise definition. No one has ever been able to fence off clearly who belongs to the American middle class and who does not. Partly this is because of the refusal of Americans to stay put in any category. My label refers to those who have climbed up out of the slums and out of the poverty of the depression to middle-income levels and who are striving to mount to the next rung of the ladder. The dynamics of this climb, as pointed out in my earlier book, are those of an urban frontier, performing for our industrial civilization many of the functions which the old agrarian frontier performed in an earlier period.

10. My full "solution" of the mystery of why Philadelphia was the one major city to give Stevenson a higher percentage than Truman was published in the Philadelphia *Bulletin*, Jan. 18, 1953.

Two main factors were involved. First, in the eleven wards most heavily Negro Eisenhower drew only 26 per cent against 45 per cent for Dewey in 1948. Second, in the non-Negro part of the city, Eisenhower's percentage matched quite closely the vote for 1940 or 1944, ward by ward. In short, the real "freak" year for voting in Philadelphia was 1948.

This freak 1948 showing can be explained by the death of Roosevelt and the fact that the Republican machine, fighting for its life, made an all-or-nothing effort to win votes. By 1952, the Republican machine had been routed locally and the voting pattern of the Roosevelt years reasserted itself.

11. The close party balance puts a considerable premium on the quality of the candidates, since so large a part of the electorate seems ready to cross party lines "for the best man." Paradoxically, it also puts a premium on effective party organization and on vote stealing. With victory in a state hinging on a few thousand ballots, it will be remarkable if vote frauds do not increase.

SIX   *The Education of George Humphrey*

1. The shift to a managed monetary policy actually began in 1951 while Truman was President. During the Eisenhower years, the

"Fed" and Treasury have worked together so closely that the Fed's actions can be viewed as part of the Eisenhower-Humphrey fiscal policy.

2. The historical evidence indicates that business generally has thrived on inflation not economy. In his monumental *A Study of Saving in the United States,* Raymond W. Goldsmith shows that nearly half of the increase in the value of our national wealth since 1897 reflected price rises. The rise in net worth because of higher price levels was far greater for corporations than for any other segment of the economy.

3. Within the business community the most articulate advocates of a new spending philosophy are men like Paul Mazur and the editors of *Fortune.* In *The Changing American Market, Fortune's* editors, with a pithiness that would do credit to Poor Richard, declare, "A nation that wants to have money to spend must spend money." Reviewing Roosevelt's efforts to lift the economy out of the depression, *Fortune* concluded that Roosevelt's "deficits were too small to counter-act the decline in private spending." None of the advocates of spending have yet come around to praising high taxes, although they are one of the more powerful stimulants to more abundant spending.

4. Part of the conflict between government and business reflects the fact that business itself has become a form of government, ruling the lives and activities of millions. See pp. 31–34 in A. A. Berle's stimulating *The Twentieth Century Capitalist Revolution.*

5. The concept of the strategic gap in our foreign economic policy is developed in my book *The Revolution in World Trade,* Chapter 3.

6. The estimates of the proportion of national income devoted to defense in different years are drawn from M. Slade Kendrick's *A Century and a Half of Federal Expenditures,* put out by the National Bureau of Economic Research.

7. What is often overlooked is that one main reason our defense establishment costs so much is the nature of our civilization, with its emphasis on high wages and labor-saving machinery. American industrialists boast $12,500 in capital has been invested for every worker, a higher investment than in any other country. Similarly, every American soldier commands a heavier investment of firepower than in any other army.

8. My comments on the importance of stand-by mobilization legislation should be viewed in the light of my being associated with Baruch in his fight for such legislation.

9. In *American Income and Its Use* Elizabeth Hoyt comments, "Technology provides us with more leisure and more technological ways for spending that leisure. We use our leisure not for a quieter life but for a more complex and speedier life."

10. The extent to which our economy has become a make-spend operation may defy exact measuring, but almost it might be said we have developed our own equivalent for the Roman "bread and circuses" in credit and TV.

11. So much scarehead publicity has been given labor's political efforts that it is often overlooked that labor never has been able to command anything like the vote Roosevelt pulled before the PAC and similar organizations were set up. This does not mean labor's political role is insignificant, but it does mean its influence is limited. Labor has been most effective in Michigan, where the Auto Workers have built what some politicians regard as the most effective Democratic organization in the country.

SEVEN *Divided We Plow*

1. The description of the visit of the Soviet farm experts to Alleman's farm is drawn from the Des Moines *Register and Tribune* whose files were made available by Kenneth MacDonald, the executive editor. The idea of inviting the Russians to visit this country originated with the *Register and Tribune*.

2. The farmer's dependence on cash income has been sharpened by a spectacular rise in what he regards as adequate living. In 1930, while hitchhiking around the country, I was given a ride by a salesman who apparently made a living by victimizing farmers. "You can always sell farmers a cheap pair of glasses," he boasted. "They've all ruined their eyesight reading by kerosene lamps and they don't believe in going to doctors."

Contrast that with the attitude toward medical care reflected in the complaint one Minnesota farmer voiced in 1954. In listing the higher expenses he had to deal with, he cited a $500 dentist bill: "I just had to pay to get my daughter's teeth straightened."

In 1930 only about a third of the nation's farmers lived along roads which didn't turn into bogs after a rain. Less than a sixth of our farmers had electricity or running water and only a fifth had radios. Currently, more than nine of every ten farms are electrified, nearly half have running water, while two-thirds enjoy access to all-weather roads.

3. For a historical survey of the farmers' efforts to adjust to a commercial economy see Carl Taylor's *The Farmers' Movement.* Lowry Nelson's *American Farm Life* and *American Agriculture* by Ronald L. Mighell are good for changes in farming since 1940.

4. Through most of the New Deal, farm legislation was dominated by Congressmen from wheat and cotton districts, supported by big-city Democrats. The flexible price support bill in 1954 upset this alliance. Among the Republicans the vote was 182 for and 23 against, among the Democrats 45 for and 147 against.

The Democrats who broke from their general party attitude to support Secretary Benson were mainly in the non-cotton South, notably Florida, New Mexico and some of the bigger cities. Among the Republicans, the principal opposition to lower price supports came from wheat and dairying areas—particularly Iowa, Kansas, Minnesota and the Dakotas. In short, the wheat and cotton Congressmen held together but they were isolated by the splitting away of legislators from other agricultural districts and from the cities.

5. The variation in attitude toward a government program among different farming areas parallels what happened during the 1920's. In the voting on the successive McNary-Haugen bills the strongest initial support came in the wheat-growing states. Fifty of the fifty-seven Congressmen from Minnesota, Iowa, Missouri, the Dakotas, Kansas and Nebraska favored the 1924 McNary-Haugen Bill, which lost 161 to 221.

As the depression spread to other crops, McNary-Haugenites won new support. By 1927 a majority of Southern Congressmen favored the legislation. Their shift enabled the bill to pass the House in 1927. For a breakdown of the Congressional vote the four times the bill came up see John D. Black's *McNary-Haugen Movement* pp. 408–9 and his article in the *American Economic Review,* September, 1928, pp. 410–11. Gilbert C. Fite's biography *George W. Peek and the Fight for Farm Parity* is a masterly account of the politics of the farm problem after World War I.

6. In his 1954 Senate race Guy Gillette suffered his heaviest losses from 1948—of 17 and 14 per cent—in the Western livestock and cash corn areas of Iowa. In the Northeastern dairy counties he dropped only 8 per cent, while his smallest loss of 6 per cent came in Southern Iowa, traditionally the most Republican part of the state, but also the poorest economically.

EIGHT   *The Three-Party South*

1. In judging the shape being given politics in the South one problem arises: what criteria to employ in measuring how much— or how little—progress has been made toward a two-party system?

The best single yardstick, it seems to me, is the degree to which voting returns stratify along impersonal lines like income, type of farming, industrialization, urbanization, or proportion of Negroes in the population.

That the racial and economic conflicts reflected in Eisenhower's vote have developed primarily since the New Deal is corroborated by his winning 118 Southern counties and 11 Virginia cities which stayed Democratic in both 1920 and 1928. He lost 32 of the counties which Harding and Hoover both won.

2. Another measure of the prospects of a two-party South will be found in the extent to which alignments in Presidential voting get projected into state primary races. In Texas and Louisiana the projection seems sufficiently strong to justify describing the struggle for Democratic control in those states as a rehearsal for two-party politics.

Of the 254 counties in Texas, 112 were won by both Eisenhower and Allan Shivers in his 1954 governor's race. Another 82 counties were lost by both men. How rooted in economics is the cleavage in Texas is indicated by how closely the vote for Shivers in Houston scales with home valuations.

Economic Vote for Shivers in Houston in 1954

Precincts with Home Value of	% 1st Primary	% Runoff Primary	Precincts with Home Value of	% 1st Primary	% Runoff Primary
$30,000	81	81	9,000	55	56
19,000	79	80	8,000	53	42
15,000	79	77	7,000	45	45
13,000	73	73	5,000	36	31
10,000	59	68	Under 5,000	37	35

In Louisiana, as well, a strong and consistent economic conflict seems at work. In New Orleans I was able to classify economically all but 19 of the city's 307 precincts with the help of the *Times-Picayune* and Rudolf Heberle and Perry Howard of Louisiana State University. The basic classification of precincts, which I had updated, was done by Carmela Graffagnini, a former student of Dr. Heberle.

The correlation between Eisenhower's vote and economic status is striking. For 11 of the 146 precincts Eisenhower won or tied, I have no economic description. Of the other 135, only 6 are classed as low income:

Economic Voting in New Orleans

Economic Class	No. of Precincts Eisenhower Won	No. of Such Precincts in City
Upper Income	32	32
Low Upper	3	4
Middle Income	89	115
Low Middle	5	11
Low Income	6	126
Totals	135	288

Almost as impressive is how closely the Eisenhower vote parallels that cast for Governor Robert F. Kennon in the February, 1952, primary. Of 115 precincts where Kennon got at least 70 per cent, Eisenhower won all but 17. In 35—including all 32 highest income precincts—he drew better than 70 per cent of the vote.

In the 9 precincts where Kennon was weakest, pulling under 30 per cent, Eisenhower drew 14 per cent of the vote.

Generally, as well, the Eisenhower-Kennon vote polarizes in opposition to the vote for Earl Long in his primary race for governor. In 1948 Long drew more than 60 per cent in 13 precincts. Eisenhower got only 36 per cent in these precincts. In the weakest Long precincts Eisenhower drew 79 per cent of the vote.

This alignment projects back at least to 1940. Fifty-two precincts cast a majority for both Eisenhower and Kennon in 1952 and for Sam H. Jones in his races against Earl Long in both 1948 and 1940. Thirty-three of these precincts rate as upper income and the other 19 as middle income. None falls in the lower income rungs.

The voting for Earl Long, as V. O. Key has pointed out in his excellent *Southern Politics,* reflected to a considerable degree how people felt about his fabulous brother Huey. A sampling of scattered counties outside of New Orleans shows that Eisenhower's highest vote came in areas where Huey Long was weakest. In turn, Long's strongest areas were where Eisenhower ran worst.

In other Southern states the tendency of national conflicts to be projected into state primary votes seems weaker but is not absent.

3. *The Savannah* by Tom Stokes recounts the historical significance of the Augusta area.

4. In all eleven Southern states the Republican Presidential vote rose from 1,361,000 in 1948 to 4,413,000 in 1952. In the 157 counties at least 50 per cent Negro the G.O.P. jumped from 19,700 to 158,600.

The urban concentration of Eisenhower's gains is detailed in the table below, giving the per cent of the total state vote cast by the leading urban counties and their share of Eisenhower's gains in the state. The table raises one puzzle which is worth further study. The widest spread between Eisenhower's gains in the cities and their proportion of the state vote comes in neither the most nor least urbanized states but in those almost evenly divided between rural and urban influences.

Republicanism in Urban South [1]

	% Urban 1950	% State Vote Cast, 1952	% Total State Rep. Gain Over 1948	Vote-gains Difference
Florida	65	55	58	3
Texas	62	32	33	1
Louisiana	54	39	40	1
Virginia	47	21	23	2
Georgia	45	33	46	13
Tennessee	44	39	49	10
Alabama	43	27	40	13
S. Carolina	36	25	31	6
N. Carolina	33	26	34	8
Arkansas	33	16	21	5
Mississippi	27	11	14	3

[1] Includes urban counties casting at least 4% of the state vote. Where this yielded one or two cities in a state, counties with cities of at least 40,000 population were added. The cities covered are:

Miami, Jacksonville, Tampa, St. Petersburg, Orlando and West Palm Beach in Florida; Dallas, Houston, Fort Worth and San Antonio in Texas; New Orleans, Baton Rouge and Shreveport in Louisiana; Richmond, Norfolk, Alexandria, Roanoke, Lynchburg and Portsmouth in Virginia; Atlanta, Augusta, Savannah, Macon, Columbus, Brunswick, and Decatur in Georgia; Memphis, Nashville, Knoxville and Chattanooga in Tennessee; Birmingham, Mobile and Montgomery in Alabama; Charleston, Columbia and Greenville in S. Carolina; Charlotte, Greensboro, Raleigh, Durham, Wilmington, Winston-Salem and Asheville in N. Carolina; Little Rock and Fort Smith in Arkansas; Jackson and Meridian in Mississippi.

In *The Journal of Politics* (Aug., 1953) Donald S. Strong stratifies the Eisenhower vote by calculating the change between 1936 and 1952. He draws much the same picture as emerges from my using the G.O.P. gains between 1948 and 1952.

5. For the table on page 181, contrasting the vote on segregation with the most heavily Negro counties, the cities used were: Charleston and Columbia in South Carolina; Macon, Savannah, Decatur, Atlanta, Columbus, Brunswick, and Augusta in Georgia; Jackson, Biloxi, Gulfport and Meridian in Mississippi; Baton Rouge, New Orleans and Shreveport in Louisiana. In Virginia, where the city vote is reported separately, all thirty-two independent cities are included. The six largest Virginia cities voted 58 per cent for segregation.

6. In deciding which precincts can be classed Negro, labor and silk stocking (see p. 184), I relied on descriptions furnished by local newspapermen. Although somewhat impressionistic, this method is quite reliable in judging how the vote polarizes.

7. The comment of the young wife of a Richmond lawyer reveals how long was the build-up of middle-class resentment which finally broke loose in the Eisenhower vote. "I was born and raised a Democrat," she told me in 1952. "But as long as I can remember my father and mother have been against the things going on in Washington. I'm ready to join the Republican party openly."

8. In 1891, four of the nine South Carolinians in Congress were said to have killed people. Dueling itself was not outlawed until 1881. In *South Carolina: A Brief History*, David D. Wallace attributes the action to "the shock to public opinion" of the duel between Colonel E. B. C. Cash and Colonel W. M. Shannon. It was this duel which caused the family of Bernard M. Baruch to leave South Carolina for New York.

9. My sketch of Tillman draws heavily on Francis Simkins' *Pitchfork Ben Tillman*.

10. In March, 1955, Edgefield opened a new $600,000 school for Negroes.

11. Many Augustans feel Watson's hatreds were inspired by the fact that when he ran for re-election to Congress in 1894 he was flagrantly counted out. Negroes were hauled across the Savannah River from South Carolina, liquored up and paid to vote. C. Vann Woodward, in *Tom Watson, Agrarian Rebel*, recounts that with 11,240 eligible voters, Richmond County (which includes Augusta) gave Watson's opponent a *majority* of 13,780. The political boss in

Augusta was a Catholic, Patrick Walsh. Watson's followers in Augusta started the Cracker Party largely to break the hold of the Catholics on the city government.

12. The school referendums in Virginia, South Carolina, Georgia, Mississippi and Louisiana may not be precise tests of feeling on segregation since the proposals voted on were indirectly phrased. Still, the vote can be taken as an accurate picture of the conflicting alignments over the issue.

Of 451 counties in the five states, only 58 opposed the segregation proposals. Thirty-one of these counties were in Georgia; 15 in Mississippi; 8 in Virginia; 5 in South Carolina and none in Louisiana. In addition 6 Virginia cities opposed the proposal. Of these 58 counties 33 are strung along the mountain highlands. All but one of these are three-fourths white.

In Mississippi a clear correlation shows up between the school vote and the size of the city in the Delta counties but, curiously enough, not in the rest of the state.

School Vote of Delta Cities

Population	% for School Amendment	Population	% for School Amendment
Over 20,000 (Jackson, Greenville, Vicksburg, Waterbury)	67	9,000 (Yazoo City)	91
16,000 (Clarksdale)	84	6,000 (Cleveland)	94
		Under 5,000 (11 towns)	91

In all the cities a large part of the vote against segregation was cast by Negroes. The deep South cities also show a greater measure of tolerance among upper-income elements than among white worker precincts. In Richmond, though, no variation by income shows up, the worker and well-to-do areas voting roughly the same.

In Virginia, outside of the mountain counties, opposition to the segregation proposal centered in suburban Arlington and Fairfax, which lie across the Potomac from Washington, and in Norfolk.

13. Progress in tolerance is likely to be held back by the heavy overrepresentation in state legislatures given rural areas, which are strongest against desegregation. In Georgia this disparity is aggravated by the system of electing officials by county units. The 8 counties with the most population are allotted six units each; the 30 next most populous counties get four units each, while the remain-

ing 121 counties get two units each. With 13 per cent of the state's population the 40 Georgia counties 50 per cent or more Negro account for 88 unit votes, against 48 units for the eight most populous counties with 35 per cent of the state's population.

What this means to a candidate like Herman Talmadge can be seen by comparing the school segregation vote with that of the two contests lost by Talmadge's father, for the Senate in 1938 against Walter George, and for Governor in 1942 against Ellis Arnall. In both these contests Eugene Talmadge ran worst in the big-city counties and strongest among the most rural counties. The balance of victory lay with the four-unit counties, two-thirds of which voted for the school amendment.

	Total units	For School Segre-gation	Won by			Won by	
			Tal-madge [1]	George	Camp	Tal-madge	Ar-nall
8 biggest cities	48	6	40	48	0	0	48
30 four-unit cos.	120	80	40	72	8	16	104
121 two-unit cos.	242	214	110	120	12	132	110

[1] Vote taken from *Southern Primaries and Elections 1920–49* by Alexander Heard and Donald S. Strong.

NINE *The Anatomy of Congress*

1. The workings of Congress have been given considerable study but the psychology of how people vote for Congress remains largely unexplored. In *Congressional Elections,* Cortez A. M. Ewing plots the sectional shifts in Congress from 1896 to through 1944. The relation of Presidential to Congressional voting is explored by both Malcolm Moos in *Politics, Presidents and Coattails* and Louis H. Bean in *The Midterm Battle.*

2. New York City holds twelve of the seats outside the South which have been Democratic since at least 1940; Chicago another five; Detroit and Los Angeles three each; Boston, Jersey City, Baltimore, Pittsburgh and Cleveland, two apiece.

3. The difficulties the Republicans face in winning a sizable majority in Congress can also be seen in the 61 seats they picked up in their 1946 sweep. Eight are no longer comparable because of redistricting. Of the remaining 53 districts the Republicans still hold 24 which leaves only 29 seats to be gained if the 1946 sweep were repeated.

In 1952 Eisenhower carried only fifteen of these. Twelve of the

29 seats gave the Democrats 60 per cent or more of their vote in 1954.

4. Just why the Democratic solidarity of the Negro should be increasing when every other political element is registering some Republican gain is an intriguing speculation. One influence is a greater tendency of Negroes to vote a straight ticket. Another is the segregation in which Negroes live. There are so few Republicans among Negroes that group pressures tend to reinforce their Democratic loyalty. A third factor is that Negroes have identified their economic welfare so strongly with the labor movement. Significantly, the peak Democratic percentages among Negroes have been registered in Detroit.

Chicago's second district, which shifted parties every two years between 1944 and 1952, is being turned into a safe Democratic seat by an increasing Negro population. Chicago's third district, which the Republicans won in 1946, 1950 and 1952, has also been gaining rapidly in Negro numbers.

5. In judging the tensions within the Democratic party one should bear in mind that the political influence of Southern traditions is not confined to the South. Many counties, like Holmes in Ohio, which were settled from the South have been realigning toward the Republicans. The Eastern Shore of Maryland, Democratic through the 1920's, sent a Republican to Congress in 1946 and has stayed Republican since. In 1952 Eisenhower's heaviest gains in Maryland came in this district.

In New Mexico, the "East Side" counties bordering Texas gave Eisenhower his heaviest gains in the state. This same "Texas effect" can be seen in Oklahoma. Migration has also put sizable numbers of "hillbillies" in the Northern cities, which is one main source of the popularity of Estes Kefauver.

6. Of the 123 districts which have been Republican since 1940, New York State has 17; Pennsylvania 14; Ohio 12; Illinois and Michigan 10 each; Massachusetts, New Jersey and Iowa 6 each; Kansas and Wisconsin 5 apiece. California is not ranked with these states because district lines have changed so often, but 7 Republican seats in California were held by 60 per cent or better in 1954.

7. The fifteen seats which have shifted between the parties at least twice between 1948 and 1954 are: Cal. 12, Ida. 1, Ill. 2, and 3; Ind. 8; Kan. 1, N.Y. 1, Md. 5; Mo. 4 and 6; Wis. 5; Pa. 11 and 19; Va. 9 and W. Va. 4. All but Kan. 1 and N.Y. 1 were Democratic in 1954.

8. The seventeen districts won by less than 1 per cent of the vote

in 1954 are: Calif. 6; Conn. 2 and at large; Fla. 1; Ill. 11; Ind. 3; Mass. 10; Mont. 2; N.H. 1; N.Y. 17; Pa. 6, 10, 11 and 19; W. Va. 4 and Ky. 3.

9. The shifting balance in many hybrid districts raises doubts as to whether rural interests are as overrepresented in Congress as generally believed. A detailed study of the vote shows that in many part-rural and part-urban districts the seats swing with the shift in the *urban* pluralities—as in Colo. 3 and 4; Ind. 3 and 7; Mo. 6; Ohio 3; Pa. 9; W. Va. 1; and the at large seats in Dela., Wash. and Conn. This would indicate divisions among the urban elements are growing more important politically than rural-urban differences.

10. Gerrymandering takes too many varied forms to be quickly summarized. In California the Republicans got the same percentage of the total state vote for Congress in 1952 as in 1950. The Republicans, though, gained six seats as a result of the reapportionment after 1950 while the Democrats gained only one. In 1954 the Democrats actually got a majority of the total Congressional vote in the state but emerged with only eleven of the thirty seats. They drew the same number of seats in 1952 with only 42 per cent of the total state vote.

New Jersey, which has not been redistricted since 1932, seems even more distorted in its representation. The table below shows how the Democrats, although never falling below 40 per cent of the state total for Congress, have gotten as few as 14 per cent of the seats. Only once, with 55 per cent in 1936, did the Democrats gain an even split in the delegation.

Year	Dem. % of total Cong. vote	Seats D.	R.	Year	Dem. % of total Cong. vote	Seats D.	R.
1932	49	4	10	1944	46	2	12
1934	51	4	10	1946	40	2	12
1936	54	7	7	1948	48	5	9
1938	47	3	11	1950	44	5	9
1940	47	4	10	1952	42	5	9
1942	45	3	11	1954	48	6	8

11. As a result of the 1952 redistricting, New York has become one of the most rigidly drawn states. Of its 43 districts, 31 were won by 60 per cent or better in 1954. These and other rigidities embedded in Congress should cause some second-thinking among those who would amend the Constitution to count the electoral vote for President by each separate Congressional District rather than by the state as a whole (see Mundt-Coudert bill).

The change would not only project all the evils of Congressional gerrymandering into the Presidency but would tend to replace the unifying effect of Presidential voting with the rigid divisions of Congress. The obstacle to a decisive party realignment would be increased. At present, as was shown in 1952, the people can unite behind a President, even while letting Congress serve as caretaker for old feuds.

12. Penrose's remarks to Matt Quay are reported in Walter Davenport's *Power and Glory: the Life of Boies Penrose.*

13. Much of the post-Civil War deadlock reflected a politics of revenge. In her excellent *Veterans in Politics,* Mary R. Dearing describes how the G.A.R. kept alive the antagonisms and loyalties of the Civil War. When sworn into the G.A.R., veterans would kneel blindfolded before a coffin, drapped in an American flag hung in mourning. On the coffin were an open Bible, crossed swords and the name of that most notorious of Southern prisons, Andersonville.

TEN   Democracy as an Arena

1. The political upsurge of the middle class in recent years certainly vindicates Arthur Holcombe's thesis as to the stabilizing role of the middle class in American politics. The departure from the past in the current role of the middle class will be found in the fact that today's middle class in urban areas is the product of two distinct historical streams, which have still to be completely reconciled.

2. If my emphasis on the decisive importance of nationalizing forces is valid, both the Democrats and Republicans will tend to become *more truly national* parties. In that event sectionalism will be transformed to where its real motivation will be opposition to these nationalizing trends.

That is largely what the "states' rights" movement now being agitated amounts to—an attempt to bring into coalition those who feel their interests hurt by the trends toward national unification. The states' rights philosophy is less an effort to cling to a tradition of the past than a weapon for fighting current political developments.

3. One feature of the continuous arena that our American democracy provides is that the same fight need not necessarily be fought from the same battle stations. People may favor "leaving things to the states" on one issue and federal control on another. Also over a period of time the most extreme advocates of states' rights may become ardent unionists or vice versa, as happened with John C. Calhoun and Daniel Webster in the pre-Civil War period.

Again, when the Republic was founded, agrarian spokesmen

saw a weak government as a protection against the encroachments of commercial interests who championed a strong government. By Bryan's time, the agrarian interests were clamoring for government intervention while business spokesmen were talking the language of Jefferson. The general American practice has been to use whatever "philosophy" or branch of government fitted one's practical interests.

4. For a good recent analysis of the constitutional conflict between the White House and Capitol Hill see Sidney Hyman's *The American President*; also W. E. Binkley's *The Powers of the President*.

5. In *Grand Inquest* (p. 125) Telford Taylor stresses how loyalty investigations serve as an "extra-legal means of inflicting punishment." Taylor writes: "Statutes cannot make it criminal to have been a member of the Young Communist League at college, or of the American League for Peace and Democracy in the late thirties or to have supported the Spanish Loyalists because they were fighting Franco, or to have spoken favorably of the Chinese Communists because they were fighting the Japanese. Yet past associations and opinions such as these have become hateful to millions of Americans who, since the criminal law is useless for the purpose, have come to rely on Congressional and state legislative investigations to expose, discredit and, so far as possible, to render unemployable individuals who held and acted upon those or similar opinions during the thirties and forties, or who now oppose this use of the investigatory process."

6. One aid in keeping a sense of balance about desegregation is to remember that Jim Crow laws have been in force only since the turn of the century. In *The Strange Career of Jim Crow*, C. Vann Woodward attributes the enactment of these laws to a relaxation of opposition to intolerance in the South and North. As he writes (p. 51): "All the elements of fear, jealousy, proscription hatred and fanaticism had long been present. . . . What enabled them to rise to dominance was . . . a general weakening and discrediting of the numerous forces that had hitherto kept them in check."

As late as 1898 the Charleston *News and Courier* argued against Jim Crow street cars: "As we have got on fairly well for a third of a century, including a long period of reconstruction, without such a measure, we can probably get on as well hereafter without it. . . ."

7. Much of the progress in civil rights in recent years was brought about by the coming of age of the children of the immigrants who came to this country in the decade before World War I. A whole generation grew up which, having suffered discrimination in childhood, was determined to end such discrimination. If the suburbs re-

main constituted as now, a new generation may arise without having had day-to-day contact with any minority elements.

8. J. K. Galbraith's *American Capitalism,* with its theory of countervailing power, argues strongly the advantages of the dispersal of economic power.

9. For stimulating discussions of what ails Western civilization see Walter Lippmann's *The Public Philosophy;* Russell Kirk's *Program for Conservatives* and Russell W. Davenport's *The Dignity of Man.* The idea that government should be entrusted to an elite with a sense of aristocratic responsibility is attractive but who is to choose the aristocrats? The choice soon would turn to either nepotism or advertising. For better or worse we have no alternative but to learn to govern through the people.

10. The crucial problem of bridging the gap between the totalitarian nature of modern war and our normally relaxed ways has received less scholarly attention than any other problem of comparable importance. The best exposition of the issue will be found in the writings of Bernard M. Baruch: *A Philosophy for Our Time,* or "What of the Future?" in the *Saturday Evening Post* of April 23, 1949. My book *The Revolution in World Trade* is also a stab at the problem.

11. The balance that now prevails as to the role of government reflects a curious "compromise" of forces. During the New Deal "liberal" elements favored strengthening government to advance welfare state objectives. As this drive lost force, with the rise in the dangers of inflation, the needs of the cold war have created new pressures and support for a stronger government. As a result the pendulum swing away from "too much government" has been slowed and the actual authority wielded by the government has remained stable for a whole decade.

Party loyalty seems another factor in maintaining this balance. In foreign aid, for example, the loss of Southern support with a Republican President has been offset by a rise in Republican support. One is tempted to conclude that the balance of partisanship fluctuates with what is needed to carry through workable policies. Somehow the necessary majorities in Congress to prevent default get mustered, but once the danger of failure is taken care of, individual members of Congress give priority to the political needs of their home districts.

In short, for all the free play given to conflict on the fringes, the American political system seems admirably constructed to achieve the minimum balance of unity that serves as the binding core.

Election Returns: 1916-1952

States carried by:

- ■ Democrats
- □ Republicans
- ▨ La Follette Progressives
- ▨ Dixiecrats

1916

1920

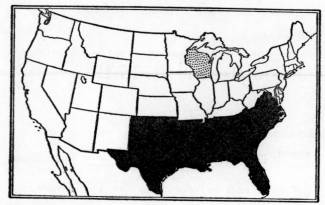

1924

1928

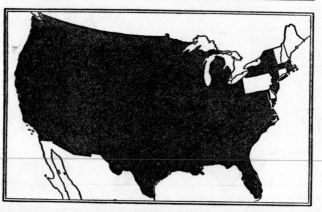

1932

1936

1940

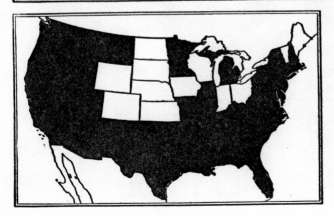

1944

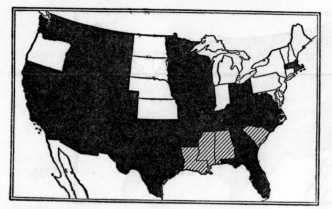

1948

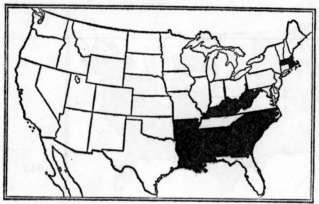

1952

INDEX